TREATISE ON CONSTITUTIONAL LAW

SUBSTANCE AND PROCEDURE

Second Edition

1997 Pocket Part

By

RONALD D. ROTUNDA

Albert E. Jenner, Jr. Professor of Law,
University of Illinois

JOHN E. NOWAK

David C. Baum Professor of Law,
University of Illinois

Volume 4

Sections 20.1 to End
APPENDICES
TABLES
INDEX

Replacing prior Pocket Part in back of Volume

ST. PAUL, MINN.
WEST PUBLISHING CO.
1996

WESTLAW® ELECTRONIC RESEARCH GUIDE

Coordinating Legal Research With WESTLAW

The *Treatise on Constitutional Law* is an essential aid to legal research. WESTLAW provides a vast, online library of over 8000 collections of documents and services that can supplement research begun in this publication, encompassing:

- Federal and state primary law (statutes, regulations, rules, and case law), including West's editorial enhancements, such as headnotes, Key Number classifications, annotations

- Secondary law resources (texts and treatises published by West Publishing Company and by other publishers, as well as law reviews)

- Legal news

- Directories of attorneys and experts

- Court records and filings

- Citators

Specialized topical subsets of these resources have been created for more than thirty areas of practice.

In addition to legal information, there are general news and reference databases and a broad array of specialized materials frequently useful in connection with legal matters, covering accounting, business, environment, ethics, finance, medicine, social and physical sciences.

This guide will focus on a few aspects of WESTLAW use to supplement research begun in this publication, and will direct you to additional sources of assistance.

Databases

A database is a collection of documents with some features in common. It may contain statutes, court decisions, administrative materials, commentaries, news or other information. Each database has a unique identifier, used in many WESTLAW commands to select a database of interest. For example, the database containing cases decided by the United States Courts of Appeal has the identifier CTA; the cases of a specific state are contained in a database having identifier XX-CS, where XX is the state's postal code.

The WESTLAW Directory is a comprehensive list of databases with information about each database, including the types of documents each contains. The first page of a standard or customized WESTLAW Directory is displayed upon signing on to WESTLAW, except when prior, saved research is resumed. To access the WESTLAW Directory at any time, enter DB.

For information as to currentness and search tips regarding any WESTLAW database, enter the SCOPE command SC followed by the database identifier (e.g., SC CTA). It is not necessary to include the identifier to obtain scope information about the currently selected database.

WESTLAW Highlights

Use of this publication may be supplemented through the WESTLAW Bulletins (WLB and WSB-XX), the WESTLAW Supreme Court Bulletin (WLB-SCT), and various Topical Highlights Federal Practice & Procedure (WTH-FPP) Highlights. Highlights, including databases contain summaries of significant judicial, legislative and administrative developments and are updated daily; they are searchable both from an automatic list of recent documents and using general WESTLAW search methods for documents accumulated over time. The full text of any judicial decision may be retrieved by entering FIND.

Consult the WESTLAW Directory (enter DB) for a complete, current listing of other highlights databases.

Retrieving Cases Citing This Publication

To retrieve cases citing this publication, sign on to a case law database and enter a query, in the following form:

1 /s Rotunda /s 13.2

Retrieving a Specific Case

The FIND command can be used to quickly retrieve a case whose citation is known. For example:

FI 5 F.3d 1412

Updating Case Law Research

There are a variety of citator services on WESTLAW for use in updating research.

Insta-Cite® may be used to verify citations, find parallel citations, ascertain the history of a case, and see whether it remains valid law. References are also provided to secondary sources, such as Corpus Juris Secundum®, that cite the case. To view the Insta-Cite history of a displayed case, simply enter the command IC. To view the Insta-Cite history of a selected case, enter a command in this form:

IC 985 F.2d 1565

Shepard's® Citations provides a comprehensive list of cases and publications that have cited a particular case, with explanatory analysis to indicate how the citing cases have treated the case, e.g., "followed," "explained." To view the Shepard's Citations about a displayed case, enter the command SH. Add a case citation, if necessary, as in the prior Insta-Cite example.

For the latest citing references, not yet incorporated in Shepard's Citations, use Shepard's PreView® (SP command) and Quick-Cite™ (QC command), in the same way.

To see a complete list of publications covered by any of the citator services, enter its service abbreviation (IC, SH, SP or QC) followed by PUBS. To ascertain the scope of coverage for any of the services, enter the SCOPE command (SC) followed by the appropriate service abbreviation. For the complete list of commands available in a citator service, enter its service abbreviation (IC, SH, SP or QC) followed by CMDS.

Retrieving Statutes, Court Rules and Regulations

The United States Code and United States Code - Annotated are searchable databases on WESTLAW (identifiers USC and USCA, respectively), as are federal court rules (US-RULES) and regulations (CFR).

Annotated and/or unannotated versions of state statutes (XX-ST and XX-ST-ANN, respectively) and state court rules (XX-RULES) are also searchable on WESTLAW, as are the administrative codes of many states (XX-ADC).

In addition, the FIND command may be used to retrieve specific provisions by citation, obviating the need for database selection or search. To FIND a desired document, enter FI, followed by the citation of the desired document, using the full name of the publication, or one of the abbreviated styles recognized by WESTLAW.

If WESTLAW does not recognize the style you enter, you may enter one of the following, using US or any other state code in place of XX:

FI XX-ST	Displays templates for compiled statutes
FI XX-LEGIS	Displays templates for legislation
FI XX-RULES	Displays templates for rules
FI XX-ORDERS	Displays templates for court orders

Alternatively, entering FI followed by the publication's full name or an accepted abbreviation will normally display templates, useful jump possibilities, or helpful information necessary to complete the FIND process. For example:

FI USCA	Displays templates for United States Code - Annotated
FI FRAP	Displays templates for Federal Rules of Appellate Procedure
FI FRCP	Displays templates for Federal Rules of Civil Procedure
FI FRCRP	Displays templates for Federal Rules of Crimina Procedure
FI FRE	Displays templates for Federal Rules of Evidence
FI CFR	Displays templates for Code of Federal Regulations
FI FR	Displays templates for Federal Register

To view the complete list of FINDable documents and associated prescribed forms, enter FI PUBS.

Updating Research in re Statutes, Rules and Regulations

When viewing a statute, rule or regulation on WESTLAW after a search or FIND command, it is easy to update your research. A message will appear if relevant amendments, repeals or other new material are available through the UPDATE feature. Entering the UPDATE command will display such material.

Documents used to update federal statutes, rules, and regulations are searchable in the United States Public Laws (US-PL), Federal Orders (US-ORDERS) and Federal Register (FR) databases, respectively. For many states, similar material is contained in Legislative Service (XX-LEGIS), Court Orders (XX-ORDERS) and Administrative Register (XX-ADR) databases. Consult the WESTLAW Directory for availability in a specific state.

When documents citing a statute, rule or regulation are of interest, Shepard's Citations on WESTLAW may be of assistance. That service covers federal constitutional provisions, statutes and administrative provisions, and corresponding materials from many states. The command SH PUBS displays a directory of publications which may be Shepardized on WESTLAW. Consult the WESTLAW manual for more information about citator services.

Using WESTLAW as a Citator

For research beyond the coverage of any citator service, go directly to the databases (cases, for example) containing citing documents and use standard WESTLAW search techniques to retrieve documents citing specific constitutional provisions, statutes, standard jury instructions or other authorities.

Fortunately, the specific portion of a citation is often reasonably distinctive, such as 22:636.1, 301.65, 401(k), 12-21-5, 12052. When it is, a search on that specific portion alone may retrieve applicable documents without any substantial number of inapplicable ones (unless the number happens to be coincidentally popular in another context).

Similarly, if the citation involves more than one number, such as 42 U.S.C.A. § 1201, a search containing both numbers (e.g., 42 +5 1201) is likely to produce mostly desired information, even though the component numbers are common.

If necessary, the search may be limited in several ways:

A. Switch from a general database to one containing mostly cases within the subject area of the cite being researched;

B. Use a connector (&, /S, /P, etc.) to narrow the search to documents including terms which are highly likely to accompany the correct citation in the context of the issue being researched;

C. Include other citation information in the query. Because of the variety of citation formats used in documents, this option should be used primarily where other options prove insufficient. Below are illustrative queries for any database containing federal cases:

> amend! const.amend! /7 8 VIII Eighth

will retrieve cases citing the Eighth Amendment to the U.S. Constitution;

> Fed.R.Civ! F.R.Civ! F.R.C.P! R.Civ! Civil Civ.! /7 16

will retrieve cases citing Federal Civil Procedure Rule 16; and

> Bankruptcy Bankr.! /7 Rule Procedure Proc. Proc.Rule /7 1007

will retrieve cases citing Bankruptcy Procedure Rule 1007.

Alternative Retrieval Methods

WIN® (WESTLAW Is Natural™) allows you to frame your issue in plain English to retrieve documents:

> Challenging (striking removing) or exempting (excluding) minority (black hispanic asian jewish) juror based on intelligence or educational qualifications (graduate scholar).

Alternatively, retrieval may be focused by use of the Terms and Connectors method:

> DI(CHALLENG*** STRIK*** STRUCK REMOV! SELECT*** EXEMPT! EXCLUD! EXCLUSION /8 JUROR JURY /P EDUCATION GRADUAT*** SCHOLAR** INTELLIGEN** /P BLACK MINORITY ASIAN HISPANIC JEWISH)

In databases with Key Numbers, either of the above examples will identify Jury ⌖33(5.15) and ⌖42 as Key Numbers collecting headnotes relevant to this issue if there are pertinent cases.

Since the Key Numbers are affixed to points of law by trained specialists based on conceptual understanding of the case, relevant cases that were not retrieved by either of the language-dependent methods will often be found at a Key Number.

Similarly, citations in retrieved documents (to cases, statutes, rules, etc.) may suggest additional, fruitful research using other WESTLAW databases (e.g., annotated statutes, rules) or services (e.g., citator services).

Key Number Search

Frequently, case law research rapidly converges on a few topics, headings and Key Numbers within West's Key Number System that are likely to contain relevant cases. These may be discovered from known, relevant reported cases from any jurisdiction; Library References in West publications; browsing in a digest; or browsing the Key Number System on WESTLAW using the JUMP feature or the KEY command.

Once discovered, topics, subheadings or Key Numbers are useful as search terms (in databases containing reported cases) alone or with other search terms, to focus the search within a narrow range of potentially relevant material.

For example, to retrieve cases with at least one headnote classified to Jury ⌖42, sign on to a caselaw database and enter

230k42   [use with other search terms, if desired]

The topic name (Jury) is replaced by its numerical equivalent (230) and the ⌖ by the letter k. A list of topics and their numerical equivalents is in the WESTLAW Reference Manual and is displayed in WESTLAW when the KEY command is entered.

Other topics of special interest are listed below.

Arrest (35)	Intoxicating Liquors (223)
Bail (49)	Military Justice (258A)
Citizens (77)	Monopolies (265)
Civil Rights (78)	Municipal Corporations (268)
Commerce (83)	Officers and Public Employees (283)
Corporations (101)	Schools (345)
Counties (104)	Searches and Seizures (349)
Criminal Law (110)	States (360)
Elections (144)	Statutes (361)
Eminent Domain (148)	Taxation (371)
Exemptions (163)	Towns (381)
Habeas Corpus (197)	Witnesses (410)
Indictment and Information (210)	

Using JUMP

WESTLAW's JUMP feature allows you to move from one document to another or from one part of a document to another, then easily return to your original place, without losing your original result. Opportunities to move in this manner are marked in the text with a JUMP symbol (▶). Whenever you see the JUMP symbol, you may move to the place designated by the adjacent reference by using the Tab, arrow keys or mouse click to position the cursor on the JUMP symbol, then pressing Enter or clicking again with the mouse.

Within the text of a court opinion, JUMP arrows are adjacent to case cites and federal statute cites, and adjacent to parenthesized numbers marking discussions corresponding to headnotes.

On a screen containing the text of a headnote, the JUMP arrows allow movement to the corresponding discussion in the text of the opinion,

▶ (3)

and allow browsing West's Key Number System beginning at various heading levels:

▶ 230   JURY
▶ 230III   Qualifications of Jurors and Exemptions
▶ 230k42   k. Intelligence and educational qualifications.

To return from a JUMP, enter GB (except for JUMPs between a headnote and the corresponding discussion in opinion, for which there is a matching number in parenthesis in both headnote and opinion). Returns from successive JUMPs (e.g., from case to cited case to case cited by cited case) without intervening returns may be accomplished by repeated entry of GB or by using the MAP command.

General Information

The information provided above illustrates some of the ways WESTLAW can complement research using this publication. However, this brief overview illustrates only some of the power of WESTLAW. The full range of WESTLAW search techniques is available to support your research.

Please consult the WESTLAW Reference Manual for additional information or assistance or call West's Reference Attorneys at 1-800-REF-ATTY (1-800-733-2889).

For information about subscribing to WESTLAW, please call 1-800-328-0109.

*

SUMMARY OF CONTENTS

(Including New and Retitled Sections or Subsections)

Volume 1

Volume 2

Volume 3

II.   CLASSIFICATIONS BASED ON RACE OR NATIONAL ORIGIN

VII.   THE RIGHT TO PRIVACY

SUMMARY OF CONTENTS

TREATISE ON CONSTITUTIONAL LAW

Volume 4

SUBSTANCE AND PROCEDURE

Chapter 20

FREEDOM OF SPEECH

WESTLAW Electronic Research

See WESTLAW Electronic Research Guide preceding the Summary of Contents.

II. HISTORICAL BACKGROUND

§ 20.2 Introduction

Page 5, add to note 1:

1. See Chief Judge H. Franklin Waters, citing this Treatise in Knights of Ku Klux Klan v. Arkansas State Highway and Transportation Dept., 807 F.Supp. 1427, 1433 (W.D.Ark.1992); Coar, J., citing Treatise, in Makula v. Village of Schiller Park, 1995 WL 755305, *10 (N.D.Ill.1995).

III. SOME BASIC TESTS AND ATTITUDES

§ 20.7 Balancing versus Absolutism

(b) Is Free Speech an Absolute?

Page 24, add to note 15:

15. Robert Post, Meiklejohn's Mistake: Individual Autonomy and the Re- form of Public Discourse, 64 U. of Colo. L.Rev. 1109 (1993).

Page 25, add new footnote to the end of the first full sentence:

. . . of free speech problems.[17.5]

17.5 See Judge Coyne, citing the Treatise in State v. Casino Marketing Group, 491 N.W.2d 882, 887 (Minn. 1992), cert. denied sub. nom.; Hall v. Minnesota, 507 U.S. 1006, 113 S.Ct. 1648, 123 L.Ed.2d 269 (1993), cert. de- nied 507 U.S. 1006, 113 S.Ct. 1648, 123 L.Ed.2d 269 (1993).

1

§ 20.8   The Overbreadth Doctrine

Page 26, add to note 1:

1. Gerber, J., quoting Treatise in, State v. Jones, 177 Ariz. 94, 99, 865 P.2d 138, 143 (App.1993); In re Advisory From the Governor, 633 A.2d 664, 674 (R.I.1993), quoting Treatise; Jesson, C.J., citing Treatise, in McDougal v. State of Arkansas, 324 Ark. 354, 359, 922 S.W.2d 323, 326 (1996).

Page 26, add to note 2:

2. Fidel, P.J., quoting Treatise, in State v. Baldwin, 184 Ariz. 267, 269, 908 P.2d 483, 485 (App.1995).

Page 30, add to end of note 37:

37. See Chief Judge Haden, citing Treatise in West Virginia Pride, Inc. v. Wood County, West Virginia, 811 F.Supp. 1142, 1148 (S.D.W.Va.1993).

Page 33, add to note 54:

54. Ehrlich, J., citing Treatise, in State v. McLamb, ___ Ariz. ___, ___ P.2d ___, 1996 WL 523566 (App.1996).

See, Madsen v. Women's Health Center, Inc., 512 U.S. 753, ___, 114 S.Ct. 2516, 2530, 129 L.Ed.2d 593 (1994), on remand 644 So.2d 86 (Fla.1994). The Court held that the petitioners did not have standing to challenge a court order as vague and overbroad because it applied to those "acting in concert" with the parties named in the injunction. The injunction applied to conduct (interfering with an abortion clinic), not pure speech. Those people "acting in concert" with petitioners are not parties to this dispute. The petitioners have no standing to attack the portion of the order that does not apply to them. The Court also rejected the claim that the "in concert" prohibition interfered with the petitioners' freedom of association, because the injunction did not forbid the petitioners from associating with others and expressing their viewpoints. The injunction only banned them from acting in concert with others to deprive third parties of their lawful rights.

§ 20.9   The Void-for-Vagueness Doctrine

Page 36, add to note 1:

1. Ridgely, J., citing Treatise in, United Video Concepts, Inc. v. City of Dover, 1994 WL 682321, *3 (Del.Super.1994).

Page 36, add to text after note 2:

To the extent that a threat is greater and its prohibition or regulation cannot be expressed more concretely, the Court will tolerate comparatively more vagueness. For example, a statute forbidding reckless *walking* would be unconstitutional as too vague, while a statute forbidding reckless *driving* is not void for vagueness.

§ 20.11 Government Prescribed Speech, Government Subsidies for Speech, Unconstitutional Conditions, and Equal Protection Analysis

Page 41, add to note 2:

2. Martin H. Redish & Daryl I. Kessler, Government Subsidies and Free Expression, 80 Minn.L.Rev. 543 (1996);

Robert C. Post, Subsidized Speech, 106 Yale L.J. 151 (1996).

Page 44, add to note 10:

10. **Loyalty Oaths.** Note that *Barnette* was really based on the first amendment principle that the state may not compel *students* to recite the Pledge of Allegiance. *Barnette* did not preclude the state from starting the school day with the Pledge; it merely prohibited the state from requiring the students to recite or participate in the Pledge. *Barnette* does not preclude state loyalty oaths of state employees. Public school teachers are state employees, but public school children are not state employees. The constitutionality of loyalty oaths and other restrictions on state employ-

ees are judged by other standards. See §§ 20.42(a).

The Pledge of Allegiance Led by Public School Teachers. While the state may not require students to recite the pledge, the state may continue to start the school day with the pledge so long as no student is forced to participate. School teachers may constitutionally continue to lead the students in the Pledge. Sherman v. Community Consolidated School District, 980 F.2d 437 (7th Cir.1992), cert. denied, 508 U.S. 950, 113 S.Ct. 2439, 124 L.Ed.2d 658 (1993).

Page 52, add to note 34:

34. See generally, Dennis Baron, The English Only Question: An Official Language for Americans? (Yale U. Press, 1990); George A. Martinez, Legal Indeterminacy, Judicial Discretion and the Mexican–American Litigation Experience: 1930–1980, 27 U.C.Davis L.Rev. 555, 574–611 (1994)(discussing cases on bilingual education).

Comparison to France. France traditionally has asserted state power to protect the French language and keep it pure. In 1994 the French Parliament, for example, banned 3,500 "foreign" words, such as "cheeseburger," "chewing gum," and "bulldozer." The law pre-

vents not only schools and government agencies and officials but also advertisers and corporations from using these foreign words instead of a corresponding word from French. Thus, one should say "logiciels" instead of "software." The new French law is accompanied by various penalties, such as fines. AP Wire Service, "New French Law Guillotines English, Other Foreign Words," reprinted in, Champaign–Urbana News Gazette, July 2, 1994, at B6, col. 1–2. Cf. Leila Sadat Wexler, Official English, Nationalism and Linguistic Terror: A French Lesson, 71 Wash.L.Rev. 285 (1996).

IV. "CLEAR AND PRESENT DANGER" AND THE ADVOCACY OF VIOLENCE OR OTHER ILLEGAL CONDUCT

§ 20.12 Introduction

Page 52, add to note 1:

1. Cardine, J., citing Treatise in, McCone v. Wyoming, 866 P.2d 740, 745 (Wyo.1993); Borden, J., citing Treatise

in, Connecticut v. Indrisano, 228 Conn. 795, 833, 640 A.2d 986, 1005 (1994).

§ 20.13   The Holmes–Brandeis "Clear and Present Danger" Test

Page 53, add to note 1:

1. Cf. J. Gregory Sidak, War, Liberty, and Enemy Aliens, 67 N.Y.U.L.Rev. 1043 (1992).

V.   PRIOR RESTRAINT OF POLITICAL SPEECH

§ 20.16   The Distinction Between Prior Restraint and Subsequent Punishment of Speech

Page 73, add to note 34:

34. **Tort Claims Against the Media, Because of What They Broadcast.** See, Thomas G. Krattenmaker & L.A. Powe, Jr., Televised Violence: First Amendment Principles and Social Science Theory, 64 Va. L. Rev. 1123 (1978); Comment, View At Your Own Risk: Gang Movies and Spectator Violence, 12 Loyola Entertainment L.J. 477 (1992); Kevin W. Saunders, Media Violence and the Obscenity Exception to the First Amendment, 3 Wm. & Mary Bill of Rights J. 107 (1994).

Page 80, add new footnote 30.5 at end of last full sentence of the page:

"It should be generally noted ... constitutes a prior restraint." [30.5]

30.5 Daniel J., quoting Treatise, in Local Organizing Committee, Denver Chapter, Million Man March v. Cook, 922 F.Supp. 1494, 1497, 109 Ed. Law Rep. 223 (D.Colo.1996); Colins, President Judge, quoting Treatise, in Brighton Management Serv. v. City of Philadelphia Tax Review Board, 667 A.2d 757, 759 (Commonwealth Court 1995), *appeal denied*, 544 Pa. 685, 679 A.2d 230 (1996).

Page 82, add to text after note 38:

Distinguishing Injunctions That Are Prior Restraints From Those That Are Not. Obviously, if a court enjoins speech, there is a prior restraint of that speech. But what if the court issues an injunction that restricts conduct and that also has an incidental and limited effect, on speech? The Supreme Court briefly considered this issue in *Madsen v. Women's Health Center, Inc.*[38.10] The divided Court upheld portions of a Florida state court injunction involving an abortion clinic that was being subjected to protests and demonstrations that made it difficult for patients and staff to enter the clinic. Given the facts before it, the Court upheld an injunction that created a 36 foot buffer zone prohibiting picketing by demonstrators who objected to the clinic performing abortions; the purpose of this buffer zone was to allow access to the clinic. It invalidated various other portions of the injunction.

Madsen rejected the argument of the petitioners that the injunction amounted to a prior restraint. The injunction did not

4

prevent the petitioners "from expressing their messages in any one of several different ways; they are simply prohibited from expressing it within the 36–foot buffer zone. Moreover, the injunction was issued not because of the content of petitioners' expression, as was the case in *New York Times Co. [v. United States].* ... but because of their [petitioners'] prior unlawful conduct." [38.15] The buffer zone, which the Court called a "speech–free buffer zone," required that the petitioners move to the other side of the street and "away from the driveway of the clinic, where the state court found that they repeatedly had interfered with the free access of patients and staff." [38.20] Because the demonstrators could not protest in the 35 foot buffer zone, they were not there to speak within the limited zone. However, they were not enjoined from demonstrating and speaking outside of a limited zone. The Court thus declined to treat the injunction in *Madsen* as a prior restraint.

38.10　512 U.S. 753, 114 S.Ct. 2516, 129 L.Ed.2d 593 (1994), on remand 644 So.2d 86 (Fla.1994).

38.15　512 U.S. at __ n. 2, 114 S.Ct. at 2524 n. 2.

38.20　512 U.S. at __, 114 S.Ct. at 2526.

§ 20.17　From *Near* to the Pentagon Papers and Beyond

Page 82, add to note 2:

2. **Heavy Presumption Against Prior Restraint.** In the years both before and since *New York Times,* the Court has emphasized that "any prior restraint on expression comes to this Court with a 'heavy presumption' against its constitutional validity." Organization for a Better Austin v. Keefe, 402 U.S. 415, 419, 91 S.Ct. 1575, 1578, 29 L.Ed.2d 1 (1971), quoting, Carroll v. President and Commissioners of Princess Anne, 393 U.S. 175, 181, 89 S.Ct. 347, 351, 21 L.Ed.2d 325 (1968); Nebraska Press Association v. Stuart, 427 U.S. 539, 559, 96 S.Ct. 2791, 2802, 49 L.Ed.2d 683 (1976); CBS, Inc. v. Davis, 510 U.S. 1315, 114 S.Ct. 912, 127 L.Ed.2d 358 (1994) (Blackmun, J., in Chambers, staying preliminary injunction of a CBS broadcast of a videotape that allegedly was procured by trespass, and aiding and abetting a violation of the South Dakota's Trade Secrets Act).

Business Week Prior Restraint. In McGraw–Hill Companies, Inc. v. Procter & Gamble Co., __ U.S. __, 116 S.Ct. 6, 132 L.Ed.2d 892 (1995), Stevens, J., as a Circuit Justice, denied an application to stay a district court order that restrained a publisher from publishing an article containing any disclosure of any documents filed under seal, or the contents thereof without the prior consent of the district court. Subsequently, the Sixth Circuit reversed the trial court and rebuked the trial court, saying that the prior restraint was "patently invalid," and that it should never have been entered. Procter & Gamble Company v. Bankers Trust Company, 78 F.3d 219 (6th Cir.1996). See also, Milo Geyelin, "Business Week Wins Big Victory As Restraint Ruling Is Reversed," Wall St. Jrl., March 6, 1996, at B6, col. 4–5 (midwest ed.).

Page 88, add to note 32:

32. Over the years, Justice Blackmun appeared to have changed his views. In his chambers opinion in, Nebraska Press Association v. Stuart, 423 U.S. 1327, 1329, 96 S.Ct. 251, 254, 46 L.Ed.2d 237 (1975)(Blackmun, J., in chambers), he said, in words that echoed those of Justice Black "Where ... a direct prior restraint is imposed upon the reporting of news by the media, each

passing day may constitute a separate and cognizable infringement of the First Amendment." In CBS, Inc. v. Davis, 510 U.S. 1315, ___, 114 S.Ct. 912, 914, 127 L.Ed.2d 358 (1994), Blackmun, J., in Chambers, stayed a preliminary injunction of a CBS broadcast of a videotape that allegedly was procured by trespass, a breach of a duty of loyalty, and aiding and abetting a violation of the South Dakota's Trade Secrets Act. Relying on *New York Times,* he said: "Nor is the prior restraint doctrine inapplicable through the 'calculated misdeeds' of CBS." And, even if "significant economic harm" can justify a prior restraint, courts cannot rely on such speculative predictions.

VI. THE OTHER SIDE OF THE COIN FROM PRIOR RESTRAINT OF THE PRESS— ACCESS TO AND BY THE PRESS

§ 20.18 A Right of Access to the Press

(a) The Fairness Doctrine and the Regulation of the Broadcast Media

Page 91, add to note 1:

1. L.A. Powe, Jr., Mass Communications and the First Amendment: An Overview, 55 Law & Contemp.Problems 53 (1992). Jonathan Weinberg, Broadcasting and Speech, 81 Calif.L.Rev. 1101 (1993).

Page 106, add after first full paragraph:

Economic Regulations of Cable. In contrast, *FCC v. Beach Communications, Inc.*[76.05] the Court applied the rational basis test to a rule that it considered a mere economic regulation, even though it affected the cable television industry. When Congress regulated the cable television industry, it drew a distinction between facilities that serve separately owned and managed buildings versus those that serve one or more buildings under common ownership or management. The statute exempted from regulations those cable facilities that fell in the latter category, so long as they provided services without using the public rights-of-way. The District of Columbia Circuit had held that this distinction was irrational and thus violated the implied equal protection component of the Fifth Amendment. The Supreme Court, without dissent, reversed.

In this case, it is "plausible," said the Court, for Congress to assume that systems under common ownership would typically be limited in size or would share some other attribute such that regulations were not needed. A legislator could "rationally" assume that subscribers who can negotiate with one voice through a common owner or manager may have greater bargaining power relative to the cable operator and therefore less need for regulatory protection. Secondly, the statutory distinction may reflect a concern over the potential for effective monopoly power: the first operator of a satellite master antenna television system (SMATV) to gain a foothold by installing a dish on one building in a block of separately owned buildings would have significant cost advantages in competing for the remaining subscribers, because it could connect additional buildings for the cost of a length of cable while its competitors would have to recover the cost of their own satellite facilities.

Needless to say, because the Court considered the issues in this case to involve an area of economic regulation, the legislators need not articulate their reasons for enacting this statute. As economic regulation it is entirely irrelevant for constitutional purposes whether the legislature was actually motivated by the conceived reason for the challenged distinction. Thus the Court concluded that the exemption under the Cable Communications Policy Act for a system serving multiple unit dwellings under common ownership or management had a rational basis.

The "Must Carry Provisions" of Cable Regulation. In *Turner Broadcasting System, Inc. v. FCC*,[76.10] the Court continued its tentative exploration of the free speech rights of cable operators in light of the developing technology. In 1992, Congress enacted, over President Bush's veto, the Cable Television and Consumer Protection and Competition Act. Sections 4 and 5 required cable television systems to devote a portion of their channels to the transmission of local broadcast stations, in an effort, according to the sponsors of the legislation, to aid the competitive viability of broadcast television. In the view of the Court, the law regulated cable speech in two major ways: first, it reduced the number of channels over which the cable operators exercised unfettered control; and, second, it made it more difficult for cable programmers to compete for carriage on the limited number of channels remaining.

Cable operators sued, claiming that these "must–carry" provisions violated the first amendment. The three–judge district court, over dissent, granted summary judgment for the United States, but Justice Kennedy, for the Court, vacated that judgment and remanded for further proceedings.

First, the *Turner* Court ruled that it should not use the less rigorous standard of review reserved for broadcast regulation because the problems of scarcity of broadcast frequencies and signal interference does not apply in the context of cable; "soon there may be no practical limitation on the number of speakers who may use the cable medium." [76.15] Second, the Court would not apply strict scrutiny to the must–carry rules because they are content–neutral: the must–carry rules, on their face, impose burdens and confer benefits without reference to the content of speech. Although the rules burden cable by interfering with cable operator's editorial discretion by compelling them to offer to carry a certain minimum number of broadcast stations, the extent of the interference does not depend upon the content of the cable operators' programming. The number of channels that the cable operators must set aside depends on capacity, not the content of the program. The law favors broadcast television over cable operators regardless of the station's programming.

7

Justice Kennedy conceded that, unlike cable programming, "broadcast programming, is subject to certain limited content restraints imposed by statute and FCC regulations." [76.20] But, he rejected the argument that the preference for broadcast stations *automatically* entails content requirements." [76.25] In his view, the Congressional purpose was to ensure that broadcast television will retain a large enough potential audience to earn necessary advertising revenue, not to control content: "Congress' overriding objective in enacting must–carry was not to favor programming of a particular subject matter, viewpoint, or format, but rather to preserve access to free television programming for the 40 percent of Americans without cable." [76.30]

The Court then determined that it should use the intermediate level of scrutiny that applies to content–neutral restrictions that impose an incidental burden on speech. Government need not impose the least restrictive means of advancing its interests, but the regulation must promote "a substantial government interest that would be achieved less effectively absent the regulation." [76.35]

In a portion of Justice Kennedy's opinion that was a plurality opinion and not an opinion of the Court, Justice Kennedy emphasized that on remand the Government "must demonstrate that the recited harms are real, not merely conjectural, and that the regulation will in fact alleviate these harms in a direct and material way." [76.40] The Government must show, for example, that the economic health of local broadcasting is in genuine jeopardy and in need of the protection afforded by "must–carry." While Congress' predictive judgments are entitled to "substantial deference," they are not "insulated from meaningful review altogether." [76.45]

Justice O'Connor, joined by four members of the Court, filed an opinion concurring in part and dissenting in part. She was more protective of the free speech rights of the cable operators, concluding that the "must–carry" are content based and a violation of the first amendment.[76.50] Justice Ginsburg also filed an opinion concurring in part and dissenting in part, and concluding that the "must–carry" provisions are unconstitutional, "an unwarranted content–based preference" that "hypothesizes a risk to local stations that remains imaginary." [76.55]

Cable Television and the Regulation of Sexually Oriented Material. The fluidity of this area of the law is illustrated by *Denver Area Educational Telecommunications Consortium, Inc. v. FCC.*[76.60] In this case, the Court considered challenges to three sections of the 1992 Cable Act designed to regulate cable television broadcasting of "patently offensive" sex-related material. The very fragmented Court invalidated two provisions and upheld one provision. Justice Breyer announced the Judgment of the Court and delivered the Opinion of the Court with respect to Part III.[76.65]

8

First the Justices turned their attention to the regulation of *leased cable channels*. A leased cable channel is a channel that the relevant federal law required a cable system operator to reserve for commercial lease by unaffiliated third parties.

Section 10(b) of the law in question required cable system operators to segregate "patently offensive" sex-related material that appears on leased channels (but not on other channels) to a separate channel, to block that channel, to unblock that channel within 30 days of a subscriber's written request, and to re-block it within 30 days of a subscriber's written request. Justice Breyer, for the Court, invalidated this provision under the First Amendment. The delays of up to 30 days would require subscribers to engage in significant advanced planning, and the writing would adversely affect viewers who would fear for their reputations if the list were inadvertently made public. Other viewers might want to watch only a few of the programs on the patently offensive channel. These restrictions were not the "least restrictive alternative" nor "narrowly tailored" to protect children. Congress used less restrictive means to deal with non-leased cable channels, and the record offered no explanation for the difference in treatment. For example, the Court wondered why blocking alone—without written access-requests—adequately protected children from exposure to regular sex-dedicated channels, but could not adequately protect those same children from programming on similarly sex-dedicated channels that are leased.

Section 10(a) of the law permitted (but did not require) cable system operators to prohibit "patently offensive" or "indecent" programming transmitted over leased channels. Between 1984 and 1992, other law prohibited cable system operators from exercising editorial control. Breyer (joined only by Stevens, O'Connor, and Souter) upheld this provision, in a ruling that was self-described as narrow. This industry is dynamic, and the Court, Breyer argued, should not impose "a rigid single standard, good now and for all future media and purposes," which may "straightjacket" the Government's ability to respond to serious problems.

Section 10(c) permitted a cable operator to prevent transmission of "patently offensive" programming on public access channels. The law defined a *public access channel* as channel capacity that cable operators agreed to reserve for public, governmental, and educational access as part of the consideration that municipalities obtained in exchange for awarding a cable franchise. Breyer (joined only by Stevens and Souter) ruled that this section, unlike section 10(a), is unconstitutional. Breyer argued that cable operators did not historically exercise editorial control over these channels, and therefore section 10(c), unlike section 10(a), "does not restore to cable operators editorial rights that they once had, and the counter-vailing First Amendment interest is nonexistent, or at least diminished." In addition, Breyer argued that section 10(c) was less necessary to protect children because public access channels "are normally subject to complex supervisory systems of various sorts, often with both public and private elements." The municipality itself, or a nonprofit body, may be the access channel manager.

Justice Kennedy, joined by Justice Ginsburg, agreed with the opinion of the Court invalidating section 10(b), but they would invalidate the other two sections as well. Sections 10(a) and (c), Kennedy pointed out, disadvantaged nonobscene, indecent programming, which is a protected category of expression. Sections 10(a) and (c) apply to access channels, each of which is a "designated public forum," which the government has opened for expressive activity by the public. Kennedy frankly criticized the plurality's narrow focus and its "evasion of any clear legal standard in deciding this case." [76.70] He argued that, at a minimum, the proper standard for reviewing the law is strict scrutiny. He elaborated:

> The plurality opinion, insofar as it upholds § 10(a) of the 1992 Cable Act, is adrift. When confronted with a threat to free speech in the context of an emerging technology, we ought to have the discipline to analyze the case by reference to existing elaborations of constant First Amendment principles. This is the essence of the case-by-case approach to ensuring protection of speech under the First Amendment, even in novel settings. Rather than undertake this task, however, the plurality just declares that, all things considered, § 10(a) seems fine. I think the implications of our past cases for this one are clearer than the plurality suggests, and they require us to hold § 10(a) invalid.[76.75]

Justice Thomas, joined by Chief Justice Rehnquist and Justice Scalia, concurred in the judgment in part and dissented in part. Thomas would uphold all three sections, based on *Turner Broadcasting System v. FCC*. While the Justices in *Turner* disagreed whether the "must-carry" rules were content-based, "there was agreement that cable operators are generally entitled to much the same First Amendment protection as the print media." [76.80] Like a free-lance writer seeking a paper in which to publish newspaper editorials, a television programmer is protected in searching for an outlet to publish cable programming, but the programmer has no free-standing First Amendment right to have that programming transmitted.[76.85] While viewers have a general right to see what a willing operator transmits, they have no right to force an unwilling operator to speak, any more than a print author can force a bookstore to carry his or her books.

By recognizing the general primacy of the cable operator's editorial rights over the rights of programmers and viewers, *Turner* raises serious questions about the merits of petitioners' claims. None of the petitioners in these cases are cable operators; they are all cable viewers or access programmers or their representative organizations. It is not intuitively obvious that the First Amendment protects the interests petitioners assert, and neither petitioners nor the plurality have adequately explained the source or justification of those asserted rights.[76.90]

76.05 508 U.S. 307, 113 S.Ct. 2096, 124 L.Ed.2d 211 (1993). Thomas, J., wrote the opinion for the Court. There were no dissents, but Stevens, J., did file an opinion concurring in the judgment.

76.10 512 U.S. 622, 114 S.Ct. 2445, 129 L.Ed.2d 497 (1994).

76.15 512 U.S. at ___, 114 S.Ct. at 2457. Contrast Hurley v. Irish–American Gay Lesbian and Bisexual Group of Boston, ___ U.S. ___, 115 S.Ct. 2338, 132 L.Ed.2d 487 (1995). In *Turner,* the Court treated cable television as a conduit for broadcast signals. There was little risk that the cable viewers would assume that the broadcast stations carried on a cable system convey ideas or messages that the cable operator necessarily endorsed. In contrast, people do not assume that parades and demonstrations are neutrally presented by the organizers of the parade or demonstration. Thus, in *Hurley* the Court ruled, unanimously, that a state may not constitutionally require private individuals who organize a parade to include among the marchers a group imparting a message that the parade organizers do not wish to convey. In this particular case, the group advocated gay rights and gay solidarity.

76.20 512 U.S. at ___, 114 S.Ct. at 2462 (footnote 7 omitted, giving examples, such as the requirement that broadcasters serve "educational and informational needs of children;" offer reasonable access to candidates for federal elective office; restrict "indecent programming;" and air programs that serve "the public interest, convenience or necessity").

76.25 512 U.S. at ___, 114 S.Ct. at 2462 (emphasis in original).

76.30 512 U.S. at ___, 114 S.Ct. at 2461.

76.35 512 U.S. at ___, 114 S.Ct. at 2469.

76.40 512 U.S. at ___, 114 S.Ct. at 2470 (plurality opinion).

76.45 512 at ___, 114 S.Ct. at 2471 (plurality opinion).

76.50 512 U.S. at ___, 114 S.Ct. at 2479 (O'Connor, J., concurring in part and dissenting in part, and joined, as to this part of her opinion, by Scalia, Ginsburg, & Thomas, JJ.).

76.55 512 U.S. at ___, 114 S.Ct. at 2481 (Ginsburg, J., concurring in part and dissenting in part).

76.60 ___ U.S. ___, 116 S.Ct. 2374, 135 L.Ed.2d 888 (1996).

76.65 Justices Stevens, O'Connor, Kennedy, Souter, & Ginsburg joined the Opinion of the Court. Breyer also delivered an Opinion with respect to Parts I, II, & V (which Stevens, O'Connor & Souter, JJ., joined), and an Opinion with respect to Parts IV & VI (which Stevens & Souter, JJ., joined). Stevens, J., and Souter, J., filed concurring opinions. O'Connor, J., filed an Opinion concurring in part and dissenting in part. Kennedy, J., filed an Opinion concurring in part, concurring in the judgment in part, & dissenting in part (which Ginsburg, J., joined). Thomas, J., filed an Opinion concurring in the judgment in part & dissenting in part (which Rehnquist, C.J., & Scalia, J., joined).

76.70 ___ U.S. at ___, 116 S.Ct. at 2405.

76.75 ___ U.S. at ___, 116 S.Ct. at 2404.

76.80 ___ U.S. at ___, 116 S.Ct. at 2420.

76.85 Justice Thomas would give to the cable operators the same free speech rights that the First Amendment gives to operators of newspapers. See, Miami Herald Publishing Co. v. Tornillo, 418 U.S. 241, 94 S.Ct. 2831, 41 L.Ed.2d 730, on remand, 303 So.2d 21 (Fla.1974).

76.90 ___ U.S. at ___, 116 S.Ct. at 2421–22.

(b) The Fairness Doctrine and the Regulation of Traditional Print Media

Page 107, add to note 82:

82. Lucas A. Powe, Jr., The Fourth Estate and the Constitution: Freedom of the Press in America (1991); Lee C. Bollinger, Images of a Free Press (1991); Gerald N. Rosenberg, The Hollow Hope:

Can Courts Bring About Social Change? (1991); L.A. Powe, Jr., The Supreme Court, Social Change, and Legal Scholarship, 44 Stan.L.Rev. 1615 (1992).

§ 20.19   A Right of Access by the Press—Speech in a Restricted Environment

Page 112, add to note 1:

1. Roth, J., citing Treatise in United States v. Antar, 38 F.3d 1348, 1360, Fed.Sec.L.Rep. ¶ 98,436, 40 Fed.R.Evid. Serv. 1006, 22 Media L.Rep. 2417 (3d Cir.1994).

Page 113, add to note 2:

2. Fisher, J., citing Treatise in, Mid–America Mailers, Inc. v. State Board of Tax Commissioners, 639 N.E.2d 380 (Ind.Tax 1994).

Page 117, replace last sentence of this page with the following:

However, the seven justices did agree that the press has no greater right of access to prisons than the public generally. The Court, once again, rejected the notion that the institutional press has greater first amendment rights than the public generally.

Page 119, add new note 33.10 to end of third full paragraph:

33.10 **Gulf War.** During the War in the Persian Gulf, in 1991, some journalists unsuccessfully challenged the Pentagon restrictions on journalists, such as the limitations on access to combat zones and the so-called security review by the military of all reports. See, The Nation Magazine v. The United States Department of Defense, 762 F.Supp. 1558 (S.D.N.Y.1991), holding that: (1) plaintiffs had standing to raise First and Fifth Amendment claims; (2) the political question doctrine did not bar claims; (3) for purposes of mootness challenge, the claims were generally capable of repetition yet evading review but the claims requesting injunctive relief were moot and the court would decline to grant application for declaratory relief on right of access and equal access claims. The television networks and the major newspapers did not join in these suits, which were filed by a number of writers and smaller publications, such as The Nation, and the Village Voice. Garry Sturgess, Media Powers Oppose War Rules But Shun Suit, Legal Times of Washington, D.C., Feb. 4, 1991, at 2.

VII.   OTHER REGULATIONS OF THE PRESS— ANTITRUST, LABOR RELATIONS, AND TAXATION

§ 20.20   The Antitrust Laws

Page 120, add to note 1:

1. Roth, J., citing Treatise in United States v. Antar, 38 F.3d 1348, 1360, Fed.Sec.L.Rep. ¶ 98,436, 40 Fed.R.Evid. Serv. 1006, 22 Media L.Rep. 2417 (3d Cir.1994).

§ 20.22   Tax Laws

Page 125, add after first full paragraph:

The "Son of Sam" Law. *Simon & Schuster, Inc. v. Members of the New York State Crime Victims Board*,[14.5] relied on *Leathers* to invalidate New York's "Son of Sam" statute, so-called because it was enacted in response to a criminal who called himself the "Son of Sam." This law required that an accused or "convicted" criminal's income derived from works describing his crime be deposited in an escrow account; these funds were then made available to victims of the crime and the criminal's creditors. The statute treated as "convicted" any person who admitted to a crime, even if that person had not been prosecuted.

The law did not place a tax on the publications describing the crime, but the result of the law was the functional economic equivalent of a tax. The law imposed a financial disincentive to create or publish works with a particular content. Justice O'Connor, for the Court, ruled that the law singled out and placed a financial burden on speech on a particular subject. The statute was overbroad and regulated speech based on content.

A statute that imposes a financial burden on speakers because of the content of their speech is "presumptively inconsistent with the First Amendment.... " In order for the state to justify such differential treatment, the regulation must be "necessary to serve a compelling state interest and [be] narrowly drawn to achieve that end." [14.10]

The state has a compelling interest to insure that criminals do not profit from their crimes and in compensating victims by using the fruits of the criminal's crime; however, the statute is not narrowly tailored to achieve that objective. The law singled out certain speech as disfavored.[14.15] The law is "significantly overinclusive" because it applies to works on any subject, provided that the author expresses thoughts or recollections about a crime, however tangentially. The law, as written, would even apply to the *Confessions of Saint Augustine,* where Saint Augustine, the author, deplores his "past foulness," including his theft of pears from a neighbor's vineyard. Similarly, it would cover *The Autobiography of Malcolm X,* which described crimes committed before Malcolm X became a public figure.

The Court explicitly did not comment on the statutes of other jurisdictions designed to serve similar purposes. If these laws are narrowly tailored, then *Simon & Schuster* does not purport to preclude their application.

In reaction to the *Son of Sam* decision, prosecutors have written large fines into plea bargains, in an effort to prevent criminal defendants from profiting from their crimes. Judges have also imposed large fines, even on paupers, to make sure that if they sell their story to the media, they still would not be able to walk away with a net profit, after having paid the fine.[14.20]

14.5 502 U.S. 105, 112 S.Ct. 501, 116 L.Ed.2d 476 (1991).

See generally, Note, Simon & Schuster, Inc. v. Fishetti: Can New York's Son of Sam Law Survive First Amendment Challenge?, 66 Notre Dame L.Rev. 1075 (1991).

Blackmun, J. and Kennedy, J., each filed separate opinions concurring in the judgment. Kennedy argued that it is "both unnecessary and incorrect to ask whether the State can show that the statute 'is necessary to serve a compelling state interest and is narrowly drawn to achieve that end.' "The Court should only consider the "straightforward question whether the State may enact a burdensome restriction of speech based on content only, apart from any consider-

ations of time, place, and manner or the use of the public forum."

14.10 502 U.S. at 117, 112 S.Ct. at 509.

14.15 As Cohen v. Cowles Media Co., 501 U.S. 663, 668, 111 S.Ct. 2513, 2518, 115 L.Ed.2d 586 (1991), on remand 479 N.W.2d 387 (Minn.1992) remanded on rehearing 481 N.W.2d 840 (1992), acknowledged: "enforcement of . . . general laws against the press is not subject to stricter scrutiny than would be applied against other persons or organizations."

14.20 Junda Woo, Big Fines Are Replacing Son of Sam Laws, Wall Street Journal, April 26, 1994, at B1, col. 3–5 (midwest ed.).

VIII.   THE PRESS AND THE CRIMINAL JUSTICE SYSTEM

§ 20.25   Judicial Protective Orders and the Press

Page 143, add to end of note 39, on the "Noriega Tapes":

39. Noriega Tapes. CNN never paid the fine that the district court had imposed for broadcasting taped phone conversations of Noriega. The district court, after it found CNN guilty of criminal contempt, gave CNN the choice of (1) paying a large, but unspecified, fine, or (2) apologizing on the air for broadcasting the tapes and only paying the

costs of prosecution. CNN took the second choice and said, on the air, that "on further consideration, CNN realizes it was in error in defying the order of the court and publishing the Noriega tapes while appealing the court's order." See, "CNN Issues Apology Over Tapes of Noriega," Wall Street Journal, Dec. 20, 1994, at B7, col. 2 (midwest ed.).

Page 146, add to text after note 51:

Attorney Discipline Cases. The attorney discipline cases enforcing the requirement that lawyers not engage in extrajudicial statements that raise a "substantial likelihood of material prejudice" are rare. As the Chief Counsel of the first judicial department of New York has explained, in addition to the first amendment problems, the typical discipline office—both underfunded and understaffed—has more than enough to do investigating charges of theft of client funds.[51.10] When disciplinary counsel prosecute publicity cases anyway, that exercise of prosecutorial discretion may (as in the *Gentile* case) be suspect.

Many lower courts (reflecting the concerns that Justice Kennedy expressed in *Gentile*)have been reluctant to find that there is a "substantial likelihood" of prejudice. Thus, in the decision, *In the*

Matter of Sullivan,[51.15] the state court refused to find that the lawyer subject to discipline knew or should have known that his extrajudicial statements would have a substantial likelihood of materially prejudicing the trial, even though, in that particular case, the defense lawyer participated in a television interview where he discussed the testimony of various people who had not testified at trial. One of the people whose "testimony" was discussed was the defendant, who had not taken the stand. Another was an expert witness whom the judge had excluded. The jury was not sequestered and the local television station broadcast and rebroadcast this interview many times.

The "Public Record" Exception and the Safe Harbor of ABA Model Rule 3.6. In *Gentile,* discussed above, Nevada's Rule 177(3) contained what is often called a "safe harbor." This subsection lists statements that can be made "notwithstanding" the previous prohibitions. This safe harbor is derived from ABA Model Rule 3.6(c), of ABA Model Rules of Professional Conduct.[51.20] Subsection 2 of this rule provides that attorneys may reveal "the information contained in a public record."

As a constitutional matter, it is difficult to justify a prohibition against an attorney or the press revealing what is already in a public record. However, this exception—an inherent byproduct of the first amendment—has provided an important exception that is big enough to drive a tractor trailer through. This exception exists because of the tendency of prosecutors and defense counsel to tell a story when they file pleadings. An indictment, for example, need not be limited to the bare bones. The prosecutor may describe the alleged crime in detail, may refer to unindicted alleged co-conspirators and what they may have said or done, and so forth. One defendant claimed that "he had never known that his nickname was 'The Snake' until he saw it stated as an alias in an indictment—and then heard the prosecutor repeatedly calling him that on television." [51.25] It should not be too controversial to suggest that "the Snake" has pejorative connotations.

Defense counsel, as well, can file pleadings (such as bail motions or other pretrial motions) that tell a detailed story and make detailed allegations that then become part of the public record.

51.10 Quoted in, Monroe Freedman, Muzzling Trial Publicity: New Rule Needed, Legal Times (of Washington, D.C.) April 5, 1993.

51.15 185 A.D.2d 440, 586 N.Y.S.2d 322 (3d Dept.1992). See also, Monroe Freedman, Muzzling Trial Publicity: New Rule Needed, Legal Times (of Washington, D.C.) April 5, 1993, discussing this case. See also Ronald D. Rotun-da, Can You Say That?, 30 Trial Magazine 18 (Dec. 1994).

51.20 (ABA, 1983, as amended), reprinted in, Thomas D. Morgan & Ronald D. Rotunda, 1993 Selected Standards on Professional Responsibility (1993), at 3, 70.

51.25 See, Monroe Freedman, Muzzling Trial Publicity: New Rule Needed, Legal Times (of Washington, D.C.) April 5, 1993.

Page 151, add to end of note 76:

76. El Vocero de Puerto Rico (Caribbean International News Corp.) v. Puerto Rico, 508 U.S. 147, 113 S.Ct. 2004, 124 L.Ed.2d 60 (1993) (per curiam). In a brief *per curiam* opinion, the Court, without dissent, reversed the Puerto Rico's Superior Court and its Supreme Court and then held that Puerto Rico's requirement of a private preliminary hearing (similar to the private hearing involved in *Press–Enterprise II*)violates the First Amendment. The concern that publicity will prejudice the accused's right to a fair trial is valid, but it is a concern that courts must address on a case-by-case basis, not on the basis of a general requirement of a private hearing. The U.S. Supreme Court also rejected the Puerto Rico Supreme Court's argument that Puerto Rican tradition and experience justified a closed hearing: one should not look to the experience or practice of any particular jurisdiction but to the experience of the type or kind of hearing throughout the United States; the "established and widespread tradition of open preliminary hearings among the States was canvassed in *Press–Enterprise* and is controlling here."

IX. REGULATION OF COMMERCIAL SPEECH

§ 20.29   What Is "Commercial" Speech?

Page 160, add to text after note 8:

Speech That Proposes a Commercial Transaction. The Courts have, at times, said that speech is commercial if it does no more than propose a commercial transaction.[9] On one level, this definition seems simple enough. A newspaper editorial would not be commercial speech, but an advertisement urging consumers to buy the New York Times would be commercial speech because it is urging the recipient of the message to buy a product.

However, if we accept this definition, we must realize that it logically could exclude a great deal of modern day advertising. For example, many typical advertisements do not urge anyone to buy something at a particular price. An advertisement might simply show a celebrity stating: "Pepsi Cola; It's the right one, baby. Uh huh!" Or, "When you drive a Lexus, people will know that you have really arrived." Such advertisements simply make statements that are difficult or impossible to verify. They do not advertise a sale, or directly urge any specific action. Rather, they serve to create a mood, just like some political advertisements try to create a mood.

And, along the same lines, some political advertisements share some of the attributes of commercial speech. The same agencies that create advertisements to sell soft drinks or soap also hire themselves out to politicians. And some political advertisements say something very close to: "Vote for me, and I'll lower your taxes," or, "Vote for me and I'll raise the taxes on the other fellow, not on you."

9. E.g., Central Hudson Gas & Electric Corporation v. Public Service Commission, 447 U.S. 557, 566, 100 S.Ct. 2343, 2351, 65 L.Ed.2d 341 (1980).

§ 20.31   The Modern Commercial Speech Doctrine

Page 163, add to note 1:

1. Daniel A. Farber, Free Speech without Romance: Public Choice and the First Amendment, 105 Harv.L.Rev. 554 (1991); Rodney A. Smolla, Information, Imagery, and the First Amendment: A Case for Expansive Protection of Commercial Speech, 71 Tex.L.Rev. 777 (1993); Ronald K.L. Collins & David M. Skover, Commerce & Communication, 71 Tex.L.Rev. 697 (1993); Alex Kozinski & Stuart Banner, The Anti–History and Pre–History of Commercial Speech, 71 Tex.L.Rev. 747 (1993); Martin H. Redish, Tobacco Advertising and the First Amendment, 81 Iowa L. Rev. 589 (1996) . .

Page 169, Replace Bold Heading at Bottom of Page with the Following:

Truthful Advertising of Harmful Substances, Such as Cigarettes.

Page 173, add to end of page, in lieu of last sentence:

In a later case, the Court made clear that whatever this statement means—the greater power includes the lesser—it is inapplicable outside of the commercial speech context.[41]

A few years later the Court went further and specifically rejected the "greater includes the lesser" argument even in the commercial speech context, and even when the Government is regulating the advertising of harmful (but lawful) products. In *Rubin v. Coors Brewing Co.*[41.10] the Court (with no dissent) invalidated, under the First Amendment, a law that prohibited beer labels from displaying alcohol content. The Government argued that the labeling ban was necessary to suppress "strength wars," whereby brewers would brag, in their advertisements, about the alcohol content of their beers. In a footnote that may overshadow the rest of the opinion,[41.15] the Court acknowledged *Posadas,* found that the "greater includes lesser" argument to be mere dictum, and then specifically rejected the Government's claim that "legislatures have broader latitude to regulate speech that promotes socially harmful activities, such as alcohol consumption than they have to regulate other types of speech." [41.20]

41. Meyer v. Grant, 486 U.S. 414, 424–25, 108 S.Ct. 1886, 1893–94, 100 L.Ed.2d 425 (1988).

41.10 517 U.S. ___, 115 S.Ct. 1585, 131 L.Ed.2d 532 (1995).

41.15 David O. Stewart, Supreme Court Continues To Struggle with Commercial Speech Doctrine, ABA Journal, Sept. 1995, at 40.

41.20 517 U.S. at ___ n. 2, 115 S.Ct. at 1589–90, n. 2.

Page 175, add to text after third full paragraph:

Radio and Television Broadcasts of Lottery Results. *United States v. Edge Broadcasting Co.*[54.5] upheld the constitutionality of Federal statutes that prohibit the broadcast of lottery advertising by a broadcaster licensed in a state that does not allow

17

lotteries; however, the federal statutes allowed such broadcasting by a broadcaster licensed in a state that sponsors a lottery, even if that signal reached into a state where lotteries were illegal. Reversing both the federal trial and appellate courts, a divided Supreme Court held that, as applied to respondent, these statutes do not violate the First Amendment.

Edge Broadcasting is a radio station licensed in North Carolina, which has no state-sponsored lottery. Indeed, participating or advertising any nonexempt raffle or lottery is a crime in that state. However, over 90% of Edge Broadcasting's listeners live in Virginia, which does sponsor a lottery. The Edge radio station, on the border between the two states, wanted to broadcast Virginia lottery advertisements.

Justice White, for the Court, specifically did not consider the Government's argument that *Central Hudson* was inapplicable on the theory that the "greater power" to prohibit "vices" such as gambling "necessarily includes the lesser power" to ban advertisements about them.[54.10] Instead the Court applied the four-part test of *Central Hudson,* and upheld the law.

First, the majority assumed, like the courts below, that Edge, if permitted, would broadcast nonmisleading information about the Virginia lottery, a legal activity. Second, the Court was "quite sure" that the federal government has a substantial interest in supporting the policies of nonlottery states while also not interfering with the policies of lottery states. The third and fourth factors under *Central Hudson* basically require the court to consider the fit between the legislature's ends and the means chosen to accomplish those ends. In this case, the majority said that "[w]e have no doubt that the statutes directly advanced the governmental interest at stake in this case." Indeed, the majority announced, without elaboration, that Congress "might have continued to ban all radio or television lottery advertisements, even by stations in States that have legalized lotteries." The congressional desire to balance the interests of the antigambling policy of states like North Carolina, while not unduly interfering with the lotteries sponsored by states like Virginia, is the substantial governmental interest that satisfies *Central Hudson,* and is also the interest directly served by applying the statutory restriction to all stations in North Carolina, even if, as applied to respondent, "there were only marginal advancement of that interest."

Applying the fourth prong of *Central Hudson,* the majority concluded that the regulations at issue were not more extensive than necessary to serve the governmental interest because, as in *Posasdas,* the fit, while "not necessarily perfect," was "reasonable." If the respondent's broadcast signals reached a portion of the North Carolina audience, then "this would be in derogation of the substantial federal interest in supporting North Carolina's laws making lotteries illegal."

The majority also concluded that the lower courts were in error in concluding that the statutory restrictions, as applied to the respondent, were ineffectual in that 11% of Edge Broadcasting's audience (the North Carolina residents) also listened to Virginia radio and television advertisements and read Virginia newspapers, all of which carried the lottery advertisements: "Even if all of the residents of Edge's North Carolina service area listened to lottery advertisements from Virginia stations, it would still be true that 11% of radio listening time in that area would be free of such material." [54.15]

Liquor Advertisements. In *Rubin v. Coors Brewing Co.*[54.20] the Court invalidated a federal law that prohibited beer labels from displaying alcohol content. (This labeling law provided that it was inapplicable if state law required disclosure of alcohol content.) The trial court, the Tenth Circuit, and the Supreme Court (without dissent) all invalidated that ban under the First Amendment. Justice Thomas, for the Court found that the commercial speech concerns a lawful activity and is not misleading. Next, the Government argued that the federal labeling law served a substantial interest—it supported state laws that banned display of alcohol content. The Court rejected that argument as well, because there was no evidence that states were in need of federal assistance. "Unlike the situation in *Edge Broadcasting,* the policies of some States do not prevent neighboring States from pursuing their own alcohol related policies within their respective borders." States could directly ban disclosure of alcohol content, "subject, of course, to the same First Amendment restrictions that apply to the Federal Government." [54.25]

The Court did agree that the Government has a substantial interest in the health, safety, and welfare of citizens by preventing "strength wars," among brewers competing based on the potency of their beers. However, the federal law did not "directly and materially advance" that interest because of its "overall irrationality." For example, the federal law allows disclosure of alcohol content on the labels of wine and hard liquor, and even compels disclosure for wines of more than 14% alcohol. The law also allows brewers to signal high alcohol content by using the term "malt liquor." The Government's labeling ban also is not sufficiently tailored to its goal. Instead of the restriction on speech, the Government, e.g., could directly limit the alcohol content of beer. Even a ban on marketing efforts emphasizing high alcohol strength (assuming that is constitutional) would be less intrusive of free speech rights.

In *44 Liquormart, Inc. v. Rhode Island,*[54.30] the Court invalidated a state law banning advertisements of accurate information about retail liquor prices except at the point of sale. The Court was fragmented as to its reasoning, but no Justice dissented. Part of Justice Stevens' opinion was the opinion of the Court and part was a plurality opinion. Stevens (joined by Kennedy, Souter & Ginsburg) recognized that bans on "truthful, nonmisleading commercial messages rarely protect consumers" from deception or overreaching, but often serve only to obscure an "underlying governmental policy" that could be implemented without regulating speech. For example, in this case, the state could have promoted temperance by imposing higher taxes on liquor or by instituting educational campaigns to promote temperance. Under either alternative, there would have been no need to restrict any speech. Stevens cautioned: "The First Amendment directs us to be especially skeptical of regulations that seek to keep people in the dark for what the government perceives to be their own good." [54.35]

Justice Thomas, concurring in the judgment and in parts of the Opinion of the Court, warned that when "the government's asserted interest is to keep legal users of a product or service ignorant in order to manipulate their choices in the marketplace, the balancing test" of *Central Hudson Gas* should not be applied. That asserted interest is "*per se* illegitimate" and should not be able to justify regulation of commercial speech any more than it can justify regulation of noncommercial speech.[54.40]

For example, if the Government had been able to show that restrictions on advertising of liquor actually did reduce consumption significantly, that showing should not justify the ban. The theory that restrictions on advertising are permissible if they are effective in manipulating people is contrary to the central principle justifying *Virginia Pharmacy Board*—that all attempts to machinate consumers and dissuade them from making legal choice by keeping them in the dark are impermissible under the First Amendment. If the Government admits that the purpose of its prohibition of truthful speech is to keep the public in the dark about the truth, the admission should spell the death knell for the policy, not justify it.

54.5 509 U.S. 418, 113 S.Ct. 2696, 125 L.Ed.2d 345 (1993), on remand 5 F.3d 63 (4th Cir.1993).

Cf. Martin H. Redish, Tobacco Advertising and the First Amendment, 81 Iowa L. Rev. 589 (1996) for a thoughtful analysis of these issues.

54.10 509 U.S. at 426, 113 S.Ct. at 2703.

54.15 509 U.S. at 432, 113 S.Ct. at 2706.

In a portion of the opinion, Part III-D, that was not the opinion of the Court, Justice White also said: "Nor need we be blind to the practical effect of adopting respondent's view of the level of particu-larity of analysis appropriate to decide its case. [T]he piecemeal approach it advocates would act to vitiate the Government's ability generally to accommodate States with differing policies." 509 U.S. at 435, 113 S.Ct. at 2708. See, Part III-D, where White, J. was joined by Rehnquist, C.J. & Scalia & Thomas, JJ.

Stevens, J., joined by Blackmun, J., dissented, arguing that the fit between the government's ends and means was not good. The means were not in proportion to the proposed end of protecting the antilottery policies of nonlottery states. "Even assuming that nonlottery States desire such assistance from the Federal Government—an assumption

that must be made without any supporting evidence—I would hold that suppressing truthful advertising regarding a
neighboring State's lottery, an activity
which is, of course, perfectly legal, is a
patently unconstitutional means of ef-
fectuating the Government's asserted
interest in protecting the policies of nonlottery States. Indeed, I had thought
that we had so held almost two decades
ago [in] Bigelow v. Virginia," 509 U.S.
at 437, 113 S.Ct. at 2709.

54.20 ___ U.S. ___, 115 S.Ct. 1585,
131 L.Ed.2d 532 (1995). Stevens, J., concurring in the judgment, argued that the
statute's unconstitutionality is "more
patent than the Court's opinion indicates." The Government should not be
able to suppress truthful speech merely
because it happens to appear on the
label of a product for sale. Brewers
should be able to tell their customers
that their beverages "are stronger—or
weaker—than competing products." The
Government could impose some regulations that "increase consumer aware-
ness," but the law in this case "is nothing more than an attempt to blindfold
the public. 517 U.S. at ___, 115 S.Ct. at
1595 (Stevens, J., concurring in the
judgment).

54.25 ___ U.S. at ___, 115 S.Ct. at
1591.

54.30 ___ U.S. ___, 116 S.Ct. 1495,
134 L.Ed.2d 711 (1996).

54.35 ___ U.S. at ___, 116 S.Ct. at
1508.

**The Application of the Twenty-
First Amendment.** Part VII of the Stevens Opinion in 44 Liquormart (which
was an Opinion of the Court) rejected
any notion that the Twenty–First
Amendment affects the reach of the
First Amendment. ___ U.S. at ___, 116
S.Ct. at 1514. The Court specifically disavowed the reasoning (but not the conclusion) of the Court in California v.
LaRue, 409 U.S. 109, 93 S.Ct. 390, 34
L.Ed.2d 342 (1972), which used the
Twenty–First Amendment to support its
conclusion that the First Amendment
did not invalidate California's prohibition of grossly sexual exhibitions in
places licensed to serve alcohol. The
Court similarly rejected the reasoning of
cases that had relied on LaRue, such as
New York State Liquor Authority v. Bellanca, 452 U.S. 714, 101 S.Ct. 2599, 69
L.Ed.2d 357 (1981)(per curiam); Newport v. Iacobucci, 479 U.S. 92, 107 S.Ct.
383, 93 L.Ed.2d 334 (1986)(per curiam).

54.40 ___ U.S. at ___, 116 S.Ct. at
1515–16.

Page 176, add to text after note 58:

With Linmark one should compare City of Ladue v. Gilleo.[58.10]
Justice Stevens, for a unanimous Court, invalidated a city ordinance that banned all residential signs subject to certain exceptions: the law, for example, allowed small residential signs advertising that the property is for sale, signs for churches and schools,
commercial signs in commercially zoned districts. The ordinance in
question did not allow Margaret Gilleo to display an 8.5 by 11 inch
sign in her window, stating: "For Peace in the Gulf." Gilleo
opposed the Persian Gulf War of 1990 to 1991. The City justified
the ordinance as an effort to prevent "ugliness, visual blight and
clutter," because signs "tarnish the natural beauty of the landscape," and so forth.

The Court assumed that the ordinance was viewpoint and
content–neutral and that the various exemptions in the ordinance
reflected legitimate differences among the side of effects of various
kinds of signs. The Court invalidated the law, not because of its
various exemptions—that is, not because the law discriminated on
the basis of the content of speech—, but because the law simply
prohibited too much speech. Even content–neutral restrictions are
invalid if they unduly limit one's ability to engage in free expression:

The impact on free communication of Ladue's broad sign prohibition ... is manifestly greater than in *Linmark*.... Here, in contrast, Ladue has almost completely foreclosed a venerable means of communication that is both unique and important. It has totally foreclosed that medium to political, religious, or personal messages. [R]esidential signs play an important part in political campaigns, during which they are displayed to signal the resident's support for particular candidates, parties, or causes.... Although prohibitions foreclosing entire media may be completely free of content or viewpoint discrimination, the danger they pose to the freedom of speech is readily apparent—by eliminating a common means of speaking, such measures can suppress too much speech. Displaying a sign from one's own residence often carries a message quite distinct from placing the same sign someplace else, or conveying the same text or picture by other means. Precisely because of their location, such signs provide information about the identity of the "speaker." [58.15]

In a footnote, the Court explained that different considerations might apply "in the case of signs (whether political or otherwise) displayed by residents for a fee, or in the case of off–site commercial advertisements on residential property. We also are not confronted here with mere regulations short of a ban." [58.20] For the Court to invite such distinctions make sense. An individual's on–site residential sign indicating his or her political viewpoints offer a very inexpensive free speech outlet for individuals, while a commercial advertiser of, for example, bacon, has many other outlets in addition to his front porch window. Even a political advertiser who is paying a fee has many choices, because he is paying a fee. In the case of commercial signs, the advertiser may also care less where the sign is located (whether on residential or commercial property) if the expected audience is approximately the same.

58.10 512 U.S. 43, 114 S.Ct. 2038, 129 L.Ed.2d 36 (1994). O'Connor, J., also filed a concurring opinion.

58.15 512 U.S. at ___, 114 S.Ct. at 2045–46 (footnotes omitted).

58.20 512 U.S. at ___ n.17, 114 S.Ct. at 2047 n. 17.

Page 178, add to text after second full paragraph:

Targeted Direct Mail Within 30 Days of an Accident. The ethics rules in Florida prohibited personal injury lawyers from sending targeted direct mail soliciting employment to victims and their relatives until 30 days have passed following an accident or disaster. This rule prevented the personal injury *plaintiff's* attorney from contacting the accident victim or a relative, but it imposed no restrictions on the *defense* attorney from contacting either the victim or the relative. In *Florida Bar v. Went for It, Inc.*,[67.10] the

22

Court did not disturb *Shapero,* but held (5 to 4) that, even though targeted mailing is constitutionally protected, Florida may ban targeted mailing by plaintiffs' attorneys for 30 days after the cause of action has occurred. Justice O'Connor, who dissented in *Shapero,* wrote the majority opinion in *Went for It.*[67.15]

Justice O'Connor, for the Court, applied the basic test advanced in *Central Hudson,*[67.20] and claimed that the state bar had substantial interests to protect and that its restrictions were narrowly tailored to directly and substantially advance that interest. She told us that the Florida rule was necessary to protect the privacy of the victims and preventing invasive conduct by lawyers. However, an airline crash or similar misfortune is not a private act. It is widely reported in the newspapers, television, and radio. The recipient of the letter does not have to respond; he or she can just throw it away. The Florida rule does nothing about invasive conduct by defense counsel or insurance adjusters.

O'Connor also argued that the Florida rule was necessary in order to prevent "the erosion of confidence in the profession that such repeated invasions have engendered." [67.25] She emphasized that the situation in *Went For It* was unlike the situation in *Shapero,* because *Shapero* only dealt "with a broad ban on *all* direct-mail solicitations, whatever the time frame and whoever the recipient," and, unlike *Shapero,* the Florida State Bar had collected evidence that it was important to have this 30 day ban on plaintiff-lawyers in order to protect the public perception of lawyers.

What was this evidence that is of constitutional significance? The State Bar's evidence was both statistical and anecdotal. O'Connor, for example, regarded as particularly "[s]ignificant" a poll showing that "27% of direct-mail recipients reported that their regard for the legal profession and for the judicial process as a whole was 'lower' as a result of receiving the direct mail." [67.30] One does not have to be a rocket scientist to figure out that if 27% did not like the mailing, then for the remaining 73%, the direct mail did not lower their respect for the profession. But O'Connor says that the state can keep everyone in the dark because 27% of the people might think better of us if they did not know what was going on.

In a significant passage, the Court said:

> Florida permits lawyers to advertise on prime-time television and radio as well as in newspapers and other media. They may rent space on billboard. They may send *untargeted letters* to the general population, *or to discrete segments thereof.*[67.35]

So, it appears that lawyers can still send letters, as long as they also send them to people who are less interested in receiving them. As for the recipients, one wonders how they will know if the letters are targeted or not. With modern computers, one can receive magazines that print the recipient's name on the magazine instead of pasting on a label. Similarly, a mass mailing can begin the letter with the phrase, "Dear Mr. Smith," rather than, "Dear Occupant." Unless the letter refers to a very specific fact (e.g., a particular accident rather than the problem of accidents generally) the recipient will not know from the letter whether it was sent only to him or to others, such as his neighbor.

If people really do not like to receive targeted mailing, then this problem should be self-policing. That is, people who do not like to hire lawyers who send letters seeking employment will not hire such lawyers. If most people do not like these letters, lawyers who send them will learn the hard way not to waste money on them. In fact, these letters must have been useful for the majority of recipients because otherwise the lawyers (who were not sending out the letters for their own health or amusement) would not have sent them.

However, now that the Florida Bar rule is in effect, a client may find out that he or she has hired the type of lawyer who (but for the Florida rule) would have sent a targeted letter. Therefore, by keeping people ignorant of the facts, the Florida rule takes away from clients the right to refuse to hire a lawyer who would send this type of targeted mailing. Meanwhile, under the Florida rule, clients are kept in the dark for 30 days while being fair game for defense lawyers, who can contact them.

The majority justified the Florida prohibition as a means to protect the public perception of lawyers. People might think better of lawyers if only they did not know the type of people that many of the lawyers are. As Justice Kennedy pointed out in his dissent, "for the first time since *Bates v. State Bar of Arizona*,[67.40] the Court now orders a major retreat from the constitutional guarantees for commercial speech in order to shield its own profession from public criticism."[67.45]

67.10 518 U.S. ___, 115 S.Ct. 2371, 132 L.Ed.2d 541 (1995), on remand 66 F.3d 270 (11th Cir.1995).

67.15 O'Connor's dissent in *Shapero* was joined by Rehnquist, C.J. and Scalia, J. Both of these Justices, along with Thomas & Breyer, JJ., joined the five person majority. The majority in *Shapero* included Kennedy, J. (who joined all of the Brennan plurality) & Stevens, J. (who joined Parts I and II of the Brennan plurality). In *Went For It*, Kennedy, J. filed a dissenting opinion joined by Stevens, Souter, & Ginsburg, JJ.

67.20 Central Hudson Gas & Electric Corp. v. Public Service Commission,

447 U.S. 557, 100 S.Ct. 2343, 65 L.Ed.2d 341 (1980).

67.25 518 U.S. at ___, 115 S.Ct. at 2381.

67.30 518 U.S. at ___, 115 S.Ct. at 2377.

67.35 518 U.S. at ___, 115 S.Ct. at 2380 (emphasis added).

67.40 433 U.S. 350, 51 Ohio Misc. 1, 97 S.Ct. 2691, 53 L.Ed.2d 810 (1977), rehearing denied 434 U.S. 881, 98 S.Ct. 242, 54 L.Ed.2d 164 (1977).

67.45 518 U.S. at ___, 115 S.Ct. at 2386 (Kennedy, J., dissenting).

Page 180, add to text after note 72:

Lawyer's Designation as Certified Public Accountant and Certified Financial Planner. In *Ibanez v. Florida Department of Business and Professional Regulation, Board of Accountancy*,[72.10] Justice Ginsburg, for the Court, held that it violated free speech when the Florida Board of Accountancy reprimanded Silvia Ibanez, an attorney, because she truthfully stated in her advertising, that she was a Certified Public Accountant (CPA) and a Certified Financial Planner (CFP). The state Board of Accountancy licensed her as a CPA, and a bona fide private organization, not the state, licensed her as a CFP. Attorney Ibanez argued her own case.

Justice Ginsburg, for a unanimous Court, upheld Ms. Ibanez's right to use the CPA designation. "[W]e cannot imagine how consumers could be misled by her truthful representation" that she is a CPA.[72.15]

The Court, seven to two, also rejected sanctions based on the fact that Ms. Ibanez had truthfully stated that she was a CFP. The Board relied on a Florida rule that prohibits the use of "specialist" unless accompanied by a disclaimer "in the immediate proximity of the statement that implies formal recognition as a specialist." It must also state that "the recognizing agency is not affiliated with or sanctioned by the state or federal government," and must set out the requirements for recognition, "including, but not limited to, education, experience[,] and testing." Justice Ginsburg, for the Court, remarked on the "failure of the Board to point to any harm that is potentially real, not purely hypothetical," and criticized the detail required on the disclaimer, which would effectively rule out use of the designation on a business card, letterhead, or yellow pages listing. She then concluded, "We have never sustained restrictions on constitutionally protected speech based on a record so bare as the one on which the Board relies here." [72.20]

O'Connor, J., joined by Rehnquist, C.J., dissented on this point, arguing that the CFP designation is both inherently and potentially misleading because a private organization, not the state, confers the designation of Certified Financial Planner.

72.10 512 U.S. 136, 114 S.Ct. 2084, 129 L.Ed.2d 118 (1994).

72.15 512 U.S. at ___, 114 S.Ct. at 2089.

72.20 512 U.S. at ___, 114 S.Ct. at 2089–91.

Page 181, add to note 74:

74. Brickley, C.J., citing Treatise, in Michigan State AFL–CIO v. Employ- ment Relations Commission, 453 Mich. 362, 375, 551 N.W.2d 165, 170 (1996).

Page 186, add to end of page:

Comparison of Lawyer Solicitation Cases With Accountant Solicitation Cases. The Court's deference to state regulation that limits the power of lawyers to engage in face to face, in-person solicitation of clients should be contrasted with the strict limits the Court has placed on the state powers to limit face to face, in person solicitation by accountants. In *Edenfield v. Fane*,[99.10] the Court invalidated a Florida ban on in-person, uninvited, direct *face-to-face* or telephone contact by Certified Public Accountants soliciting business in the business context. The Court held that, as applied, the Florida ban on CPA solicitation in the business context violated free speech. The CPA who is soliciting business intends to communicate truthful, nondeceptive information proposing a lawful commercial transaction.

This Florida law need only be reasonably tailored to serve a substantial state interest. Yet even under this intermediate standard of review, the Court found that the law is unconstitutional as applied. Although the state's interest in protecting consumers from fraud and overreaching, in protecting their privacy, and in maintaining the fact and appearance of CPA impartiality is substantial, Florida did meet its burden to show that the rule is reasonably tailored to meet those interests, that its serves these purposes in a direct and material manner. For example, the state offered no studies or even anecdotal evidence that personal solicitation by CPA's creates dangers of fraud, overreaching, or compromised independence.

Ohralik does not support the CPA restriction. It's "narrow" holding—said the Court in *Edenfield*—depended on "unique" features of in-person solicitation by lawyers. The CPA, unlike a lawyer, is not trained in the art of persuasion. The CPA, in contrast to the lawyer, is trained in "independence and objectivity, not advocacy." In addition, the CPA's prospective clients, unlike the young accident victim in *Ohralik,* are sophisticated experienced business executives. The people whom the CPA wishes to solicit meet the CPA in their own offices, and there is no pressure to retain the CPA on the spot. *Ohralik,* in short, does not relieve the state of the obligation to prove that the preventative measures that it proposes will contribute "in a material way" to relieving a "serious" problem.

99.10 507 U.S. 761, 113 S.Ct. 1792, 123 L.Ed.2d 543 (1993). Kennedy, J., delivered the opinion of the Court, which voted 8 to 1 to invalidate the state restrictions. Only O'Connor, J., dissented.

Page 196, add after carryover paragraph:

News Racks on Sidewalks. In *City of Cincinnati v. Discovery Network, Inc.*,[134.10] the Court considered a Cincinnati ordinance that prohibited the distribution of commercial handbills on public property. The City applied this ordinance to require the removal of those news racks on the city sidewalks that contained so-called "commercial" publications (such as free magazines advertising real estate sales), but the city did not extend the ban to similar news racks containing newspapers. The city called the commercial publications "commercial handbills" and argued that the purpose of its prohibition was to make the sidewalks more attractive and promote safer streets (e.g., people might trip over the news racks). However, while the city sought to remove the 62 news racks distributing these commercial publications, it did not apply its prohibition to news racks (numbering about 1,500 to 2,000) that sold regular *newspapers,* which the City deemed to be publications published daily or weekly and *primarily* covering or commenting on current events.

Applying *Central Hudson* and *Fox,* the Court invalidated the city's ban. It concluded, first, that the city had the burden to establish a "reasonable fit" between its legitimate interests in safety and esthetics and its choice of a limited and selective prohibition of news racks as the means chosen to serve those legitimate interests. Second, Cincinnati did not meet its burden of establishing a "reasonable fit." Cincinnati's equivocal distinction that it attempted to draw between newspapers and commercial handbills "bears no relationship *whatsoever* to the particular interests that the city has asserted." [134.15]

The city has a valid concern with the aggregate number of news racks on the streets, but not with their contents, because each news rack, whether it contains "newspapers" or "commercial handbills" is equally unattractive. There is, in short, no basis of distinction between "newspapers" and "handbills" that is relevant to any interest that the city has asserted. Even if it were assumed that the city could ban all news racks on public property, that would not justify the discriminatory ban (based on the content of the news racks) that the city imposed. This content-based restriction is also not a valid time, place, or manner restriction.[134.20]

134.10 507 U.S. 410, 113 S.Ct. 1505, 123 L.Ed.2d 99 (1993).

134.15 507 U.S. at 424, 113 S.Ct. at 1514 (emphasis in original).

134.20 Blackmun, J., concurring, stated that he believed that "the analysis set forth in *Central Hudson* and refined in *Fox* affords insufficient protection for truthful, noncoercive commercial speech concerning lawful activities." Intermediate scrutiny is appropriate for time, place, or manner restrictions (without regard to content) or when the restraint on commercial speech is designed to protect the consumer from misleading or coercive speech, but not for a regulation that suppresses truthful commercial speech to serve some other government purpose. He concluded by stating that he hoped that the Court "ultimately will come to abandon *Central Hudson's* analysis entirely" in favor of giving "full protection for truthful, noncoercive commercial speech about lawful activities." 507 U.S. at 430–33, 113 S.Ct. at 1517–18 (Blackmun, J., concurring).

Rehnquist, C.J., joined by White & Thomas, JJ., filed a dissenting opinion.

X. LIBEL AND INVASION OF PRIVACY

§ 20.32 Introduction

(a) The Problem of Values in Conflict

Page 196, add to note 1:

.1. See generally, Holderman, J., citing §§ 20.32–20.35 of Treatise, in Air Line Pilots Association, International, v. Department of Aviation of the City of Chicago, 1993 WL 462834, *3 (N.D.Ill. 1993).

Page 197, add to text after note 4:

A 1992 study discovered six jury verdicts of over $10 million. During the entire decade of the 1980s, there were only four awards in excess of $10 million. During the 1980s, there were 158 libel judgments, totaling $231.9 million in damages. For 1990 and 1991, there were 21 libel awards, totaling $190.4 million. The median libel verdict for 1990 and 1991 was $2.5 million, more than 12 times the median during the 1980s. However, about 75% of the jury awards are reduced or thrown out on appeal.[4.5]

The average jury libel award in 1994–1995 was $1.5 million, up 57% from 1992–1993, a period when the average jury libel award was $929,422. However, the number of cases going to trial declined, from 34 trials in 1992–1993 to 21 trials in 1994–1995. The news media lost over half of the trials (13 out of 21 trials) in 1994–1995. Four of these 13 verdicts resulted in a damage award of more than $1 million, and one verdict exceeded $10 million. On average, about 70% of the libel awards are thrown out or reduced on appeal.[4.6]

4.5 Junda Woo, Juries' Libel Awards Are Soaring, With Several Topping $10 Million, Wall St. Journal, Aug. 26, 1992, at B6, col. 1–2 (midwest ed.) This study was supported by the Libel Defense Resource Center. See also, "A Winning Record for Libel Defendants, ABA Journal, Jan., 1996, at 21.

4.6 Alexanrda Peers, Libel Awards Are Growing, Wall St.Jrl., Feb. 9, 1996, at B2, col. 4.

Page 198, add to note 6:

6. Paul T. Hayden, Reconsidering the Litigator's Absolute Privilege to Defame, 54 Ohio State L.J. 985 (1993)(discussing competing values).

§ 20.33 New York Times v. Sullivan and Libel of a Public Official

(b) New York Times Scienter

Page 203, add to note 11:

11. Following the decision in Harte-Hanks, the Minnesota Supreme Court, on remand, reinstated the $200,000 damage award. From 1988 to the early part of 1992, about six cases similar to this lawsuit have been filed by various parties claiming that other news publications breached a promise of confidentiality. Wall Street Journal, Feb. 7, 1992, at B2, col. 3 (midwest ed.).

See Per Curiam opinion, quoting this Treatise in Bryant v. Harris, 985 F.2d 559, n. 3 (6th Cir.1993).

(c) Burden of Proof

Page 204, add to note 17:

17. And see, Judge Arnold, citing Treatise, in Mueller v. Abdnor, 972 F.2d 931, 936 (8th Cir.1992), distinguishing the "clear and convincing" standard from the "preponderance" standard applicable on a slander of title claim.

Page 205, add to text after note 21:

The requirement of an independent appellate review of libel verdicts has benefitted libel defendants. The empirical experience during the 1980's showed that less than a third of libel verdicts against media defendants survived undisturbed after an independent appellate review.[21.10]

21.10 Independent Appellate Review. A study of 112 libel appeals over the past decade showed that media defendants were quite successful on appeal because of the requirement of an independent appellate review: only 28.3% of the damage awards made it through the appeal process undisturbed; 41.3% of the libel verdicts against media defendants were reversed entirely; 14.1% were reversed in part, with new trials ordered; and in 16.3% of the libel verdicts against media defendants, the courts of appeal upheld the verdicts but threw out or reduced the damages. Milo Geylelin, Libel Defendants Fare Well on Appeal, Research Finds, Wall St. Journal., May 31, 1994, at B10, col. 1 (midwest ed.).

Page 209, add to end of note 29:

29. Erickson, J., citing Treatise in, Keohane v. Stewart, 882 P.2d 1293, 1296 (Colo.1994) (en banc), cert. denied ___ U.S. ___, 115 S.Ct. 936, 130 L.Ed.2d 882 (1995).

(d) Public Officials

Page 213, add new note 46.10 to end of first full paragraph:

. . . considered a public official.[46.10]

46.10 See Chief Judge Mihm, citing this Treatise in Grossman v. Smart, 807 F.Supp. 1404, 1408 (C.D.Ill.1992).

§ 20.35   Private Individuals

(d) Dun & Bradstreet, Inc. v. Greenmoss Builders, Inc.

Page 228, add new note 52.10 to end of last full paragraph:

. . . applying their subjective judgments.[52.10]

52.10 See Chief Judge Mihm, citing this Treatise in Grossman v. Smart, 807 F.Supp. 1404, 1411 (C.D.Ill.1992).

Page 230, add to note 56:

56. Ronald D. Rotunda, The Warren Court and Freedom of the Press 85, 90–103, in The Warren Court: A Retrospective (Bernard Schwartz, ed. Oxford University Press 1996).

§ 20.36   Rights of Privacy and Rights of Publicity

Page 233, add to end of note 5 (which began at page 231):

5. Ronald D. Rotunda, The Warren Court and Freedom of the Press 85, 87–88, in The Warren Court: A Retrospec- tive (Bernard Schwartz, ed. Oxford University Press 1996).

XI. FIGHTING WORDS AND HOSTILE AUDIENCES

§ 20.37   Introduction

Page 240, add new note to end of first sentence of this section:

"Government regulation of speech . . . was to proscribe 'fighting words.' " [0.05]

0.05 Taylor, P.J., quoting Treatise, in South v. City of Mountain Brook, 1996 WL 342264, *2 (Ala.Crim.App. 1996).

". . . situation of the individual shouting 'fire' in a crowded theater." [.06]

.06 McMillan, J., citing Treatise in, Conkle v. State, 677 So.2d 1211, 1220 (Ala.Crim.App.1995).

Page 240, add to end of note 1:

1. The question of "hate speech" is more fully discussed in § 20.39, below.

For an historical discussion of the efforts to suppress abolitionist speech as "seditious," and an analysis of why this suppression effort led to protection for such speech in the Fourteenth Amend- ment, see, Michael Kent Curtis, The 1859 Crisis Over Hinton Helper's Book, The Impending Crisis: Free Speech, Slavery, and Some Light on the Meaning of the First Section of the Fourteenth Amendment, 68 Chicago–Kent L.Rev. 1113 (1993).

Page 241, add a new paragraph after the end of carryover paragraph:

The rationale behind the "fighting words" doctrine is that some words are a particularly intolerable and socially unnecessary way or manner of expressing an idea or thought. The prohibition of "fighting words" is not on the thought or idea itself but on the *manner* or mode of expressing it. The fighting words doctrine allows the state to prohibit an intolerable technique or manner of expressing an idea, but does not authorize the state to ban the idea itself. The reason why fighting words are a category of expression excluded from the protection of the first amendment is not that their content communicates any particular idea, but rather "that their content embodies a particularly intolerable (and socially un- necessary) *mode* of expressing *whatever* idea the speaker wishes to convey." [2]

2. R.A.V. v. City of St. Paul, 505 U.S.   120 L.Ed.2d 305 (1992) (emphasis in
377, 391–95, 112 S.Ct. 2538, 2548–49,   original).

§ 20.38   The Doctrine Emerges

Page 241, add to note 1:

1. Parker, J., citing Treatise in, Shell
v. Host International Corp., 513 N.W.2d
15, 18 (Minn.App.1994).

§ 20.39   Subsequent Modifications

Page 246, add after the end of carryover paragraph:

Content Based Fighting Words—the Problem of *"Hate Speech."* *R.A.V. v. City of St. Paul*,[19.5] is a significant decision explaining and limiting the "fighting words" doctrine. In this case the City of St. Paul enacted an ordinance that provided:

> "Whoever places on public or private property a symbol, object, appellation, characterization or graffiti, including, but not limited to, a burning cross or a Nazi swastika, which one knows or has reasonable grounds to know arouses anger, alarm or resentment in others on the basis of race, color, creed, religion or gender commits disorderly conduct and shall be guilty of a misdemeanor."

The City alleged that R.A.V. and several other teenagers burned a cross *inside* the privately owned, *fenced* yard of a black family, who lived across the street from where R.A.V. was staying. R.A.V., of course, intended to terrorize the black family.

The Court noted that the only question was the constitutionality of this ordinance. The defendant, R.A.V., was also charged with violation of a state law that prohibited racially motivated assault,[19.10] but there was no Constitutional challenge to that count.

The state supreme court had ruled that the ordinance only reached expressions that constituted "fighting words," within the meaning of *Chaplinsky,* and that it was a "narrowly tailored means toward accomplishing the compelling governmental interest in protecting the community against bias-motivated threats to public safety and order." [19.15] Thus, in the view of the state court, the ordinance was constitutional. The U.S. Supreme Court disagreed.

Justice Scalia, for the majority, accepted this interpretation by the state court, but explained that the problem with the ordinance is that it is unconstitutional on its face, because it "prohibits otherwise permitted speech solely on the basis of the subject [that] the speech addresses." [19.20] The Court, for example, in the flag burning decisions,[19.25] has made clear that content-based restrictions on speech are presumptively unconstitutional. In *R.A.V.* the Court applied this principle to the "fighting words" doctrine: the government may not regulate even fighting words "based on hostility—or favoritism—towards the underlying message expressed." [19.30]

This case is best understood by turning to a hypothetical that Justice Scalia used to explain the ruling of the Court. The problem with the St. Paul ordinance is that, under its provisions—

> "One could hold up a sign saying, for example, that all 'anti-Catholic bigots' are misbegotten; but not that all 'papists' are, for that would insult and provoke violence 'on the basis of religion.' St. Paul has no such authority to license one side of a debate to fight freestyle, while requiring the other to follow Marquis of Queensbury Rules." [19.35]

Justice Stevens, in his separate opinion concurring in the judgment, sought to distinguish this hypothetical regarding the anti-Catholic/anti-papist signs, but in order to distinguish the hypothetical, he first had to change it! He recited exactly the above-indented quotation, and then stated the following, including the bracketed language:

> "This may be true, but it hardly proves the Court's point. The Court's reasoning is asymmetrical. The response to a sign saying that 'all [religious] bigots are misbegotten' is a sign saying that 'all advocates of religious tolerance are misbegotten.' " [19.40]

The problem with Justice Stevens's reasoning[19.45] is that the hypothetical ordinance, in fact, does make it a crime to state that "all papists are misbegotten," but not a crime to state that "all anti-Catholic bigots are misbegotten." The ordinance, by its own terms, only seeks to ban certain types of fighting words: it seeks to ban words that would insult and provoke on the basis of religion, but not similar words that do not fit within that content. In order for Justice Stevens to criticize Justice Scalia's hypothetical, he first had to modify it, and then criticize a hypothetical different than the one that Justice Scalia had advanced.

The Minnesota Supreme Court, in upholding the ordinance, emphasized that the ordinance was directed against "bias-motivated" hatred, and messages "based on virulent notions of racial supremacy." [19.50] The brief of St. Paul, filed in the juvenile court, explicitly stated that the "burning of a cross does express a message which the St. Paul Ordinance attempts to legislate." [19.55] This content-based purpose was the fatal flaw of the statute.

The rationale behind the "fighting words" doctrine is that some words consist of a particularly intolerable and socially unnecessary way or manner of expressing an idea or thought. The prohibition is not on this thought or idea but on the way that it is expressed. The fighting words doctrine allows the state to prohibit an intolerable technique or manner of expressing an idea, but does not authorize the state to ban the idea itself. As the Court explained, "the reason why fighting words are categorically excluded from the protection of the First Amendment is not that their content communicates any particular idea, but that their content embodies a particularly intolerable (and socially unnecessary) *mode* of expressing *whatever* idea the speaker wishes to convey." [19.60]

In short, when the Court holds that "fighting words" are a category of speech excluded from the protection of the first amendment, it really means that the state may ban intolerable *means* of expressing an idea, no matter what idea the speaker wishes to express. This doctrine does not give the state power to ban speech solely on the basis of the subjects that the speech addresses.

For example, the state can ban a *noisy* sound truck, as an improper means of expressing an idea,[19.65] but the state has no power to ban noisy sound trucks expressing Republican (but not Democratic) *ideas.* Nor could the state ban sound trucks expressing political as opposed to nonpolitical messages. The sound truck may be prohibited only because it is noisy, not because of the ideas it is promoting.

Similarly, the state can ban setting fires in the public streets, but it cannot ban burning the flag as a means of protest. If one decided to burn the flag on the public streets, the state could punish the act of burning (no matter what it was that one was burning), because it would be justified by a neutral statute that prohibited only an act without regard to what one was seeking to express. A law that made it a crime to disgrace the flag by burning it, however, would be improper, because it requires the state to prove a certain mental attitude in connection with the burning.

R.A.V. v. City of St. Paul does not impose an "underinclusiveness" requirement on the "fighting words" doctrine. Rather, it imposes the familiar requirement that the state prohibition on proscribable speech must not be based on the content of speech. Selective regulation of speech is presumptively unconstitutional.[19.70]

Some speech can be prohibited because of its content, in the sense that we must look at the content of speech to see what category the speech is in. For example, is the speech at issue "fighting words" or "obscene"? But that does not mean that the state has *carte blanche* to do as it wishes merely because speech falls in the category of "fighting words" or "obscene."

Thus, the state could ban *all* obscene speech because it is all proscribable or able to be forbidden, notwithstanding the first amendment. Or the state could ban all obscene speech *in a certain media or market,* such as all obscene speech on the telephone.[19.75] The latter prohibition is not based on any viewpoint expressed by the speech, so it is not prohibited by any principle found in *R.A.V.* There is no danger that the state is really interested in suppressing particular ideas. It is only suppressing prurience in a particular market. But it would be improper for the state to ban that obscenity because it includes an offensive *political* message.[19.80] The power of the government to ban obscenity, or fighting words, does not give it the power to drive certain ideas or viewpoints from the marketplace.

Consistent with *R.A.V.,* the Federal Government can ban speech that threatens the President.[19.85] As the majority in *R.A.V.* explained, the reason why threats of violence are not protected by the first amendment is that such threats engender fear, disrupt activities, and cause apprehension; all these reasons apply with special force when the Federal Government prohibits threats that specify the President. But even here, "the Federal Government may not criminalize only those threats against the President that mention his policy on aid to inner cities." [19.90]

Title VII and Sexually Derogatory "Fighting Words." Under the principle of *R.A.V.,* the state can forbid fraud in one type of industry but not another, simply because the state believes that the risk of fraud is greater in one industry than another. There is no danger that the state is really seeking to ban the content of certain types of speech or suppress certain viewpoints in such circumstances. But the state "may not prohibit only that commercial advertising that depicts men in a demeaning fashion." [19.95] That would fail the requirement that there must be "no realistic possibility that official suppression of ideas is afoot." [19.100] Advertising that depicts men (or women) in a demeaning fashion is not to be admired, but it is protected by the first amendment nonetheless. The Government cannot seek to drive out or disfavor this particular viewpoint. Similarly, a law may not forbid a white man from hurling a racist anti-black fighting word at a black man if it permits a black man to hurl a racist anti- white word at a white man.

Correspondingly, the state can ban certain discriminatory *conduct.* One cannot immunize one's self from a ban on conduct merely by accompanying that conduct by speech. A murderer does not cloak himself with the first amendment merely because he shouts, "Death to Tyrants," while pulling the trigger. Pursuant to Title VII, Congress has banned sexual discrimination in employment practices.[19.105] Such conduct (a refusal to promote someone to a better job because of sexism) is not immune from prohibition merely because the practitioner accompanies the bad conduct with sexually disparaging statements. Sexually derogatory fighting words, "among other words, may produce a violation of Title VII's general prohibition against sexual discrimination in employment practices," because where "the government does not target conduct on the basis of its expressive content, acts are not shielded from regulation merely because they express a discriminatory idea or philosophy." [19.110] The words may even amount to admissions of the offensive conduct. Proof that the individual uttered sexist remarks may be useful evidence to impeach his claim that he would never say such a thing.[19.115] But the power to criminalize conduct is quite a bit different than the power to criminalize mere speech, even offensive speech.

R.A.V. is an important case. It forbids the state from making mere words a crime because the words are politically incorrect, or because the state wishes to drive certain ideas from the marketplace. Even when prohibiting "fighting words," the state may not engage in an effort to suppress unpopular or even offensive ideas. The state may forbid "fighting words," as long as it does so in a viewpoint neutral manner. There must be, in short, no realistic possibility that the state is trying to officially suppress ideas. The government may not regulate "fighting words" based on hostility towards the underlying message expressed.

In contrast to *R.A.V.*, the Court a year later was unanimous in *Wisconsin v. Mitchell,*[19.120] which held that a Wisconsin statute that provides for enhancement of a defendant's sentence whenever he intentionally selects his victim based on the victim's race does not violate defendant's speech rights by purporting to punish his biased beliefs. The statute at issue in *R.A.V.* was explicitly directed at speech; however, the statute at issue in *Mitchell* is aimed at *conduct* (aggravated battery by Mitchell, who selected and beat up his victim—"a white boy"—on the grounds of color). The first amendment does not protect this conduct. The trial court in a case such as this only looked at the defendant's motives in determining what sentence to impose. Although the sentencing judge may not constitutionally take into account the defendant's *abstract* beliefs,[19.125] the first amendment does not prevent the court looking at the defendant's motive in a case such as this.

It is not unusual for the sentencing judge to look at motive in determining punishment. It is common for a defendant to receive a minimum sentence because he was acting with good motives, or a high sentence because of bad motives.[19.130] For example, the state may consider as an aggravating circumstance a murder committed for monetary gain. It is proper for the sentencing judge to take into account that the murder was premeditated, and that the murderer's motive was money, a "murder for hire" case, because a paid hitman is particularly dangerous. The more purposeful the offense, the more severely it may be punished.[19.135] Thus it is proper, in a murder case, for the trial judge (in deciding to sentence the defendant to death) to take into account the racial hatred of the defendant towards the victim, and the desire of the defendant to provoke a race war.[19.140]

Wisconsin singled out bias-inspired *conduct* for disfavored treatment and enhancement of criminal penalty simply because the state concluded that this type of conduct inflicted greater individual and societal harm; crimes motivated by violence are more likely to provoke retaliatory crimes; such crimes inflict emotional distress on their victims and incite community unrest; those who injure for racist reasons are often thought to be unbalanced and thus more dangerous.

The Court also rejected the argument that a penalty enhancement on a criminal *act* may somehow chill free speech. It is unlikely that a bigot will suppress his or her bigoted beliefs on the theory that if the bigot commits an admittedly criminal act (such as assault, or murder), then the state might seek to discover and then introduce evidence of that bigotry. The chain of events is too speculative to justify a conclusion that the Wisconsin statute chills free speech.

In short, the first amendment does not prohibit the evidentiary use of speech to establish elements of a criminal *act* or to prove motive or intent. Assuming that a statement passes the normal evidentiary rules of relevance, admissibility, and reliability, the state may introduce the defendant's prior speech to prove motive or intent or to establish the elements of a crime.[19.145]

19.5 505 U.S. 377, 112 S.Ct. 2538, 120 L.Ed.2d 305 (1992). Scalia, J., delivered the opinion of the Court, joined by Rehnquist, C.J., and Kennedy, Souter, and Thomas, JJ. White, J., filed an opinion concurring in the judgment, in which Blackmun and O'Connor, JJ., joined, and in which Stevens, J., joined except as to Part I–A. Blackmun, J., filed an opinion concurring in the judgment. Stevens, J., also filed an opinion concurring in the judgment, in Part I of which White and Blackmun, JJ. joined.

See, Suzanna Sherry, Speaking of Virtue: A Republican Approach to University Regulation of Hate Speech, 75 Minn. L.Rev. 933 (1991); Symposium: Hate Speech After R.A.V., 18 Wm. Mitchell L.Rev. 889 (1992); Akhil Amar, The Case of the Missing Amendments, 106 Harv.L.Rev. 124 (1992); Nat Hentoff, Free Speech for Me—But Not for Thee: How the American Left and Right Relentlessly Censor Each Other (1992); Paul T. Hayden, Religiously Motivated "Outrageous" Conduct: Intentional Infliction of Emotional Distress as a Weapon Against "Other People's Faiths," 34 Wm. & Mary L.Rev. 579 (1993); Alex Kozinski & Eugene Volokh, A Penumbra Too Far, 106 Harv.L.Rev. 1639 (1993); Ronald D. Rotunda, A Brief Comment on Politically Incorrect Speech in the Wake of R.A.V., 47 So. Methodist U.L.Rev. 9 (1993).

See also, Symposium, Academic Freedom and Legal Education, 43 J. of Legal Education 313–414 (1993); William Van Alstyne, The University in the Manner of Tiananmen Square, 21 Hastings Const. L. Q.1 (1993); Alan E. Brown-stein, Hate Speech and Harassment: The Constitutionality of Campus Codes That Prohibit Racial Insults, 3 Wm. & Mary Bill of Rights J. 179 (1994); John M. Blim, Undoing Our Selves: The Error of Sacrificing Speech in the Quest for Equality, 56 Ohio State L.J. 56 (1995).

19.10 Minn.Stat. § 609.2212(4), cited in R.A.V. v. City of St. Paul, 505 U.S. at 378 n. 2, 112 S.Ct. at 2541 n. 2. See also, 505 U.S. at 379 n. 1, 112 S.Ct. at 2541 n. 1, referring to other applicable laws under which R.A.V. could have been charged, such as terrorist threats, arson, and criminal damage to property.

19.15 In re Welfare of R.A.V., 464 N.W.2d 507, 510–11 (Minn.1991), reversed R.A.V. v. City of St. Paul, 505 U.S. 377, 112 S.Ct. 2538, 120 L.Ed.2d 305 (1992).

19.20 505 U.S. at 381, 112 S.Ct. at 2542 (footnote omitted).

19.25 E.g., Texas v. Johnson, 491 U.S. 397, 406, 109 S.Ct. 2533, 2540, 105 L.Ed.2d 342 (1989); United States v. Eichman, 496 U.S. 310, 110 S.Ct. 2404, 110 L.Ed.2d 287 (1990).

19.30 505 U.S. at 386, 112 S.Ct. at 2545. Thus, for example, a content-neutral ban on targeted, stationary residential picketing is constitutionally valid, on its face. Frisby v. Schultz, 487 U.S. 474, 108 S.Ct. 2495, 101 L.Ed.2d 420 (1988), on remand 857 F.2d 1175 (7th Cir.1988), appeal after remand 877 F.2d 6 (7th Cir.1989). But a similar ban that exempts *labor* picketing is not content-neutral because it exempts speech based on content; it exempts picketing that refers to labor issues, and hence violates the first amendment. Carey v. Brown, 447 U.S. 455, 100 S.Ct. 2286, 65 L.Ed.2d 263 (1980). A ban on targeted picketing prohibits an act (stationary picketing that targets a particular house), without regard to the content of that picketing. A ban on nonlabor picketing bans picketing based on its content (issues other than labor issues).

19.35 505 U.S. at 391, 112 S.Ct. at 2548.

19.40 505 U.S. at 435, 112 S.Ct. at 2571 (Stevens, J., concurring in the judgment).

Justice Stevens also stated that it "seems to me" to be "extremely unlikely" that such signs "could be fighting words." However, if Justice Scalia had substituted a more vernacular, vulgar, or colloquial term than the polysyllabic word, "misbegotten"—often fighting words are monosyllabic—it should not be difficult to conceive of the expression being placed in the category of "fighting words."

19.45 Note that Justices White and Blackmun only joined part I of Justice Stevens' separate opinion, not this part.

19.50 464 N.W.2d at 508, 511.

19.55 Quoted in, 505 U.S. at 391, 112 S.Ct. at 2548.

19.60 505 U.S. at 391–95, 112 S.Ct. at 2548–49 (emphasis in original).

19.65 Niemotko v. Maryland, 340 U.S. 268, 282, 71 S.Ct. 325, 333, 95 L.Ed. 267 (1951) (Frankfurter, J., concurring in the result).

19.70 The presumption of invalidity may sometimes be overcome. Thus, Burson v. Freeman, 504 U.S. 191, 112 S.Ct. 1846, 119 L.Ed.2d 5 (1992), with no majority opinion, upheld a Tennessee law (typical of the law of many jurisdictions) that prohibited the solicitation of votes and the display or distribution of campaign materials within 100 feet of a polling place. There was substantial history that supported the conclusion that the state had a compelling interest in preventing voter intimidation and election fraud. History supported the conclusion that the best way to preserve the secrecy of the ballot and safeguard the integrity of the election process is to limit access to the area around the voter.

19.75 Sable Communications of California, Inc. v. Federal Communications Commission, 492 U.S. 115, 109 S.Ct. 2829, 106 L.Ed.2d 93 (1989).

19.80 Kucharek v. Hanaway, 902 F.2d 513, 517 (7th Cir.1990), cert. denied 498 U.S. 1041, 111 S.Ct. 713, 112 L.Ed.2d 702 (1991). Justice Stevens, in his separate opinion, argued that obscene anti-government speech was "fantastical," because, by definition, it would not lack serious political value. 505 U.S. at 418, 112 S.Ct. at 2562 (Stevens, J., concurring in the judgment). Justice Scalia briefly responded that a hard core obscene movie, with a model sporting a political tattoo, is still obscene. 505 U.S. at 385 n. 4, 112 S.Ct. at 2544 n. 4.

19.85 Watts v. United States, 394 U.S. 705, 89 S.Ct. 1399, 22 L.Ed.2d 664 (1969) upheld the facial validity of 18 U.S.C.A. § 871, which makes criminal threats on the life of the President.

19.90 505 U.S. at 388, 112 S.Ct. at 2546.

19.95 505 U.S. at 388, 112 S.Ct. at 2546.

19.100 505 U.S. at 390, 112 S.Ct. at 2547.

19.105 E.g., 42 U.S.C.A. § 2000e–2; 18 U.S.C.A. §§ 1981, 1982.

19.110 505 U.S. at 388–91, 112 S.Ct. at 2546–47.

See generally, Kingsley R. Browne, Title VII as Censorship: Hostile–Environment Harassment and the First Amendment, 52 Ohio State L.J. 481 (1991), a thoughtful article analyzing the free speech problems of "hostile work environment" cases. Professor Browne warns:

"[It is a] fundamental *constitutional* truth that the government may not establish a fundamental *moral* truth through suppression of expression. Probably everyone reading this Article would agree that the world would be a better place without much of the expression that is described in the harassment cases. It does not follow, however, that the world would be a better place if elimination of such expression is compelled by the threat of governmental sanctions." 52 Ohio State L.J. at 550 (emphasis in original).

See also, Kingsley R. Browne, Workplace Censorship: A Response to Professor Sangree, 47 Rutgers L.Rev. 579 (1995), responding to, Suzanne Sangree, Title VII Prohibitions Against Hostile Environment Sexual Harassment and the First Amendment: No Collision in Sight, 47 Rutgers L.Rev. 461 (1995).

19.115 See, Dawson v. Delaware, 503 U.S. 159, 112 S.Ct. 1093, 117 L.Ed.2d 309 (1992).

19.120 508 U.S. 476, 113 S.Ct. 2194, 124 L.Ed.2d 436 (1993), on remand 178 Wis.2d 597, 504 N.W.2d 610 (1993).

19.125 Dawson v. Delaware, 503 U.S. 159, 112 S.Ct. 1093, 117 L.Ed.2d 309 (1992), on remand 608 A.2d 1201 (Del.1992). See § 20.40, below.

19.130 1 Wayne LaFave & Austin Scott, Substantive Criminal Law § 3.6(b), at 324 (1986).

19.135 Tison v. Arizona, 481 U.S. 137, 156, 107 S.Ct. 1676, 1687, 95 L.Ed.2d 127 (1987), rehearing denied 482 U.S. 921, 107 S.Ct. 3201, 96 L.Ed.2d 688 (1987).

19.140 Barclay v. Florida, 463 U.S. 939, 103 S.Ct. 3418, 77 L.Ed.2d 1134 (1983) (plurality opinion), rehearing denied 464 U.S. 874, 104 S.Ct. 209, 78 L.Ed.2d 185 (1983).

19.145 See, Haupt v. United States, 330 U.S. 631, 67 S.Ct. 874, 91 L.Ed. 1145 (1947), rehearing denied 331 U.S. 864, 67 S.Ct. 1195, 91 L.Ed. 1869 (1947). The Federal Government prosecuted Haupt for treason. To prove that Haupt engaged in certain acts out of "adherence to the enemy" and not (as Haupt claimed) out of a motive of "parental solitude," the government introduced evidence of statements that Haupt had made in earlier conversations that had taken place long prior to the time period relevant in the indictment. The conversations showed that Haupt had sympathy towards Hitler and hostility towards the United States. The Court rejected the argument that use of this evidence was improper. The evidence is admissible "on the question of intent and adherence to the enemy," even though the Court cautioned about the use of this evidence: "Such testimony is to be scrutinized with care to be certain the statements are not expressions of mere lawful and permissible difference[s] of opinion with our own government or quite proper appreciation of the land of [one's] birth." 330 U.S. at 642, 67 S.Ct. at 879.

§ 20.40   The Present Status of the "Fighting Words" and "Hostile Audience" Doctrines

Page 246, add to note 2:

2. Sedler, The Unconstitutionality of Campus Bans on "Racist Speech:" The View from Without and Within, 53 U.Pittsburgh L.Rev. 631 (1992).

Page 247, add to end of first full paragraph:

Similarly, *Dawson v. Delaware* [7.5] held that the first amendment prohibits the introduction, in a capital sentencing proceeding, of the fact that the defendant was a member of an organization called the Aryan Brotherhood, because the evidence had no relevance to the issues being decided. The evidence showed "nothing more" than the defendant's abstract beliefs, where those beliefs had no bearing on the issue being tried.[7.10]

7.5 503 U.S. 159, 112 S.Ct. 1093, 117 L.Ed.2d 309 (1992), on remand 608 A.2d 1201 (Del.1992). Chief Justice Rehnquist wrote the opinion for the Court. Blackmun, J. filed a concurring opinion. Thomas, J., dissented.

7.10 For example, the victim, like the defendant, was white, so no elements of racial hatred were involved in the murder. There was also no showing that the racist organization committed any unlawful or violent acts or even endorsed those acts. The Court, however-er, explained that the state might have avoided this problem if it had presented more evidence. The prosecution claimed that its expert witness (who did not testify) would have demonstrated that "the Aryan Brotherhood is a white racist prison gang that is associated with drugs and violent escape attempts at prisons, and that advocates the murder of fellow inmates." Such specific evidence might have been relevant in rebutting the defendant's mitigating evidence consisting of testimony emphasizing his kindness to family members and the good time credits that he had earned by enrolling in various drug and alcohol programs in prison.

Justice Thomas' dissenting opinion argued that the prison gang membership was relevant and admissible because it indicated that the defendant had the character of a person who engages in prison gang activities. This evidence tended to establish future dangerousness and rebutted the defendant's effort to show that he was kind to others. The majority replied that the material that the dissent advanced on the nature of prison gangs "would, if it had been presented to the jury, have made this a different case." But Delaware only presented evidence of Dawson's "mere abstract beliefs.... " The majority explained that the jurors should not be able to punish Dawson merely because they find his beliefs to be morally reprehensible. 503 U.S. at 164–69, 112 S.Ct. at 1097–99.

Page 247, replace the second sentence of the second full paragraph with the following:

R.A.V. v. City of St. Paul,[7.15] discussed in the previous section, is certainly a case where the Court rejected a prosecution that, if it had been brought under a more carefully drafted statute, would have been permissible. Justice Blackmun concurred in the judgment but not the opinion in *R.A.V.* Earlier, Justice Blackmun had complained in his dissent in *Gooding v. Wilson,* [8] that "the Court, despite its protestations to the contrary, is merely paying lip service of *Chaplinsky.*" [9] The decision in *R.A.V.* indicates that the Court will not allow content-based restrictions on speech, even if the restrictions are justified by the "fighting words" doctrine.

7.15 505 U.S. 377, 112 S.Ct. 2538, 120 L.Ed.2d 305 (1992).

8. 405 U.S. 518, 92 S.Ct. 1103, 31 L.Ed.2d 408 (1972).

9. 405 U.S. at 537, 92 S.Ct. at 1113 (Blackmun, J., dissenting).

Page 247, add new note to end of last full sentence on this page:

"Words are 'fighting words' when they are an offer to exchange fisticuffs." [11.5]

11.5 Daniel J., quoting Treatise, in Local Organizing Committee, Denver Chapter, Million Man March v. Cook, 922 F.Supp. 1494, 1500, 109 Ed. Law Rep. 223 (D.Colo.1996).

XII. FREEDOM OF ASSOCIATION

§ 20.41 Introduction—The Freedom to Associate and Not to Associate

Page 249, add to note 5:

5. Brickley, C.J., citing Treatise, in Michigan State AFL–CIO v. Employment Relations Commission, 453 Mich. 362, 375, 551 N.W.2d 165, 171 (1996); Levin, J., concurring, citing Treatise, in Michigan State AFL–CIO v. Employment Relations Commission, 453 Mich. 362, 399, 551 N.W.2d 165, 181 (1996).

Page 250, add to note 7, under "Prisons":

7. See, Rowland v. California Men's Colony, Unit II Men's Advisory Council, 506 U.S. 194, 211, 113 S.Ct. 716, 726, 121 L.Ed.2d 656 (1993), on remand 990 F.2d 519 (9th Cir.1993), where the Court applied Dictionary Act, 1 U.S.C.A. § 1, and interpreted the word "person" as used in the *in forma pauperis* statute, to prevent an association of prisoners (who were bringing a civil rights action against prison authorities) from being treated as *in forma pauperis*.

This interpretation did not violate any freedom of association. In order to file *in forma pauperis* the law would require the prisoners to give individual asset information whether these individuals were suing as individuals or through an association, an artificial entity.

Page 250, add new note to end of first full paragraph:

... to promote expressive activity.[9.10]

9.10 Cf. Madsen v. Women's Health Center, Inc., 512 U.S. 753, ___, 114 S.Ct. 2516, 2530, 129 L.Ed.2d 593 (1994), on remand 644 So.2d 86 (Fla.1994), where the Court upheld a portion of an injunction that forbade petitioners, who were protesting the operation of an abortion clinic, from violating the injunction by acting "in concert" with others. The Court rejected the argument that the "in concert" prohibition interfered with the petitioners' freedom of association. The petitioners could associate with others and express their viewpoints. The injunction only banned them from acting "in concert" with others to deprive third parties of their lawful rights.

Page 254, add to text after note 24:

One who chooses to speak also has the right to decide what not to say. This is a crucial right derived from free speech and the right of association. Nothing in *Roberts* undermines this important principle. The *Roberts* Court made quite clear that application of the state law imposed no restrictions on the right of an organization to exclude members based on their ideology. Thus, the state cannot require the organizers of a parade celebrating the NAACP to admit the KKK with its own float, anymore than the state could require a KKK parade to include a float celebrating the KKK.[24.10] The choice of a speaker to propound, or not to propound, a particular point of view is a choice that is beyond the power of government to control.

24.10 **First Amendment Right of Parade Organizers to Select Parade Marchers.** Private citizens in Boston organized an annual St. Patrick's Day parade. The parade organizers (a private group called the South Boston Allied War Veterans Council, an unincorporated association of individuals) did not want to include among the marchers in the parade a group that wished to convey a message that the organizers of the parade do not wish to convey. That group, the Irish–American Gay, Lesbian and Bisexual Group of Boston, called GLIB, wanted to march in the parade in order to express pride in their Irish heritage and in the sexual orientation of GLIB's members. GLIB filed suit, arguing that the refusal of the parade organizers to allow their marching violated a state law prohibiting discrimination on account of sexual orientation in places of public accommodation. The state court agreed with GLIB, and the U.S. Supreme Court unanimously reversed, on first amendment grounds. Hurley v. Irish–American Gay, Lesbian and Bisexual Group of Boston, ___ U.S. ___, 115 S.Ct. 2338, 132 L.Ed.2d 487 (1995).

The parade organizers in *Hurley* did not exclude homosexuals from participating in the parade, and they disavowed any intention of doing so. Openly gay individuals also could participate in various units admitted to the parade. No individual member of GLIB even claimed that he or she had been excluded from parading as a member of any group that the parade organizers had approved to march. The only question is whether state law could constitutionally require the parade organizers to admit GLIB with its own parade unit carrying its own banner. Every participating unit in a parade affects the message conveyed by the private organizers. The state law, in essence, ordered parade organizers to alter the expressive content of their parade, and this the state cannot do.

The state court argued that the parade organizers were lenient in admitting participants, but such leniency does not justify state interference. A "private speaker does not forfeit constitutional protection simply by combining multifarious voices, or by failing to edit their themes to isolate an exact message as the exclusive subject matter of the speech." __ U.S. at __, 115 S.Ct. at 2345.

Page 255, add to note 27:

27. National Organization for Women, Inc. v. Scheidler, 510 U.S. 249, 114 S.Ct. 798, 127 L.Ed.2d 99 (1994) (RICO does not require proof that either a racketeering enterprise or predicate acts of racketeering be motivated by economic purpose).

Page 256, add after carryover paragraph:

There is no violation of the freedom to associate when the Court does not allow an association of prisoners who are bringing a civil rights lawsuit against prison authorities to proceed *in forma pauperis*. There is no unconstitutional burden on the prisoners' associational rights because individual asset information would be required anyway from prisoners, regardless of whether they were suing individually or through an association.[33.10]

33.10 Rowland v. California Men's Colony, 506 U.S. 194, 113 S.Ct. 716, 121 L.Ed.2d 656 (1993), on remand 990 F.2d 519 (9th Cir.1993). In this case, the Court held (5 to 4) that an association of prison inmates, who were bringing a civil rights action under 42 U.S.C.A. § 1983, were not allowed to proceed *in forma pauperis*. The Court held that only natural persons may qualify for treatment, under 42 U.S.C.A. § 1915, which governs who may proceed *in forma pauperis*. Thomas, J., joined by Blackmun, Stevens, & Kennedy, JJ., filed a dissenting opinion. Kennedy, J., also filed a dissenting opinion.

Page 256, add to end of note 34:

34. To the same effect is: Norman v. Reed, 502 U.S. 279, 112 S.Ct. 698, 116 L.Ed.2d 711 (1992), on remand 154 Ill.2d 77, 180 Ill.Dec. 685, 607 N.E.2d 1198 (1992), cert. denied 509 U.S. 906, 113 S.Ct. 3000, 125 L.Ed.2d 693 (1993). That case struck an Illinois statute that broadly prohibited a new party from bearing the name of an established party. The "established" party in this case was a third party, called the Harold Washington Party (HWP). The state argued that the purpose of the law was to prevent persons not associated with the party to latch on to its name, causing voter confusion and denigrating party cohesiveness. But the state supreme court read this law in a very rigid and literal manner, so rigid that it was interpreted to bar candidates running in one political subdivision from ever using the name of a political party established in another, even when the Harold Washington Party had authorized the petitioners to use the HWP name. The state court's inhospitable reading of the statute sweeps broader than necessary to advance electoral order and therefore violates the First Amendment right of political association.

Page 256, add to end of note 36:

36. See, Daniel Hays Lowenstein, Associational Rights of Major Political Parties: A Skeptical Inquiry, 71 Texas L.Rev. 1741 (1993).

Page 260, add to note 50:

50. Poll Tax Exacted by Political Party Convention. Morse v. Republican Party of Virginia, ___ U.S. ___, 116 S.Ct. 1186, 134 L.Ed.2d 347 (1996). All registered voters in Virginia who declared their intent to support Republican Party nominees could become delegates to the Party's state convention to nominate candidates on payment of what was called a "registration fee." Stevens, J., in his plurality opinion, ruled that § 5 of the Voting Rights Act of 1965 required preclearance of the Party's decision to exact the fee, and that the appellants were permitted to challenge the fee as a poll tax prohibited by § 10 of the Act. The Stevens' plurali-

ty opinion [___ U.S. at ___, 116 S.Ct. at 1197] cited and relied on, Ronald D. Rotunda, Constitutional and Statutory Restrictions on Political Parties in the Wake of *Cousins v. Wigoda*, 53 Texas L.Rev. 935, 953–54 (1975). The political party argued that the statutory preclearance procedure violated the party's right of association. Given the history of discrimination that led to the Voting Rights Act, Stevens simply responded that "the minimal burden on the right of association implicated in this case is unquestionably justified." ___ U.S. at ___ n. 38, 116 S.Ct. at 1210 n. 38. The fragmented Court then remanded the case.

Page 260, add to text after note 52:

Prohibition of Write-in Votes. Until the late 1880s all votes in this country were write-in votes. Until the Australian secret ballot system, with state-prepared ballots, was introduced into this country in 1888, all voters cast ballots that they had prepared themselves, or ballots that others (such as organized political parties) prepared on their behalf.[52.5]

Approximately 100 years later, Hawaii decided that it would *ban* write-in votes. In *Burdick v. Takushi*,[52.10] the Court upheld this law. The Court ruled that a Hawaiian law that *prohibited* write-in votes in both the primary and general elections did not violate any voter's right of expression and association. The state did provide easy access to the primary ballot until the cutoff date for the filing of nominating petitions. So, only voters who fail to identify their candidates until shortly before the primary bear any burden. Justice White, for the Court, said that the interest in making a late, rather than early, choice is entitled to little weight. Whether categorized as a voting rights case or a ballot access case, the Court emphasized that reasonable, politically neutral regulations that have the effect of channeling expressive activity at the polls should be upheld.

The Court found that Hawaii has various interests to uphold, such as avoiding "unrestrained factionalism" at the general election, and permitting unopposed victors in certain primaries to be designated office holders. When a State's ballot access laws pass constitutional muster by imposing only reasonable burdens on First and Fourteenth Amendment rights, then "a prohibition on write-in voting will presumptively be valid...." [52.15]

52.5 See generally, L.E. Fredman, The Australian Ballot: The Story of American Reform (1968).

When state-printed ballots were first introduced, various state courts emphasized that a right to cast a write-in ballot was an essential constitutional right.

E.g., Sanner v. Patton, 155 Ill. 553, 562–64, 40 N.E. 290, 292–93 (1895); Patterson v. Hanley, 136 Cal. 265, 270, 68 P. 821, 823 (1902), modified 136 Cal. 265, 68 P. 975 (1902). Oughton v. Black, 212 Pa. 1, 6–7, 61 A. 346, 348 (1905).

52.10   504 U.S. 428, 112 S.Ct. 2059, 119 L.Ed.2d 245 (1992). White, J., delivered the opinion of the Court.

"None of the Above." Kennedy, J., joined by Blackmun & Stevens, JJ., dissented, noting that large numbers of Hawaiian voters cast *blank* ballots in uncontested races rather than vote for the single candidate listed. In 1990, 27% of the voters who voted for other races did not cast votes in uncontested state Senate races. These voters were not satisfied with the choices available to them, and "it is hard to avoid the conclusion that at least some voters would cast write-in votes for other candidates if given this option." 504 U.S. at 442, 112 S.Ct. at 2068 (Kennedy, J., dissenting).

One would think that the state could fulfill all of its interests and avoid the problem of voters who cast blank ballots if the state would, as a matter of course, allow the choice of "None of the Above." The state would the be providing an alternative for the voters who do not like any of the candidates. The prohibition on write-in votes would preclude stealth candidates, who appear out of no where to win the election. But the alternative of "none of the above" would allow voters to protest all of the candidates. If over half the voters chose the designation of "none of the above," then there would have to be a new election, with none of the previous candidates allowed to run, because all of them received fewer votes than "none of the above."

In one–party areas, the opportunity to vote for "none of he above," would give an alternative to voters who do not want any of the party candidates.

52.15   504 U.S. at 440, 112 S.Ct. at 2067.

Page 261, add to text at end of the page:

Inquiry into Beliefs in Capital Cases. *Dawson v. Delaware* [60] held that the first amendment prohibits the introduction, in a capital sentencing proceeding, of the fact that the defendant was a member of a racist organization called the Aryan Brotherhood, where that evidence had no relevance to the issues being decided. The introduction of this evidence in these circumstances violated the defendant's associational freedoms.

In this case, the victim, like the defendant, was white, so no elements of racial hatred were involved in the murder; there was also no showing that the organization committed any unlawful or violent acts or even endorsed those acts. The evidence showed "nothing more" than the defendant's abstract racist beliefs, where those beliefs had no bearing on the issue being tried.

The Court, however, explained that the state might have avoided this problem if it had presented more evidence. The prosecution claimed that its expert witness (who did not testify) would have demonstrated that "the Aryan Brotherhood is a white racist prison gang that is associated with drugs and violent escape attempts at prisons, and that advocates the murder of fellow inmates." [61] Such specific evidence might have been relevant in rebutting the defendant's mitigating evidence consisting of testimony about his supposed kindness to family members and the good time credits he earned by enrolling in various drug and alcohol programs in prison.

Justice Thomas filed a dissenting opinion, arguing that the prison gang membership was relevant and admissible because it indicated that the defendant had the character of a person who engages in prison gang activities. This evidence tended to establish future dangerousness and rebutted the defendant's effort to show that he was kind to others. The majority replied that the material that the dissent advanced on the nature of prison gangs "would, if it had been presented to the jury, have made this a different case." [62] But Delaware only presented evidence of Dawson's "mere abstract beliefs...." [63] The majority explained that the jurors should not be able to punish Dawson merely because they find his beliefs to be morally reprehensible.

60. 503 U.S. 159, 112 S.Ct. 1093, 117 L.Ed.2d 309 (1992), on remand 608 A.2d 1201 (Del.1992). Chief Justice Rehnquist wrote the opinion for the Court. Blackmun, J., filed a concurring opinion.

Hate Speech. See § 20.39.

61. 503 U.S. at 163, 112 S.Ct. at 1097.

62. 503 U.S. at 167, 112 S.Ct. at 1099.

63. 503 U.S. at 166, 112 S.Ct. at 1098. Cf. Texas v. Johnson, 491 U.S. 397, 414, 109 S.Ct. 2533, 2544, 105 L.Ed.2d 342 (1989), the flag burning case, where the Court said that the "government may not prohibit the expression of an idea simply because society finds the idea itself offensive or disagreeable."

§ 20.42 Public Employment Restrictions

(a) Political Affiliation

Page 273, add to note 42, after first full paragraph:

42. See also, Waters v. Churchill, 511 U.S. 661, 114 S.Ct. 1878, 128 L.Ed.2d 686 (1994). Without a majority opinion, the Court considered the question of whether the *Connick* test should be applied to what the Government employer *thought* was said, or what the trier of fact ultimately determines to have been said. The plurality opinion by O'Connor, J., joined by Rehnquist, C.J., Souter & Ginsburg, JJ., concluded that the trier of fact should determine what the government employer "reasonably" thought was said. The government decisionmaker must also reach its conclusion in good faith, rather than as a pretext. Scalia, J., joined by Kennedy & Thomas, JJ., concurred in the judgment, and objected to the plurality's adding the "new First Amendment procedural right" that the employer, in order to act reasonably, must conduct an investigation before taking disciplinary action in certain circumstances.

Page 274, add to note 46:

46. Inquiry into Beliefs in Capital Cases. Compare, Dawson v. Delaware, 503 U.S. 159, 112 S.Ct. 1093, 117 L.Ed.2d 309 (1992), on remand 608 A.2d 1201 (Del.1992). The Court held that the first amendment prohibits the introduction, in a capital sentencing proceeding, of the fact that the defendant was a member of an organization called the Aryan Brotherhood, where that evidence had no relevance to the issues being decided. The introduction of this evidence in these circumstances violated the defendant's associational freedoms. In this case, the victim, like the defendant, was white, so no elements of racial hatred were involved in the murder; there was also no showing that the organization committed any unlawful or violent acts or even endorsed those acts. The evidence showed "nothing more" than the defendant's abstract beliefs, where those beliefs had no bearing on the issue being tried. The Court, however, explained that the state might have avoided this problem if it had presented more evidence.

Page 275, add to text after note 49:

Independent Contractors of the Government. In *O'Hare Truck Service, Inc. v. City of Northlake*,[49.10] the Court refused to draw any distinction between government employees and independent contractors for the Government. Once again, the case arose in Illinois, in the Chicago area. O'Hare Truck Service was on a rotation list of companies available to perform towing services at the request of the city. It was removed from the list after its owner (John Gratzianna), refused to contribute to the respondent mayor's reelection campaign. Allegedly, the removal was in retaliation for this refusal. The Seventh Circuit dismissed the claim, arguing that *Branti v. Finkel* and *Elrod v. Burns* do not apply to independent contractors. Justice Kennedy, for the Court, reversed, holding that if the government retaliates against a contractor or regular provider of services because of its exercise of rights of political association or the expression of political allegiance, there is a violation of the guarantee of free speech.

Kennedy made some important distinctions that should be relevant in future law suits. This is not a case, he said, where O'Hare Trucking was "part of a constituency that must take its chance of being favored or ignored in the larger political process— for example, by residing or doing business in a region the government rewards or spurns in the construction of public works." Instead, the politicians imposed on Gratzianna a specific demand for political support. When he refused, the city terminated a relationship that, based on his prior longstanding practice, "he had reason to believe would continue." [49.15]

The Court said—in a further effort to caution litigants not to read this case too broadly—that it was "inevitable" that there should be case-by-case adjudication so that the courts will consider the necessity of allowing government the needed discretion in awarding contracts.[49.20] Thus, there is no First Amendment violation if the government terminates its affiliation with the contractor for reasons unrelated to free speech (e.g., the provider is unreliable) if either the asserted justification is not a pretext, or if the contractor's affiliation is an appropriate requirement for the effective performance of the job.

A companion case, decided the same day as *O'Hare Truck Service*, was *Board of County Commissioners v. Umbehr*.[49.25] The respondent, Umbehr, was a trash hauler, and an outspoken critic of the Board of County Commissioners. Umbehr alleged that the Commissioners voted to terminate or prevent the automatic renewal of his at-will contract to haul trash for the County because of his criticism of them. Justice O'Connor, for the Court, held that the First Amendment protects independent contractors from termination of at-will government contracts in retaliation for their exercise of free speech.

Umbehr is a particularly significant decision because it outlines what plaintiffs and defendants must do in order to meet their burden of proof and burden of persuasion. To win, Umbehr must demonstrate that the termination of his contract was motivated by his speech on a matter of public concern. Initially, he must prove "more than the mere fact that he criticized the Board members before they terminated him." If he shows that, the Board will win if it can show, by a preponderance of the evidence, that, in light of their knowledge at the time of the termination, the Board members would have terminated the contract regardless of the speech, or if the Board proves that "the County's legitimate interests as contractor, *deferentially viewed*, outweigh the free speech interests at stake." In accessing the appropriate remedy, it is relevant to consider evidence that the Board members discovered facts after termination that would have led to a later termination anyway, and evidence of mitigation of Umbehr's loss by means of subsequent contracts with the cities. The Court emphasized "the limited nature of our decision today." This case concerned the termination of a "pre-existing commercial relationship with the government," so "we need not address the possibility of suits by bidders or applicants for new government contracts who cannot rely on such a relationship." [49.30]

49.10 ___ U.S. ___, 116 S.Ct. 2353, 135 L.Ed.2d 874 (1996).

49.15 ___ U.S. at ___, 116 S.Ct. at 2358.

49.20 ___ U.S. at ___, 116 S.Ct. at 2358.

49.25 ___ U.S. ___, 116 S.Ct. 2342, 135 L.Ed.2d 843 (1996).

49.30 ___ U.S. at ___, 116 S.Ct. at 2352. (emphasis added). Scalia, J., joined by Thomas, J., filed a dissenting opinion to both *Umbehr* and *O'Hare Truck*: "The Democratic mayor gives the city's municipal bond business to what is known to be a solid Democratic law firm—taking it away from the solid Republican law firm that had the business during the previous, Republican, administration. What else is new? Or he declines to give the construction contract for the new municipal stadium to the company that opposed the bond issue for its construction, and that in fact tried to get the stadium built across the river in the next State." Such favoritism is common, and "no one has ever thought it violated—of all things—the First Amendment." ___ U.S. at ___, 116 S.Ct. at 2373.

(d) Restrictions on Extra–Judicial Speech of Judges

Page 278, add to note 61:

61. Abbie Baynes, Judicial Speech: A First Amendment Analysis, 6 Georgetown J. Legal Ethics 81 (1992).

Page 279, add to text after note 67:

Restrictions on a Judge's Judicial Speech. The first amendment offers protection to judges even while they are acting in their capacity as judges,[67.5] but the contours of this protection is affected by the fact that judges also have special obligations not assumed by ordinary people who do not assume the station of a judge. For example, if the judge, while acting in his or her capacity as judge, espouses racial bigotry, the judge is exercising no first amendment privilege that would immunize the judge from discipline.[67.10] Some courts, dominated by people with no strong sense of humor, have even disciplined judges for writing memoranda in limerick form.[67.15] While these appellate judges do not seem to appreciate the whimsical or droll, other judges, including U.S. Supreme Court Justices, have engaged in puns or other forms of humor, with no one even suggesting that such behavior was improper.[67.20]

In many states, judges are elected, and run for office. Many states limit the content of what a judge may say in the campaign. To regulate the content of a campaign is a like trying to take the politics out of politics. Once the state makes the decision to conduct an election for an office, even a judicial office, the first amendment comes into play to protect speech that is at the core of the free speech rights.[67.25]

67.5 See, e.g., Mosk, Judges Have First Amendment Rights, 2 Calif.Lawyer 30 (Oct.1982). Cf. Kiovsky, First Amendment Rights of Attorneys and Judges in Judicial Election Campaigns, 47 Ohio St. L.J. 201 (1986); Patrick M. McFadden, Electing Justice: The Law and Ethics of Judicial Election Campaigns (1990); Mark R. Riccardi, Code of Judicial Conduct Canon 7B(1)(c): An Unconstitutional Restriction on Freedom of Speech, 7 Georgetown J. of Legal Ethics 153 (1993); Daniel J. Burke, Code of Judicial Conduct Canon 7B(1)(c): Toward the Proper Regulation of Judicial Speech, 7 Georgetown J. of Legal Ethics 181 (1993).

67.10 Mosk, Judges Have First Amendment Rights, 2 Calif.Lawyer 30 (Oct.1982); Abbie Baynes, Judicial Speech: A First Amendment Analysis, 6 Georgetown J. of Legal Ethics 81, 104–16 (1992).

67.15 In re Rome, 218 Kan. 198, 542 P.2d 676 (1975). See also, State ex rel.

Commission on Judicial Qualifications v. Rome, 229 Kan. 195, 623 P.2d 1307 (1981), cert. denied 454 U.S. 830, 102 S.Ct. 127, 70 L.Ed.2d 108 (1981), rehearing denied 454 U.S. 1094, 102 S.Ct. 662, 70 L.Ed.2d 633 (1981).

67.20 E.g., Stevens, J., dissenting in Maine v. Taylor, 477 U.S. 131, 106 S.Ct. 2440, 91 L.Ed.2d 110 (1986), on remand 802 F.2d 441 (1st Cir.1986). This case involved a state prohibition on the importation of live bait fish from out of state. Stevens said, "There is something fishy about this case." 477 U.S. at 152, 106 S.Ct. at 2454.

67.25 Buckley v. Illinois Judicial Inquiry Board, 997 F.2d 224 (7th Cir. 1993), invalidating various restrictions imposed on judicial campaign speech. For a case rejecting this viewpoint (and described in Buckley as being "distinguishable, although precariously"), see, Stretton v. Disciplinary Board, 944 F.2d 137 (3d Cir.1991).

XIII. REGULATION OF THE TIME, PLACE, AND MANNER OF SPEECH IN PUBLIC PLACES AND THE PUBLIC FORUM

§ 20.46 Licensing Schemes Implemented by Administrators and Injunctions Issued by the Courts

Page 289, add to text after note 2:

In short, a permit scheme, first, may not constitutionally grant to the government administrator an overly broad amount of discretion, and second, the decision to grant or deny the permit may not be based on the content of the message.

Page 291, add to text after note 11:

In *Forsyth County v. The Nationalist Movement* [11.5] the Court invalidated, on its face, an ordinance permitting the administrator to vary the permit fee based on the content of the demonstration or parade. The ordinance allowed the administrator to vary the fee based on his or her estimate of the cost of maintaining public order. The fee was not to exceed $1000 per day of the parade, open air meeting, or procession.

First, the ordinance granted the administrator too much discretion. For example, it was up to the county administrator to decide whether the fee imposed would include any or all of the county's administrative expenses. The administrator could also decide to charge *no* fee.[11.10]

Second, the ordinance, in effect, required that the fee be based on the content of the demonstration, parade, or procession, because the fee charged was supposed to cover the "cost of necessary and reasonable protection of persons participating in or observing" the activity. Given this test, the administrator must, of necessity, look at the content of the message that is displayed, estimate the response of persons observing that message, and determine the number of police necessary to meet the expected response. To the extent that observers of the parade are likely to throw bottles, the organizers of the parade will have to pay more for their permit, because it is the seekers of the license, not the observers, that must pay the costs. The Court concluded that the listeners' reaction to speech is not a content-neutral basis for regulation. The fact that the speaker provokes controversy rather than is boring is not a reason to increase the permit fee. Free speech should not become more costly simply because the observers turn themselves into a hostile mob.[11.15]

Nominal License Fees. Finally, *Forsyth County* held that the $1000 maximum cap on the fee did not save it from invalidity. In fact, even a nominal fee would be unconstitutional. What makes the

Forsyth County fee unconstitutional is that the amount of the fee is a function of the content of the speech. In addition, the imposition of fee lacks procedural safeguards. Thus, in concluding its opinion, the Court held that *under these circumstances,* "no limit on such a fee can remedy these constitutional violations." [11.20]

11.5 505 U.S. 123, 112 S.Ct. 2395, 120 L.Ed.2d 101 (1992). Blackmun, J., delivered the opinion of the Court. Rehnquist, C.J., joined by White, Scalia, and Thomas, JJ., filed a dissenting opinion.

11.10 Contrast, Cox v. New Hampshire, 312 U.S. 569, 576–77, 61 S.Ct. 762, 765–66, 85 L.Ed. 1049 (1941). In that case, the language in the statute at issue granted to the administrator a great deal of discretion. However, as that statute was interpreted and applied, the discretion was not unfettered but was limited in important ways. In this case, there was no testimony or

evidence that indicated anything that would place limits on the administrator's unfettered discretion. 505 U.S. at 133 n. 11, 112 S.Ct. at 2403 n. 12.

11.15 This principle, which is hardly a new one, did not originate with this case. See, e.g., Schneider v. State, 308 U.S. 147, 162, 60 S.Ct. 146, 151, 84 L.Ed. 155 (1939); Murdock v. Pennsylvania, 319 U.S. 105, 116, 63 S.Ct. 870, 876, 87 L.Ed. 1292 (1943); Hustler Magazine v. Falwell, 485 U.S. 46, 55–56, 108 S.Ct. 876, 881–82, 99 L.Ed.2d 41 (1988).

11.20 505 U.S. at 136, 112 S.Ct. at 2405.

§ 20.47 Reasonable Time, Place, and Manner Restrictions on Speech, Without Regard to Content

(a) Introduction

Page 296, add to note 1:

1. Hoffman, J., citing Treatise in, Borchert v. State, 621 N.E.2d 657, 658 (Ind.App.3d Dist.1993).

Page 296, add new note to end of first paragraph:

". . . unrelated to content." [1.5]

1.5 Blair Arnold, joined by Corbin, J., citing Treatise and dissenting in   Hodges v. Gray, 321 Ark. 7, 17, 901 S.W.2d 1, 6 (1995).

Page 297, add to text after note 4:

If the category of speech is not always excluded from first amendment protection—for example, obscenity is a category of speech excluded from protection—then, as noted below, for the state to enforce a content-based restriction on speech, the state must show that its regulation is necessary to serve a compelling state interest and is narrowly tailored to achieve that goal.[4.5]

4.5 See § 20.47(c), below, discussing, e.g., Perry Education Association v. Perry Local Educators' Association, 460   U.S. 37, 44–46, 103 S.Ct. 948, 954–55, 74 L.Ed.2d 794 (1983), on remand 705 F.2d 462 (7th Cir.1983).

(b) Regulation of Sound and Noise

Page 300, add to note 11:

11. Madsen v. Women's Health Center, Inc., 512 U.S. 753, ___, 114 S.Ct. 2516, 2528, 2529, 129 L.Ed.2d 593 (1994), on remand 644 So.2d 86 (Fla. 1994), upholding a court injunction limiting, to certain hours, the use of sound amplification equipment in the area of an abortion clinic. The Court found that the limited noise restrictions burdened no more speech than necessary to protect the well–being of the clinic's patients. It is reasonable to have content–neutral noise control around medical facilities where patients undergo surgery and have recovery. Accord, N.L.R.B. v. Baptist Hospital, Inc., 442 U.S. 773, 783–84 n. 12, 99 S.Ct. 2598, 2604–05 n. 12, 61 L.Ed.2d 251 (1979). The Court in *Madsen* also upheld another portion of the injunction that prohibited sound amplification equipment within 300 feet of the residences of the staff of the abortion clinic, because it is reasonable for the Government to demand that the petitioners turn down the volume if the protests overwhelm the neighborhood.

(c) Where the Speech Takes Place—The Degrees of Public Forum

Page 308, add to text after first full paragraph:

In various cases the Court has made clear that if there is a public forum, the state cannot discriminate against religious speech in that forum. The fact that speech is religious certainly does not mean that the speech should have less First Amendment protection. To have freedom of speech without freedom of religious speech would be like playing *Hamlet* without the prince.[42.10]

42.10 Religious Speech and the Public Forum. Capitol Square Review and Advisory Board v. Pinette, 519 U.S. ___, 115 S.Ct. 2440, 132 L.Ed.2d 650 (1995). State law made Capitol Square, an open area next to the state capitol, the seat of government. It was used for public speeches, festivals, and celebrations advocating various causes, both secular and religious. To use the square, the applicant simply filled out a form and met several criteria concerning primarily safety, sanitation, and noninterference with other uses of this public square. The state policy was religiously neutral. However, the state refused to issue a permit to the Ku Klux Klan, which wanted to display a Latin cross. The state claimed that displaying the cross would violate the establishment clause. The Klan sued, the federal court ordered that the permit be issued, and the Supreme Court affirmed. The display was unattended. One might compare the display to a stationary parade float. The Court held that the state did not violate the establishment clause of the First Amendment when it permitted the Klan to display the cross. The case was argued on establishment clause grounds, not free speech grounds, and the Court found no establishment clause violation:

"[P]rivate religious speech, far from being a First Amendment orphan, is as fully protected under the Free Speech Clause as secular private expression." 519 U.S. at ___, 115 S.Ct. at 2446 (Scalia, J., for the Court).

Page 309, add new note 44.10 after third sentence in first full paragraph:

... for public communication).[44.10] ...

44.10 See Judge Highsmith, quoting this Treatise in Pritchard v. Carlton, 821 F.Supp. 671, 675 n. 8 (S.D.Fla. 1993).

Page 310, add to text at end of first sentence of the third full paragraph:

This type of content-based restriction on speech must also be narrowly drawn to achieve this compelling state interest.

Page 311, add note 50.5 at end of second full paragraph:

". . . public officials oppose the speaker's viewpoint." [50.5]

    50.5 Timlin, J., citing Treatise, in Baca v. Moreno Valley Unified Sch.   Dist., 936 F.Supp. 719, 730 (C.D.Cal. 1996).

Page 312, add after carryover paragraph:

    News Racks on Public Sidewalks. *City of Cincinnati v. Discovery Network, Inc.,*[55.10] held that it was unconstitutional for the City of Cincinnati to ban the distribution of "commercial" publications (such as free magazines advertising real estate sales) through the use of free-standing news racks on public property, such as city sidewalks. The City did not extend the ban to similar news racks containing newspapers. The city called the commercial publications "commercial handbills" and argued that the purpose of its prohibition was to make the sidewalks more attractive and promote safer streets (e.g., people might trip over the news racks). However, while the city sought to remove the 62 news racks distributing these commercial publications, it did not apply its prohibition to news racks (numbering about 1,500 to 2,000) that sold regular *newspapers,* which the City deemed to be publications published daily or weekly and *primarily* covering or commenting on current events.

    The Court concluded, first, that the city had the burden to "establish a 'reasonable fit' between its legitimate interests in safety and esthetics and its choice of a limited and selective prohibition of news racks as the means chosen to serve those interests." Second, Cincinnati did not meet its burden of establishing a "reasonable fit." Indeed, Cincinnati's equivocal distinction between newspapers and commercial handbills "bears no relationship *whatsoever* to the particular interests that the city has asserted." [55.15] After all, if a news rack is an eyesore, that defect does not change merely because the contents of the news rack is a daily newspaper (with real estate advertisements) rather than a listing of real estate advertisements. The likelihood that someone might trip over a news rack is not a function of whether the news rack contains newspapers or handbills.

    Admittedly, the city has a valid concern with the aggregate number of news racks on the streets, but not with their contents, which does not affect the attractiveness of the outside of the news racks. If the city wished to reduce the number of news racks, it could have done that without considering their contents. The city, for example, could have eliminated 10% of the total number by lot.

There is, in short, no basis of distinction between "newspapers" and "handbills" that is relevant to any interest that the city has asserted. Even assuming that the city could ban all news racks on public property, that would not justify the *discriminatory* ban (based on the content of the news racks) that the city imposed. This content-based restriction is also not a valid time, place, or manner restriction.[55.20]

55.10 507 U.S. 410, 113 S.Ct. 1505, 123 L.Ed.2d 99 (1993). Rehnquist, C.J., joined by White & Thomas, JJ., filed a dissenting opinion.

55.15 507 U.S. at 424, 113 S.Ct. at 1514 (emphasis in original).

55.20 Blackmun, J., concurring, stated that he believed that the Court's case law affords insufficient protection for truthful, noncoercive commercial speech concerning lawful activities. Intermediate scrutiny is appropriate for time, place, or manner restrictions

(without regard to content) or when the restraint on commercial speech is designed to protect the consumer from misleading or coercive speech, but "not for a regulation that suppresses truthful commercial speech to serve some other government purpose." He concluded by stating that he hoped that the Court will favor giving "full protection for truthful, noncoercive commercial speech about lawful activities." 507 U.S. at 430–33, 113 S.Ct. at 1517–18 (Blackmun, J., concurring).

Page 313, add to note 61:

61. Non–stationary Pickets. Following *Frisby,* the picketers in that case continued to picket, but there was no longer any stationary picketing. Eventually the doctor who was the subject of the picketing moved his practice and declared bankruptcy, which was caused in part by a malpractice suit that the doctor claimed had been sponsored by his opponents. The doctor also announced that he would no longer perform abortions. Wall Street Journal, April 7, 1993, at B10, col. 1–2 (midwest ed.).

See, Madsen v. Women's Health Center, Inc., 512 U.S. 753, ___, 114 S.Ct.

2516, 2530, 129 L.Ed.2d 593 (1994), on remand 644 So.2d 86 (Fla.1994), invalidating a portion of a court injunction that prohibited picketing and demonstrating within 300 feet of the residences of the staff of an abortion clinic. The 300 foot ban is not limited to "focused picketing" solely in front of a particular residence, but would also ban general marching. A narrower ban, limited as to time, duration of picketing, and number of pickets outside of a smaller zone would have accomplished any legitimate state purposes.

Page 316, add to text after carryover paragraph:

Aggressive Begging on the Public Streets. Is it constitutional for a state or locality to prohibit aggressive begging or panhandling on the public streets and sidewalks? Some cities and other units of government are responding to complaints that aggressive beggars are intimidating passers-by on the city streets and sidewalks by aggressively asking for handouts. Begging, that is, asking for money, is a form of speech. The supplicant is *asking* for money. As the next subsection explains, the first amendment does place limits on the government when it seeks to regulate charities when soliciting funds; the government can protect the prospective donors from fraud, but the government does not have *carte blanche* to enact excessive regulations.[69.10]

Aggressive begging should be distinguished from mere passive begging. The passive beggar simply sits on the street or sidewalk or subway platform, may have a hat in his or her hand, and by a sign or simple statement ask for money. The aggressive beggar hollers or screams at a particular person while asking for funds, will follow or may even chase after a prospective donor, often shouts obscenities if the donation is not given or is not large enough. The aggressive beggar as opposed to the passive beggar is intimidating and thus the prospective donor feels threatened. The beggar may block the sidewalk or other passage way, or ask for money in a confined space, such as in a subway tunnel, or in front of an automated teller machine.

The Supreme Court has not yet decided this specific issue. In *United States v. Kokinda*,[69.15] a case involving postal property, the Court did recognize that there is a greater role for state regulation when solicitors *impede* the normal flow of traffic and are *intrusive* in a *face-to-face* setting. In connection with lawyer advertising, it emphasized the important difference between advertising and *face-to-face solicitation*. In *Ohralik v. Ohio State Bar*,[69.20] a lawyer-solicitation case, the Court emphasized that the state had power to protect people from "those aspects of solicitation that involve fraud, undue influence, *intimidation,* overreaching, and other forms of *'vexatious conduct.'* " [69.25] And, in connection with airport terminals, the Court (while deciding that the terminal was not a public forum) upheld an anti-solicitation regulation. The Court noted that *face-to-face* solicitation creates special risks of duress.[69.30] In a separate opinion, Justice O'Connor noted:

> "As residents of metropolitan areas know from daily experience, confrontation by a person asking for money . . . is more intrusive and intimidating than an encounter with a person giving out information." [69.35]

On the other hand, in various charitable solicitation cases, the Court has not distinguished between *face-to-face* solicitation and other types of solicitation.[69.40]

One important issue to consider with respect to laws that regulate aggressive begging is whether they are unconstitutionally vague. The degree of vagueness that the Constitution tolerates is less in a free speech case than in other areas. To the extent that the regulation governs action rather than pure speech, the Court allows more vagueness.[69.45] The Court also allows more vagueness when the threat is greater. For example, a statute forbidding reckless walking would be unconstitutional, while a statute forbidding reckless driving is not void for vagueness.

69.10 See, § 20.47(d), Regulation to Prevent Fraud, below.

Aggressive Begging. See generally, Helen Hershkoff, Aggressive Panhandling Laws: Do These Statutes Violate the Constitution?, Yes: Silencing the Homeless, ABA Journal 40 (June 1993);

Roger Conner, Aggressive Panhandling Laws: Do These Statutes Violate the Constitution?, No: A Solution to Intimidation, ABA Journal 41 (June 1993).

In Roulette v. City of Seattle, 850 F.Supp. 1442 (W.D.Wash.1994), the district court held that a city ordinance

53

that prohibited sitting or lying on public sidewalks in commercial districts during certain hours did not, on its face, violate the Constitution. The court also held that the ordinance forbidding aggressive begging was not unconstitutionally overbroad or vague. The court did strike a portion of the ordinance what was vague and overbroad (listing circumstances that are to be considered to determine if begging is aggressive), so as to limit the scope of the ordinance to constitutionally permissible bounds.

69.15 497 U.S. 720, 110 S.Ct. 3115, 111 L.Ed.2d 571 (1990), a decision with no majority opinion.

69.20 436 U.S. 447, 98 S.Ct. 1912, 56 L.Ed.2d 444 (1978). Compare, In re Primus, 436 U.S. 412, 98 S.Ct. 1893, 56 L.Ed.2d 417 (1978). See generally § 20.31, above.

69.25 436 U.S. at 462, 98 S.Ct. at 1921 (footnote omitted) (emphasis added).

69.30 International Society for Krishna Consciousness, Inc. v. Lee, 505 U.S. 672, 112 S.Ct. 2701, 120 L.Ed.2d 541 (1992).

69.35 International Society for Krishna Consciousness, Inc. v. Lee, 505 U.S. 672, 690–92, 112 S.Ct. 2711, 2713–14, 120 L.Ed.2d 541 (1992) (O'Connor, J., concurring in No. 91–155 and concurring in the judgment in No. 91–339).

69.40 E.g., Schaumburg v. Citizens for a Better Environment, 444 U.S. 620, 629, 100 S.Ct. 826, 832, 63 L.Ed.2d 73 (1980), rehearing denied 445 U.S. 972, 100 S.Ct. 1668, 64 L.Ed.2d 250 (1980).

See generally, § 20.47(d).

69.45 See § 20.9, The Void-for-Vagueness Doctrine.

Page 322, add to text after note 98:

School Buildings, After Hours. In *Lamb's Chapel v. Center Moriches Union Free School District*,[98,10] the Court, without dissent, reversed the trial and appellate courts and invalidated New York regulations that were used to deny to a church access to school premises (after the regular school day was completed) because the church wished to exhibit for public viewing and for religious purposes a film that dealt with family and child-rearing issues. The school rule allowed after-hours use of school property for social, civic, and recreational uses *but not* for religious purposes. The Court, speaking through Justice White, agreed that the school had created only a limited public forum, but in this case the school had denied access to a nonpublic forum based on the viewpoint of the speaker: the rules permitted school property to be used for the presentation of all views about family planning and child-rearing except those dealing with the subject from a religious viewpoint.[98.15]

State University Funding of Student Organizations, Including Student Religious Groups. The University of Virginia, a state school, paid the printing costs of publications of student groups. The Student Activities Fund (SAF) would pay outside contractors for these printing costs. These student groups were independent of the University and not controlled by it. In administering the Student Activities Fund, the University engaged in viewpoint discrimination against a particular student newspaper; the school refused to pay the publication costs of a particular student group because it had a Christian perspective. University regulations gave funds to student groups *except* those that "promot[ed] or manifest[ed] a particular belie[f] in or about a deity or an ultimate reality."

In *Rosenberger v. Rector and Visitors of the University of Virginia* [98.20], Justice Kennedy, for the Court, held that the SAF was a limited public forum, and—in light of *Lamb's Chapel* —the University was unconstitutionally discriminating against the viewpoint advocated by this particular student publication. Providing funds to student publications on a neutral basis is no different than providing access to facilities. Public funds, or compulsory student activity fees, are involved when the school grants access, because the facility must be kept up, heated, maintained, and repaired. Just as the school in *Lamb's Chapel* could not constitutionally deny access to a public forum on the basis of religious belief, so also the University of Virginia could not constitutionally refuse to provide funding for a particular student publication because of the religious advocacy of that publication. The University realized that it could not deny funding to the publications of a student group based on the secular views of the group; religious views are deserving of no lesser status under the First Amendment.

The University of Virginia's funding of student publications, including those publications that promoted or manifested belief in a deity, did not violate the establishment clause of the First Amendment because the government program was neutral towards religion. In short, the establishment clause does not require the state to exclude an otherwise eligible student group from participation in the student activity fund on the basis of religious viewpoint if such exclusion would violate the free speech and press clauses of the First Amendment if the viewpoint were nonreligious. For example, if student organizations had access to university computers and word processing, then, a religious student organization should also have access (on a religiously neutral basis) to university computers and word processing. The student organization could use the equipment to create speech with a religious viewpoint or content. The state's action "in providing the group with access would no more violate the Establishment Clause than would giving those groups access to an assembly hall." [98.25] There is no logical, or constitutional, difference between the school using funds to operate and maintain the computer or paying a third party to operate and maintain the computer.

Justice Souter, speaking for a four-person dissent, likened the University of Virginia's payment to the third party of photocopying and publication costs to the state's payment of the salary of a clergyman. He claimed that the majority required the University of Virginia to use "public funds for the direct subsidization of preaching the word," and that is "categorically forbidden by the Establishment Clause." [98.30] One should realize that state payment of the salary of a clergyman is different because the payment cannot be neutral. The state cannot pay for clergymen, whether or not they are religious, because clergymen by definition are religious. But a school can neutrally give access to student groups,

55

whether those groups advocate religion or politics. And the state can neutrally fund student publications, whether those publications advocate religion, atheism, politics, or hedonism.

Souter did not object to earlier cases where the Court approved of government aid neutrally given to religious and nonreligious groups. But, he argued, in those cases "the aid was indirect." [98.35] However, if "directness" is so important, the aid in *Rosenberger* was indirect, because it never went directly to the student group; instead the University paid publication costs to a third party. And, if Souter is really insistent that the state cannot aid neutrally, it would, under Souter's view, be antagonistic towards religion. Surely the fire department, in putting out a blaze, should not refuse to help a local church if it were on fire, even though the church never paid property or income taxes to finance the fire department. [98.40]

98.10 508 U.S. 384, 113 S.Ct. 2141, 124 L.Ed.2d 352 (1993).

98.15 The Court also concluded that there was no establishment clause violation under the three-part test that Lemon v. Kurtzman, 403 U.S. 602, 91 S.Ct. 2105, 29 L.Ed.2d 745 (1971), had articulated, because the film would not be shown during school hours, the school was not sponsoring the test, and it was not realistic to think that the general public would think that the school was endorsing religion or any particular creed. Any benefit to religion or to the particular church was incidental. Scalia, J., joined by Thomas, J., concurred in the judgment, and objected to the majority's invocation of *Lemon*:

"Like some ghoul in a late-night horror movie that repeatedly sits up in its grave and shuffles abroad, after being repeatedly killed and buried, *Lemon* stalks out Establishment Clause jurisprudence once again, frightening the little children and school attorneys of Center Moriches Union Free School District.... Over the years, however, no fewer than five of the currently sitting Justices have, in their own opinions, personally driven pencils through the creature's heart (the author of today's opinion repeatedly), and the sixth has joined an opinion doing so.... What a strange notion, that a Constitution which *itself* gives 'religion in general' preferential treat-

ment (I refer to the Free Exercise Clause) forbids endorsement of religion in general."

Kennedy, J., filed a separate opinion concurring in part and in the judgment, agreeing "with Justice Scalia that the Court's citation of *Lemon v. Kurtzman* is unsettling and unnecessary."

98.20 519 U.S. ___, 115 S.Ct. 2510, 132 L.Ed.2d 700 (1995). See also, Board of Education of Westside Community Schools v. Mergens, 496 U.S. 226, 248, 252, 110 S.Ct. 2356, 2370–71, 2373, 110 L.Ed.2d 191 (1990); Board of Education of Kiryas Joel Village School District v. Grumet, 512 U.S. 687, ___, 114 S.Ct. 2481, 2491, 129 L.Ed.2d 546 (1994).

98.25 519 U.S. at ___, 115 S.Ct. at 2523.

98.30 519 U.S. at ___, 115 S.Ct. at 2535 (Souter, J., dissenting, joined by Stevens, Ginsburg, & Breyer, JJ.).

98.35 519 U.S. at ___, 115 S.Ct. at 2541 (Souter, J., dissenting, joined by Stevens, Ginsburg, & Breyer, JJ.).

98.40 Souter has no real answer to this problem. In a footnote he announced that police and fire protection should be provided, but he did not explain why his analysis allowed these exceptions. 519 U.S. at ___ n. 5, 115 S.Ct. at 2541 n. 5 (Souter, J., dissenting, joined by Stevens, Ginsburg, & Breyer, JJ.).

Page 324, add to carryover paragraph, after note 103:

Subsequently, the Court surprised many observers by holding that a government-owned airport is not a public forum. This conclusion is the product of two opinions, decided the same day. The first one is *International Society for Krishna Consciousness,*

Inc. v. Lee,[103.5] where Chief Justice Rehnquist wrote the opinion of the Court. The second is *Lee v. International Society for Krishna Consciousness, Inc.*[103.10] a short Per Curiam opinion, where Chief Justice Rehnquist filed a dissenting opinion, joined by Justices White, Scalia, and Thomas.

The International Society for Krishna Consciousness, Inc., a not-for-profit religious corporation, challenged the Port Authority, which had placed restrictions on the distribution and literature and the solicitation of contributions in airport terminals under its control. In *Lee,* the first case, the Court held that the airport terminal was a nonpublic forum and that the prohibition on the solicitation of contributions was reasonable and thus permissible. In the Per Curiam opinion, the second case, the Court held that the ban on the distribution of literature was protected by the first amendment.

The Krishna's practice, a ritual known as *sankirtan,* consists of going into public places, disseminating religious literature and soliciting funds to support the religion. The Port Authority controls three airport terminals servicing the New York City metropolitan area. These terminals are generally open to the public and contain various stores, snack shops, restaurants, newsstands, etc. The majority noted that nearly all the people who use the terminals are either terminal employees or visit for reasons related to air travel, such as changing planes, dropping off or picking up passengers, or taking flights.

The majority readily agreed that *sankirtan* is a form of speech, but rejected the argument that airport terminals, like the sidewalks and streets, are public fora. First, "given the lateness with which the modern air terminal has made its appearance" on the public scene, it cannot be described as "immemorially" held in the public trust.[103.15]

The majority is certainly correct that airport terminals have a relatively late appearance in an historical sense, but one might say the same thing about superhighways, or state-owned oases along side of these highways. The airplane, no less than the automobile, is also a relatively late invention. But the state-owned air terminal is a lot like state-owned streets: people use these facilities to go from one place to another, and alongside these streets and sidewalks are a lot of restaurants, newsstands, stores, etc. The public areas of the airport terminal, like the city sidewalks, are open generally, without restriction. One need not possess an airline ticket to roam freely in the public area outside the security checkpoints.

Although it may be said that the main purpose of airports is to facilitate travel, to go from point *A* to point *B,* not to promote expressive activity, it equally may be said that the main purpose of streets is to facilitate travel, to go from point *A* to point *B,* not to promote expressive activity. The sidewalk, no less than an airport terminal, serves to facilitate transportation. And, in neither case, can it be said that the main purpose of the sidewalk (or the terminal) is to promote expressive activity. An important similarity between the publicly-owned airport terminal and the city sidewalks is that in both cases, expressive activity is harmonious and compatible with the transportation uses of the facility.

Second, the majority rejected the comparison of airports with bus or rail terminals, even though all may be regarded as transportation modes. Although bus or train stations historically have allowed expressive activities such as passing out literature or the solicitation of funds, this fact is "irrelevant;" the crucial difference, according to the majority, is that "bus and rail terminals traditionally have had *private* ownership." [103.20]

One would think that if, historically, even *private* bus and train terminals have been opened up for general expressive activities, then *a fortiori*, a *public* transportation terminal should be considered a public forum. But the majority asserted:

> "The development of privately owned parks that ban speech activity would not change the public fora status of publicly held parks. But the reverse is also true. The practices of privately held transportation centers do not bear on the government's regulatory authority over a publicly owned airport." [103.25]

Unfortunately, other than asserting by *ipse dixit*—"But the reverse is also true."—the Court does not explain *why* the reverse is also true.

The majority also argued that when new methods of transportation are developed, there should be new inquiries as to whether the transportation necessities are compatible with various types of expressive activity. It was very important to the majority that state-owned airports are like privately owned airports in that they are *commercial* establishments funded by user fees and designed to make a regulated profit. This purpose may be frustrated if airports are also required to provide for the free exchange of ideas.

Anti–solicitation Prohibition. Given that state-owned airport terminals are not public fora, the majority then concluded that the prohibition on solicitation of funds was "*reasonable.*" Solicitors might slow down the pace of traffic, thus affecting passengers in a hurry to catch a flight. Passengers wishing to avoid the solicitor would have to alter their path; the very act of solicitation might slow down the harried passenger, who may already be loaded with luggage and children in tow.

The majority also noted that *face to face* solicitation[103.30] of funds creates special risks of duress and fraud. The people solicited are often too polite to tell the solicitor to just go away. The unsavory solicitor can target the most vulnerable, such as the handicapped, or those accompanied by small children, who may be on tight schedules and cannot easily avoid the solicitation. In this environment, the solicitor can more easily commit fraud, short-change the purchaser, who is too short of time to file complaints with the proper authorities.

For these reasons, the Port Authority limited solicitation to the sidewalk areas outside of the airport terminals. Because it is not necessary for the Port Authority to demonstrate that the solicitation of funds was the most reasonable or only reasonable way of dealing with what the Port Authority saw was a problem, the anti-solicitation regulations were permissible.

Distribution of Literature. In the short Per Curiam opinion following *Lee,* a different majority of the Court (composed of various judges unable to agree on a rationale) [103.35] concluded that a ban on the distribution of literature in the airport terminals is invalid under the first amendment. Justice O'Connor's separate opinion made clear that only the *free* distribution of literature, or leafletting, is protected because it does not present the same kinds of problems (other than litter) associated with face-to-face solicitation of funds.[103.40] That opinion, in connection with the views of Chief Justice Rehnquist and Justices White, Scalia, and Thomas, constitute a five person majority that would allow the Port Authority to ban the face-to-face distribution of literature *for sale.*[103.45]

Content–Based Restrictions in the Areas Surrounding Polling Places

Burson v. Freeman [103.50] represents a rare case, where the Court approved of content-based restrictions in a public forum. The Court balanced two important rights: the right to engage in political speech, which is at the heart of the first amendment, and the right to vote, the right that is preservative of all our rights and at the heart of democracy.

A Tennessee law (like the law of many other jurisdictions) prohibited the solicitation of votes and the display or distribution of campaign materials within 100 feet of the entrance to a polling place. The Tennessee Supreme Court held that the law violated the first and fourteenth amendments, but the Supreme Court, with no majority opinion, reversed.

The law was clearly content-based. It did not prohibit commercial solicitation in the area immediately surrounding the voting booth. The law not only restricted but entirely prohibited public discussion of an entire topic within the forbidden zone, in this case within 100 feet of the entrance to a polling place, which was a "campaign free" zone.

Justice Blackmun's plurality found that the section was a facially content-based restriction on speech in a public forum, and must be subjected to exacting scrutiny. However, this law survived this test.[103.55] It was necessary to serve a compelling state interest to prevent voter intimidation and election fraud. "The only way to preserve the secrecy of the ballot is to limit access to the area around the voter." The next question is *"how large* a restricted zone is permissible or sufficiently tailored." The plurality rejected the argument that the 100 foot boundary was not narrowly tailored. Admittedly, the state had no empirical proof, but "it is difficult to make specific findings about the effects of a voting regulation." The Tennessee Supreme Court had required that the boundary be reduced to 25 feet, but it takes only about 15 seconds to walk the 75 additional feet. Whatever the boundary is, the plurality concluded that a 100 foot boundary is on the constitutional side of the line. It "is the rare case in which we have held that a law survives strict scrutiny. This, however, is such a rare case." [103.60]

Justice Scalia, concurring in the judgment, argued that if the category of "traditional public forum" is to be an analytical tool rather than a conclusory label, "it must remain faithful to its name and derive its content from *tradition*." [103.65] The area around the polling booth, *"by long tradition,"* was not a public forum. He would uphold the law as a reasonable, viewpoint-neutral regulation of a *non*public forum.

Injunctions of Protests In the Public Forum: Abortion Clinics

In *Madsen v. Women's Health Center, Inc.*[103.70] the Court considered the constitutionality of a state court injunction entered against protestors at a Florida abortion clinic. A divided Court, applying the first amendment, upheld parts of the injunction and invalidated other parts.

The original state court injunction prohibited the petitioners from blocking or interfering with public access of the abortion clinic and from physically abusing persons entering or leaving the clinic. This injunction applied to protest activities in the traditional public forum, the streets and sidewalks. The state court broadened this injunction after it concluded that protestors were still interfering with access to the clinic. This broadened injunction, which the U.S. Supreme Court reviewed, applied to petitioners, Operation Rescue and various other named organizations, their agents, and "all persons acting in concert or participation with them, or on their behalf;" it prohibited them from engaging in various acts. The Court invalidated parts of the injunction and upheld other parts. The injunction appears in the margin.[103.71]

Chief Justice Rehnquist, for the Court, upheld parts of this injunction and overruled other parts. He concluded that, given the particular factual circumstances and the record before the Court, the state court's establishment of a 36 foot buffer zone on a public street from which demonstrators were excluded does not violate the first amendment because it burdened no more speech than necessary to prevent unlawful conduct. But the Court invalidated other parts of the injunction are unconstitutional under the first amendment because they were broader than necessary—a 36 foot buffer zone applied to private property, a prohibition of "images observable" from the abortion clinic, a 300 foot buffer zone around residences.

Injunctions and the Requirement of Content Neutral Speech. First, the Court turned to the question of whether the injunction was "content neutral." The majority rejected the argument that the injunction was content neutral simply because it only applied to restrict the speech of abortion protestors. An injunction, by its very nature, said the Court, applies to particular persons because of their actions in the context of a specific dispute. The injunction regulates "their activities, and perhaps their speech," because of their past actions in a specific circumstance.[103.72] Although the amended injunction did not apply to prohibit demonstrations by people supporting abortions, that fact did not make it content based. The injunction was still content neutral, because there were no such demonstrations by people favoring abortions and thus no request for relief from such demonstrations.

The majority also argued that the injunction was content neutral because the government's restriction of petitioners was without reference to the content of petitioners' antiabortion message. The trial court injunction imposed "incidental restrictions" on the petitioners' message because they had "repeatedly violated" the original injunction. The fact that the "injunction covered people with a particular viewpoint does not itself render the injunction content or viewpoint based;" it only suggests that "those in the group *who conduct* violated the court's order happen to share the same opinion regarding abortions being performed at the clinic."[103.73] Therefore the injunction does not demand the "heightened scrutiny" as provided in *Perry Education Association*.

Evaluating a Content Neutral Injunction. The Court was evaluating an injunction and not a statute. Even though it concluded that the injunction was content neutral, the injunction still limited protest activities in the traditional public forum. Thus, the Court determined that there should be a "somewhat more stringent application of general First Amendment principles" than would be applied in traditional time, place, and manner analysis.[103.74] A statute or ordinance is generally applicable and represents a choice made by the legislative processes. An injunction has a greater risk of censorship and discriminatory application because one judge imposes it, obviously without any legislative debate. However, an injunction, unlike a law, can be narrowly tailored to provide relief when a violation of law has already occurred.

In balancing these concerns, the Court ruled that the proper test is to determine whether the injunction's challenged provisions burden "no more speech than necessary" to accomplish its objective. The injunction must be narrowly drawn, "couched in the narrowest terms" necessary to accomplish its "pin–pointed objectives." [103.75]

In this case, the Court found that the governmental interests that the Florida Supreme Court had identified were "quite sufficient" to justify an appropriately tailored injunction.[103.76] The state court wished to protect a woman's right to secure a lawful abortion and receive medical counseling, protect public safety and the free flow of traffic on the city streets and sidewalks, and protect property rights and residential privacy.

36 Foot Buffer Zone to Keep Streets Open. The Court upheld the constitutionality of the 36 foot buffer zone around the clinic entrance and driveway. Even with this buffer zone, the protesters could be seen and heard from the clinic parking lots. This portion of the injunction, moreover, banned "focused picketing," and did not ban general dissemination of information, such as distributions of handbills and solicitation. The injunction, in these circumstances, burdened no more speech than necessary to accomplish its purpose of protecting access to the clinic and assisting an orderly traffic flow on the street.

Chief Justice Rehnquist said that, although the need for a complete buffer may be debatable, the Court should defer to the state court, which is more familiar with the facts and background of the disputes. Furthermore, the petitioners never certified a full record before the U.S. Supreme Court and argued against including the factual record. Significantly, the Court noted that the petitioners "are assuming, *arguendo,* that a factual basis exists to grant injunctive relief;" thus, the Court said that it must judge the case "*on the assumption* that the evidence and testimony presented to the state court supported its findings that the protesters standing, marching, and demonstrating near the clinic's entrance interfered with ingress to and egress from the clinic despite the issuance of the earlier injunction." [103.77]

36 Foot Buffer Zone as Applied to Private Property. The Court invalidated the injunction creating the buffer zone as applied to private property on the north and west sides of the clinic, because it burdened more speech than necessary. The patients and clinic staff did not have to cross the private property to reach the clinic. In addition, the record did not show that the protestors' activities on private property interfered with the clinic operation or access.[103.78]

Noise Restrictions. The Court upheld the limited noise restrictions because they burdened no more speech than necessary to protect the well–being of the clinic's patients. It is reasonable to have noise control around medical facilities where patients undergo surgery and have recovery.[103.79]

Ban on "Images Observable." The Court invalidated the broad injunction against the display of images observable from the clinic. This portion of the injunction is broader than necessary, because the clinic could simply pull the curtains on its windows if a patient is bothered by disagreeable placards. If the goal of the injunction is to reduce patients' anxiety, the court could have enjoined signs that could be interpreted as threats or veiled threats, but the injunction was much broader than that.[103.80]

300 Foot No Approach Zone. The Court invalidated the portion of the injunction that prohibited the petitioners from physically approaching anyone seeking clinic services within 300 feet of the clinic, unless the person approached indicated a desire for communication. It is difficult, said the Court, to justify prohibiting *"all* uninvited approaches" no matter how peaceful the contact might be.[103.81]

The "consent" requirement (prohibiting communication unless the person approached indicates a desire for communication)—this "requirement alone invalidates" this portion of the injunction because it burdens more speech than necessary to prevent intimidation and provide for access to the clinic.[103.82]

300 Foot Zone Residential Zone. The injunction prohibited the use of sound amplification equipment within 300 feet of the residences of the clinic staff. The Court allowed that restriction because it is reasonable for the Government to demand that the petitioners turn down the volume if the protests overwhelm the neighborhood.[103.83]

The injunction also prohibited impeding access to streets that provide the sole access to residences of the clinic staff. The Court upheld this provision as well, because it was necessary for the clinic staff to return to their residences.

The Court invalidated the prohibition against picketing and demonstrating within 300 feet of the residences of clinic staff. Although the residence is the "last citadel of the tired, the weary, and the sick," [103.84] the 300 foot ban is much larger than necessary. Also, it is not limited to focused picketing solely in front of a particular residence, but would ban general marching. A narrower ban, limited as to time, duration of picketing, and number of pickets outside a smaller zone, could have accomplished any legitimate purposes of the state.[103.85]

Standing and the "in concert" Restriction. The Court held that the petitioners did not have standing to challenge the court order as vague and overbroad because it applied to those "acting in concert" with the parties named in the injunction. Those people "acting in concert" with petitioners are not parties to this dispute. The petitioners have no standing to attack the portion of the order that does not apply to them.[103.86]

Freedom of Association. The Court rejected the claim that the "in concert" prohibition interfered with the petitioners' freedom of association. The petitioners could associate with others and express their viewpoints. The injunction only banned them from acting in concert with others to deprive third parties of their lawful rights.[103.87]

103.5 505 U.S. 672, 112 S.Ct. 2701, 120 L.Ed.2d 541 (1992). Rehnquist, C.J., delivered the opinion of the Court, joined by White, O'Connor, Scalia, and Thomas, JJ. O'Connor, J., filed a concurring opinion. Kennedy, J., filed an opinion concurring in the judgment, in part I of which Blackmun, Stevens, and Souter, JJ., joined. Souter, J., filed a dissenting opinion, in which Blackmun and Stevens, JJ., joined.

Lillian R. BeVier, Rehabilitating Public Forum Doctrine: In Defense of Categories, 1992 Supreme Court Review 79 (1992).

Government Corporations and State Action. While the Court held that airports are not public forums, a distinct question is whether there is state action. Although the government-owned airport involved state action, the Court found no public forum. The Court did not suggest that government-owned corporations do not involve state action.

Consider Lebron v. National Railroad Passenger Corp., ___ U.S. ___, 115 S.Ct. 961, 130 L.Ed.2d 902 (1995), on remand 69 F.3d 650 (2d Cir.1995). In that case, an artist sued Amtrak (the National Railroad Passenger Corp.) claiming that Amtrak violated the First Amendment when it rejected the artist's lease of billboard space because of its political content. Scalia, J., for the Court, held that Amtrak is a governmental agency or instrumentality for purposes of individual rights granted by the Constitution. The Court concluded:

"where, as here, the Government creates a corporation by special law, for the furtherance of governmental objectives, and retains for itself permanent authority to appoint a majority of the directors of that corporation, the corporation is part of the Government for purposes of the First Amendment." ___ U.S. at ___, 115 S.Ct. at 974–75.

It is true that Amtrak's authorizing statute states that it is not "an agency or establishment of the United States

Government." However, that statute settles the question of Amtrak's status as a governmental entity only for matters within the control of Congress, such as whether it is subject to statutes that impose obligations or confer powers on governmental entities (e.g., the Administrative Procedure Act, the Federal Advisory Committee Act; laws governing Government procurement), or whether Congress deprives it of sovereign immunity from suit. But Congress cannot exempt Amtrak from the restrictions of the First Amendment any more than Congress could declare by statute that the FBI is exempt from the Fourth Amendment. The Court then remanded for the lower court to decide the plaintiff's free speech claim. Only O'Connor, J., dissented. She argued that the plaintiff had earlier conceded that Amtrak was a private entity and should not be able to raise that issue before the Court.

103.10 505 U.S. 830, 112 S.Ct. 2709, 120 L.Ed.2d 669 (1992) (per curiam).

103.15 505 U.S. at 679, 112 S.Ct. at 2706.

103.20 505 U.S. at 681, 112 S.Ct. at 2707.

103.25 505 U.S. at 681, 112 S.Ct. at 2707.

103.30 Face-to-Face Solicitation. It is interesting to note that in prior cases dealing with the solicitation of funds the Court has not really distinguished between face-to-face solicitation and other types of solicitation. See, § 20.47(d). See also, Schaumburg v. Citizens for a Better Environment, 444 U.S. 620, 629, 100 S.Ct. 826, 832, 63 L.Ed.2d 73 (1980), rehearing denied 445 U.S. 972, 100 S.Ct. 1668, 64 L.Ed.2d 250 (1980); Riley v. National Federation of the Blind of North Carolina, Inc., 487 U.S. 781, 788–89, 108 S.Ct. 2667, 2673, 101 L.Ed.2d 669 (1988).

However, in commercial speech cases involving lawyers, in approving or disapproving of state regulation of lawyers, the Court has emphasized the importance of face-to-face solicitation as a justification for stricter state regulation to protect the public. See § 20.31.

103.35 Lee v. International Society for Krishna Consciousness, Inc., 505 U.S. 830, 112 S.Ct. 2709, 120 L.Ed.2d 669 (1992) (per curiam). See, O'Connor, J., concurring in No. 91–155 and concurring in the judgment in No. 91–339; Kennedy, J., joined by Blackmun, Stevens, and Souter, JJ. as to Part I, concurring in the judgment; Souter, joined by Blackmun and Stevens, JJ., concurring in the judgment in No. 91–339 and dissenting in No. 91–155.

103.40 O'Connor, J., concurring in No. 91–155 and concurring in the judgment in No. 91–339, 505 U.S. 672, 689–92, 112 S.Ct. 2711, 2713–14, 120 L.Ed.2d 541.

103.45 Kennedy, J., argued that air terminals are public fora; he was joined by Blackmun, Stevens, and Souter, JJ., on this point. In the remainder of Kennedy's separate opinion (in a portion that no one else joined), he argued that face-to-face solicitation could still be forbidden to the extent that the solicitor asked for the "immediate payment of money"; for example, he would allow the distribution of pre-addressed envelopes. Kennedy also concluded (again, with no one agreeing with him on this point) that the Port Authority's "flat ban on the distribution or sale of printed material must, in my view, fall in its entirety." International Society for Krishna Consciousness, Inc. v. Lee, 505 U.S. 672, 708, 112 S.Ct. 2711, 2723, 120 L.Ed.2d 541 (1992) (Kennedy, J., concurring in the judgment). The anomalous result of the Kennedy rule is that the solicitor cannot simply ask you for a donation, but he can ask that you pay him $15 for a one page typed brochure! Note that Justice Kennedy thinks that this distinction is constitutionally required.

While Kennedy's opinion argued that the *face-to-face sale* of literature is constitutionally protected in the airport terminals, the separate opinion of Souter, J., joined by Blackmun and Stevens, JJ. argued that all face-to-face solicitation of funds is constitutionally protected as free speech. Souter, J., joined by Blackmun and Stevens, JJ., concurring in the judgment in No. 91–339 and dissenting in 505 U.S. 672, 709–15, 112 S.Ct. 2711, 2724–26.

103.50 504 U.S. 191, 112 S.Ct. 1846, 119 L.Ed.2d 5 (1992). Blackmun, J., announced the judgment of the Court. He was joined by Rehnquist, C.J. and White and Kennedy, JJ. Kennedy, J., filed a concurring opinion; Scalia, J., filed an opinion concurring in the judgment. Kennedy, J., who joined Blackmun's opinion, also filed a concurring opinion, questioning the practice of suggesting that content-based limits on speech can be upheld if confined in a narrow way to serve a compelling state interest. The law at issue, in his view, was constitutional because it accommodated another important right, the right to vote.

Stevens, J., joined by O'Connor and Souter, JJ., dissented, arguing that the evidence that Tennessee introduced at trial to justify the 100 foot campaign-free zone was "exceptionally thin." Thomas, J., took no part in the consideration or decision of this case.

It is interesting to note that the National Labor Relations Board also restricts what would otherwise be free speech activities when they are engaged in, at, or near polling places in union representation elections. E.g., NLRB v. Carroll Contracting & Ready–Mix, Inc., 636 F.2d 111 (5th Cir.1981).

103.55 The evidence supporting the Tennessee law had historical support, both in this country and in other democracies, as Justice Blackmun recounted in his opinion. Tennessee first passed various polling regulations in 1890, as part of a switch to the Australian system, which that country had used to guarantee secret ballots and to protect the voters. By 1896, 90% of the states had adopted similar proposals, also in order to protect the voter from harassment and intimidation, and to protect the ballot from fraud. The particular regulations at issue in this case go back only to 1967, when Tennessee enacted a prohibition on the distribution of campaign literature within 100 feet of the polling place. All 50 states have similar restrictions. See, Note, Defoliating the Grassroots: Election Day Restrictions on Political Speech, 77 Georgetown L.J. 2137 (1989).

103.60 504 U.S. at 209, 112 S.Ct. at 1857 (Blackmun, J.).

103.65 504 U.S. at 213, 112 S.Ct. at 1859 (emphasis in original).

103.70 512 U.S. 753, 114 S.Ct. 2516, 129 L.Ed.2d 593 (1994), on remand 644 So.2d 86 (Fla.1994). Rehnquist, C.J., delivered the opinion of the Court, joined by Blackmun, O'Connor, Souter, & Ginsburg, JJ., and in part by Stevens, J. Souter, J., also filed a concurring opinion.

Stevens, J., filed an opinion concurring in part and dissenting in part. He would have upheld the 300 foot buffer zone around the clinic.

Scalia, J., joined by Kennedy & Thomas, JJ., filed an opinion concurring in part and dissenting in part. Justice Scalia vigorous opinion would have invalidated the entire injunction on free speech grounds and argued that the Court was creating a special rule for abortion cases, which have worked "a major distortion in the Court's constitutional jurisprudence," with the Court's "ad hoc nullification machine claim[ing] its greatest, and most surprising victim, the First Amendment." He explained:

"Because I believe that the judicial creation of a 36–foot zone in which only a particular group, which has broken no law, cannot exercise its rights of speech, assembly, and association, and the judicial enactment of a noise prohibition, applicable to that group and that group alone, are profoundly at odds with out First Amendment precedents and traditions, I dissent." 512 U.S. at ___, 114 S.Ct. at 2535.

Cf. Cheffer v. McGregor, 6 F.3d 705, 711 (11th Cir.1993), rehearing granted, opinion vacated 41 F.3d 1421 (11th Cir. 1994).

103.71 The injunction at issue provided, 512 U.S. at ___, 114 S.Ct. at 2522:

"(1) At all times on all days, from entering the premises and property of the Aware Woman Center for Choice [the Melbourne, Florida clinic]. . . .

"(2) At all times on all days, from blocking, impeding, inhibiting, or in any other manner obstructing or interfering with access to ingress into and egress from any building or parking lot of the Clinic.

"(3) At all times on all days, from congregating, picketing, patrolling, demonstrating or entering that portion of public right–of–way or private property within [36] feet of the property line of the Clinic. . . . An exception to the 36 foot buffer zone is the area immediately adjacent to the Clinic on the east. . . . The [petitioners] . . . must remain at least [5] feet from the Clinic's east line. Another exception to the 36 foot buffer zone relates to the record title owners of the property to the north and west of the Clinic. The prohibition against entry into the 36 foot buffer zones does not apply to such persons and their invitees. The other prohibitions contained herein do apply, if such owners and their invitees are acting in concert with the [petitioners]. . . .

"(4) During the hours of 7:30 a.m. through noon, on Mondays through Saturdays, during surgical procedures and recovery periods, from singing, chanting, whistling, shouting, yelling, use of bullhorns, auto horns, sound amplification equipment or other sounds or images observable to or within earshot of the patients inside the Clinic.

"(5) At all times on all days, in an area within [300] feet of the Clinic, from physically approaching any person seeking the services of the Clinic unless such person indicates a desire to communicate by approaching or by inquiring of the [petitioners]. . . .

"(6) At all times on all days, from approaching, congregating, picketing, patrolling, demonstrating or using bullhorns or other sound amplification equipment within [300] feet of the residence of any of the [respondents'] employees, staff, owners or agents, or blocking or attempting to block, barricade, or in any other manner, temporarily or otherwise, obstruct the entrances, exits or driveways of the residences of any of the [respondents'] employees, staff, owners or agents. The [petitioners] and those acting in concert with them are prohibited from inhibiting or impeding or attempting to impede, temporarily or otherwise, the free ingress or egress of persons to any street that provides the sole access to the street on which those residences are located.

"(7) At all times on all days, from physically abusing, grabbing, intimidating, harassing, touching, pushing, shoving, crowding or assaulting persons entering or leaving, working at or using services at the [respondents'] Clinic or trying to gain access to, or leave, any of the homes of owners, staff or patients of the Clinic.

"(8) At all times on all days, from harassing, intimidating or physically abusing, assaulting or threatening any present or former doctor, health care professional, or other staff member, employee or volunteer who assists in providing services at the [respondents'] Clinic.

"(9) At all times on all days, from encouraging, inciting, or securing other persons to commit any of the prohibited acts listed herein."

103.72 512 U.S. at ___, 114 S.Ct. at 2523.

103.73 512 U.S. at ___, 114 S.Ct. at 2524 (emphasis in original).

103.74 512 U.S. at ___, 114 S.Ct. at 2524. The majority noted that Justice Scalia argued that content neutral *injunctions* are *"at least* as deserving of strict scrutiny as a statutory, content–based restriction," 512 U.S. at ___, 114 S.Ct. at 2538 (emphasis in original) (Scalia, J., concurring in the judgment in part and dissenting in part). because injunctions are procedurally harder to challenge than statutes and individual judges should not be trusted in situations where they can suppress particular ideas. Stevens, J., in contrast, argued that the reviewing court should be more deferential to the court ordering the injunction. 512 U.S. at ___, 114 S.Ct. at 2531 (Stevens, J., concurring in part and dissenting in part).

103.75 512 U.S. at ___, 114 S.Ct. at 2526. See also, Carroll v. President and Commissioners of Princess Anne, 393 U.S. 175, 183, 89 S.Ct. 347, 353, 21 L.Ed.2d 325 (1968).

103.76 512 U.S. at ___, 114 S.Ct. at 2526.

103.77 512 U.S. at ___, 114 S.Ct. at 2527–28 (second emphasis added).

103.78 512 U.S. at ___, 114 S.Ct. at 2528.

103.79 512 U.S. at ___, 114 S.Ct. at 2528. See also, NLRB v. Baptist Hospital, Inc., 442 U.S. 773, 783–84 n. 12, 99 S.Ct. 2598, 2604–05 n. 12, 61 L.Ed.2d 251 (1979).

103.80 512 U.S. at ___, 114 S.Ct. at 2529.

103.81 512 U.S. at ___, 114 S.Ct. at 2529 (emphasis in original).

103.82 512 U.S. at ___, 114 S.Ct. at 2529.

See also, Boos v. Barry, 485 U.S. 312, 322, 108 S.Ct. 1157, 1164 99 L.Ed.2d 333 (1988), where the Court said that as "a general matter, we have indicated that in public debate our own citizens must tolerate insulting and even outrageous, speech in order to provide adequate breathing space to the freedoms protected by the First Amendment."

103.83 512 U.S. at ___, 114 S.Ct. at 2529.

103.84 Frisby v. Schultz, 487 U.S. 474, 484, 108 S.Ct. 2495, 2502, 101 L.Ed.2d 420 (1988). In contrast to the broad injunction in *Madsen*, the *Frisby* Court upheld an ordinance that was limited to "focused picketing taking place solely in font of a particular residence."

103.85 512 U.S. at ___, 114 S.Ct. at 2530.

103.86 512 U.S. at ___, 114 S.Ct. at 2530. See also, Regal Knitwear Co. v. N.L.R.B., 324 U.S. 9, 14–15, 65 S.Ct. 478, 481–82, 89 L.Ed. 661 (1945). In that case, a party has no standing to challenge an injunction applying to "successors and assigns" of the enjoined party, because the challenger was not a successor or assign; thus the challenge was an "abstract controversy over the use of these words."

103.87 512 U.S. at ___, 114 S.Ct. at 2530.

(d) Regulation to Prevent Fraud

Page 324, add to text after note 106:

McIntyre v. Ohio Elections Commission,[106.10] invalidated an Ohio statute that prohibited the distribution of anonymous campaign literature. Margaret McIntyre distributed leaflets objecting to a proposed school tax levy. Some of the handbills identified her only as expressing the views of "concerned parents and taxpayers." A school official complained that she was distributing unsigned leaflets in violation of the Ohio law, and the Ohio Election Commission imposed a $100 fine on her, and the Ohio Supreme Court rejected her first amendment challenge, arguing that the law was reasonable and serves to identify those who engage in fraud, libel, and false advertising.

The Supreme Court started with the proposition that an author is generally free to decide to be anonymous. Anonymity protects the author from the tyranny of the majority. She may be motivated, for example, by fear of economic, official, or social reprisal, or merely a desire to preserve her privacy. She may wish that the speech is evaluated without regard to its authorship. The decision to exclude her name is like other editorial decisions, an aspect of free speech, and this freedom is not limited to the literary realm. The Ohio law, the Court noted, has no language limiting its application to fraudulent, false, or libelous statements. While the law is limited to writings designed to influence an election ("core political speech"), it applies even if there is no hint of falsity or libel. It also regulates the speech based on its content (when the purpose of the speech is to influence an election). Because the law limits "core political expression," it must be subjected to "exacting scrutiny."

In this case, the name of the private author would probably be unknown to the recipient of the handbill, and identifying the author added little, if anything, to the reader's ability to evaluate the document's message. Ohio has other laws that prohibit fraud and libel, and a prohibition of anonymous leaflets is not its principal weapon. Moreover, the present law is overbroad. It applies not only to election of public officers but also to ballot issues. But ballot issues present neither a substantial risk of libel nor any potential appearance of corrupt advantage. The Ohio law applies to candidates and also to persons acting independently using only their own modest resources. The Court acknowledged that the State might be able to justify a limited identification requirement, but Ohio's rules go far beyond that. The state's restriction is much too broad.[106.15]

Anonymous, unidentified pamphleteering is not an evil that the state should stamp out; rather, it is a shield that protects the dissenter from the tyranny of the majority. It "not a pernicious, fraudulent practice, but an honorable tradition of advocacy and of dissent." [106.20] Ohio's blunderbuss approach violates free speech guarantees. A state, in short, may not seek "to punish fraud indirectly, by indiscriminately outlawing a category of speech, based on its content, with no necessary relationship to the danger sought to be prevented." [106.25]

106.10 517 U.S. ___, 115 S.Ct. 1511, 131 L.Ed.2d 426 (1995). Ginsburg, J., filed a concurring opinion. Thomas, J., concurred in the result. Scalia, J., joined by Rehnquist, C.J., dissented.

106.15 In other contexts, the Court has, at times, approved of narrow restrictions on anonymous speech. In First National Bank of Boston v. Bellotti, 435 U.S. 765, 792 n. 32, 98 S.Ct. 1407, 1424 n. 32, 55 L.Ed.2d 707 (1978), rehearing denied 438 U.S. 907, 98 S.Ct. 3126, 57 L.Ed.2d 1150 (1978), the Court said that

"Identification of the source of [corporate] advertising may be required as a means of disclosure so that the people will be able to evaluate the arguments to which they are being subjected." This dictum does not decide the issue involved in *McIntyre*. *Bellotti* involved corporate expenditures, which the Court has often treated as different from, and less protected than, individual communications.

In Buckley v. Valeo, 424 U.S. 1, 67, 96 S.Ct. 612, 657, 46 L.Ed.2d 659 (1976)

(per curiam), motion granted 424 U.S. 936, 96 S.Ct. 1153, 47 L.Ed.2d 727 (1976) the Court mentioned that "sources of a candidate's financial support also alert the voter to the interests to which a candidate is most likely to be responsive and thus facilitate predictions of future performance in office." This language only referred to financial contributions to a candidate or expenditures authorized by a candidate or his agent. Later in *Buckley* the Court approved of a requirement that "independent expenditures in excess of a threshold level be reported to the Federal Election Commission." 424 U.S. at 157–59, 160, 96 S.Ct. at 699–700, 701. However, that comment did not refer to any prohibition of anonymous leafleting. The disclosure rule mentioned in *Buck-*

ley only required identification to the Federal Election Commission of the amount and use of money expended in support of a candidate. The disclosure rule did not require self-identification of all writings related to elections.

Lobbying and Disclosure. In United States v. Harriss, 347 U.S. 612, 74 S.Ct. 808, 98 L.Ed. 989 (1954), the Court upheld limited disclosure requirements for lobbyists. Unlike the situation in *McIntyre*, lobbyists have direct access to elected officials, and the lack of any disclosure may cause the appearance of corruption and improper influence.

106.20 517 U.S. at ___, 115 S.Ct. at 1524.

106.25 517 U.S. at ___, 115 S.Ct. at 1524.

Page 327, add after carryover paragraph:

More recently, there is evidence that the Court has appreciated that *face-to-face* solicitation of funds raises special problems. There is a greater possibility of fraud and duress compared to mail solicitation.[113.5]

113.5 Face-to-Face Solicitation. See, International Society for Krishna Consciousness, Inc. v. Lee, 505 U.S. 672, 112 S.Ct. 2701, 120 L.Ed.2d 541 (1992), holding that the Port Authority may constitutionally ban face-to-face solicitation of funds, because such face-to-face activity raises special problems of fraud and duress. In prior cases dealing with the solicitation of funds the Court has not really distinguished between face-to-face solicitation and other types of solicitation. E.g., Schaumburg v. Citizens for a Better Environment, 444 U.S. 620, 629, 100 S.Ct. 826, 832, 63 L.Ed.2d 73 (1980), rehearing denied 445 U.S. 972,

100 S.Ct. 1668, 64 L.Ed.2d 250 (1980); Secretary of State of Maryland v. Joseph H. Munson Co., 467 U.S. 947, 959–61, 104 S.Ct. 2839, 2848–49, 81 L.Ed.2d 786 (1984); Riley v. National Federation of the Blind of North Carolina, Inc., 487 U.S. 781, 788–89, 108 S.Ct. 2667, 2673, 101 L.Ed.2d 669 (1988).

However, in cases involving lawyers, in approving or disapproving of state regulation of lawyers, the Court had earlier emphasized the importance of face-to-face solicitation as a justification for stricter state regulation. See § 20.31.

(e) Zoning Regulations

Page 335, add to note 159:

159. Compare, City of Ladue v. Gilleo, 512 U.S. 43, 114 S.Ct. 2038, 129 L.Ed.2d 36 (1994). A unanimous Court, invalidated a city ordinance that banned all residential signs, subject to certain exceptions: the law, for example, allowed small residential signs advertising that the property is for sale, signs for churches and schools, commercial signs in commercially zoned districts. The ordinance in question did not allow Margaret Gilleo to display an 8.5 by 11 inch sign in her window, stating: "For Peace in the Gulf." Gilleo opposed the Persian

Gulf War of 1990 to 1991. The City justified the ordinance as an effort to prevent "ugliness, visual blight and clutter," because signs "tarnish the natural beauty of the landscape," and so forth.

The Court assumed that the ordinance was viewpoint and content–neutral and that the various exemptions in the ordinance reflected legitimate differences among the side of effects of various kinds of signs. The Court invalidated the law, not because of its various exemptions—that is, not because the law discriminated on the basis of the content of speech—, but because the law simply prohibited too much speech. Even content–neutral restrictions are invalid if they unduly limit one's ability to engage in free expression.

In a footnote the Court explained that different considerations might apply "in the case of signs (whether political or otherwise) displayed by residents *for a fee*, or in the case of off–site commercial advertisements on residential property.

We also are not confronted here with mere regulations short of a ban." 512 U.S. at ___ n. 17, 114 S.Ct. at 2047 n. 17 (emphasis added). Such distinctions make sense. An individual's on–site residential sign indicating his or her political viewpoints offer a very inexpensive and convenient form of free speech, while a commercial advertiser, or anyone who is paying a fee for a sign, has many other effective outlets.

XIV. SYMBOLIC SPEECH

§ 20.48   Introduction

Page 336, add to note 3:

3. **Importance of Symbolic Speech.** Peter Meijes Tiersma, Nonverbal Communication and the Freedom of "Speech," 1993 Wis.L.Rev. 1525 (1993); Peter Meijes Tiersma, Linguistic Issues in the Law, 69 Language 113 (No. 1, 1993).

Page 336, add to note 4:

4. **The Pledge of Allegiance Led by Public School Teachers.** While the state may not require students to recite the pledge, the state may continue to start the school day with the pledge as long as no student is forced to partici-pate. School teachers may constitutionally continue to lead the students in the Pledge. Sherman v. Community Consolidated School District, 980 F.2d 437 (7th Cir.1992), cert. denied, 508 U.S. 950, 113 S.Ct. 2439, 124 L.Ed.2d 658 (1993).

§ 20.49   Fashioning a Test for First Amendment Protection for Symbolic Speech and the Role of Improper Legislative and Administrative Motivation

Page 347, add to note 53:

53. For a thoughtful analysis of the competing issues, see, Roger Pilon, ed., Flag–Burning, Discrimination, and the Right to Do Wrong (Cato Institute, Center for Constitutional Studies 1990).

Page 352, add to text after carryover paragraph:

The power of the state to legislate against and prosecute hate crimes does not offer the state *carte blanche* discretion whenever hate crimes are at issue. The state, in short, may not punish an individual merely for belonging to an association, even a racist one. For example, *Dawson v. Delaware* [73.5] held that the first amendment prohibited the state from introducing, in a capital sentencing proceeding, the fact that the defendant was a member of an organization called the Aryan Brotherhood, where that evidence had no relevance to the issues being decided. The evidence showed "nothing more" than the defendant's abstract beliefs, where those beliefs had no bearing on the issue being tried.[73.10] However, the state could have avoided this result by presenting evidence tying defendant's racist associations to the sentencing question. The prosecution in *Dawson* claimed that its expert witness (who did not testify) would have demonstrated that the Aryan Brotherhood, to which Dawson belongs, is a white racist prison gang associated with drugs and violent escape attempts at prisons, and which advocates the murder of fellow inmates. Such specific evidence, the Court explained, might have been relevant in rebutting the defendant's mitigating evidence consisting of testimony about his kindness to family members and the good time credits he earned by enrolling in various drug and alcohol programs in prison.[73.15]

73.5   503 U.S. 159, 112 S.Ct. 1093, 117 L.Ed.2d 309 (1992), on remand 608 A.2d 1201 (Del.1992). Chief Justice Rehnquist wrote the opinion for the Court. Blackmun, J. filed a concurring opinion. Thomas, J., dissented.

73.10   For example, the victim, like the defendant, was white, so no elements of racial hatred were involved in the murder; there was also no showing that the organization committed any unlawful or violent acts or even endorsed those acts.

73.15   503 U.S. at 167, 112 S.Ct. at 1099. Justice Thomas' dissenting opinion argued that the prison gang membership was relevant and admissible because it indicated that the defendant

had the character of a person who engages in prison gang activities. This evidence tended to establish future dangerousness and rebutted the defendant's effort to show that he was kind to others. The majority replied that the material that the dissent advanced on the nature of prison gangs "would, if it had been presented to the jury, have made this a different case." But Delaware only presented evidence of Dawson's "mere abstract beliefs. . . . " The majority explained that the jurors should not be able to punish Dawson merely because they find his beliefs to be morally reprehensible. 503 U.S. at 163–67, 112 S.Ct. at 1097–99.

Page 352, add new note to end of carryover paragraph:

". . . could not have been convicted."[73.20]

73.20   Najam, J., citing Treatise in, Board of Trustees of Hamilton Heights   School Corp. v. Landry, 638 N.E.2d 1261 (Ind.App.1st Dist.1994).

Page 359, add new note to end of first full paragraph:

"The Government . . . engaged in any public protest."[116.10]

116.10   Borman, J., citing Treatise in, Fieger v. Thomas, 872 F.Supp. 377, 387 (E.D.Mich.1994); Conlon, J., citing   Treatise in, Gomez v. Comerford, 1995 WL 23527, *10 (N.D.Ill.1995).

XV. REGULATION OF THE ELECTORAL PROCESS BY RESTRICTIONS ON CAMPAIGN FINANCING AND BY LIMITATIONS OF POLITICAL ACTIVITY OF GOVERNMENT EMPLOYEES

§ 20.51 Regulation of Campaign Financing

(b) Campaign Contributions and Expenditures

Page 367, replace first sentence of second full paragraph with the following:

The *Buckley* Court reasoned that the effective power of the Government to reduce corruption by limiting expenditures diminishes as the value of the communication increases.

Page 378, add to end of page:

The Political Party Expenditure Provision of the Federal Election Act of 1971. The Federal Election Campaign Act of 1971 included a provision that imposed dollar limits on a political party's expenditures "in connection with the general election campaign of a [congressional] candidate." In *Colorado Republican Federal Campaign Committee v. Federal Election Commission*,[60] the Colorado Republican Party (before it had selected its Senate candidate) bought radio advertisements attacking the Democratic Party's likely candidate for Senate. The Federal Election Commission claimed that this "expenditure" exceeded the dollar limits that the Federal Election Campaign Act imposed on a political party's expenditure in connection with the general election campaign. A fragmented Court, with no majority opinion, rejected the Federal Election Commission's assertion of power and ruled that the First Amendment prohibited applying that limitation on party expenditures to expenditures that the political party made "independently," that is, without coordination with any candidate.

---

60. ___ U.S. ___, 116 S.Ct. 2309, 135 L.Ed.2d 795 (1996). The particular section of the Federal Election Campaign Act at issue was § 441a(d)(3). Breyer, J., announced the judgment of the Court, and delivered an opinion joined by O'Connor & Souter, JJ. They refused to consider the broader question whether, in the special case of political parties, the First Amendment also forbids congressional efforts to limit coordinated expenditures.

Kennedy, J., joined by Rehnquist, C.J., & Scalia, J., filed an opinion concurring in the judgment and dissenting in part. They concluded that the FECA, on its face, violates the First Amendment when it restricts spending of a political party in cooperation, consultation, or concert with a candidate. Thomas, J., joined by Rehnquist, C.J. & Scalia, J., also filed an opinion concurring in the judgment and dissenting in part, concluding that § 441a(d)(3) is unconstitutional on its face. Thomas, J., in a portion of his opinion not joined by any other Justice, argued that the Court should reject *Buckley v. Valeo* because there is no constitutionally significant difference between campaign contributions and expenditures. Bribery laws and disclosure laws offer less restrictive means of preventing corruption.

§ 20.52   Regulation of Political Activity of Government Employees

Page 379, add to note 2:

2. Congress loosened the restrictions of the Hatch Act in 1993. See Public Law 103–94 (Oct. 6, 1993), 107 Stat. at Large 1001, et seq., 5 U.S.C.A. § 7321, et seq. Section 7321 provides, generally: "It is the policy of the Congress that employees should be encouraged to exer- cise fully, freely, and without fear of penalty or reprisal, and to the extent not expressly prohibited by law, their right to participate or to refrain from participating in the political processes of the Nation."

Page 382, add to text after first full paragraph:

The Burden of Proof and the Employer's Duty to Act Reasonably. If the public employee is being disciplined or discharged for speech that is not a matter of public concern and that the employer believes would disrupt the office, what test should the court use to determine what was said. In order words, should the trier of fact seek to determine what the government employer *thought* was said, or should the trier of fact seek to determine what actually was said? In *Waters v. Churchill* [18.10] the Court considered the question, and was unable to muster a majority opinion.

In *Waters*, defendants fired Plaintiff Churchill from her nursing job in a public hospital because of what she allegedly said to a co–worker on a lunch break. Defendants claimed that Churchill made disruptive statements critical of her department and of defendants. Churchill denied that she made some statements and contended that what she did say was nondisruptive, but was critical of certain hospital policy that she thought threatened patients. The Seventh Circuit ruled that if the jury believed Churchill's version of what she said, then *Connick* protected her; the issue, in the view of the Seventh Circuit, was what Churchill actually said, not what the employer thought that she had said.

The Supreme Court, with no majority opinion, vacated and remanded. Justice O'Connor, for the plurality (joined by Rehnquist, C.J., Souter & Ginsburg, JJ.), concluded that the Seventh Circuit rule was insufficiently protective of the government decisionmaker. Instead, the trier of fact should determine what the government employer "reasonably" thought was said. The government decisionmaker must also reach its conclusion in good faith, rather than as a pretext.

Justice Scalia (joined by Justice Kennedy & Thomas) concurred in the judgment, but objected to the plurality's adding the "new First Amendment procedural right" that the employer, in order to act reasonably, must conduct an investigation before taking disciplinary action in certain circumstances.[18.15]

18.10   511 U.S. 661, 114 S.Ct. 1878, 128 L.Ed.2d 686 (1994).

18.15   Stevens, J., joined by Blackmun, J., dissented because the plurality's rule is insufficiently protective of free speech: "the plurality concludes that a dismissal for speech is valid as a matter of law as long as the public employer reasonably believed that the employee's speech was unprotected." Souter, J., also filed a concurring opinion, agreeing that "a public employer who reasonably believes a third–party report that an employee engaged in constitu-tionally unprotected speech may punish the employee in reliance on that report, even if it turns out that the employee's actual remarks were constitutionally protected." He wanted to emphasize that, "in order to avoid liability, the public employer must not only reasonably investigate the third–party report, but must also actually believe it."

Page 384, add to end of carryover paragraph:

Restrictions on the Compensation Earned by Government Employees for Making Speeches and Writing Articles. In 1989 Congress enacted § 501(b) of the Ethics in Government Act, a section that broadly prohibited federal employees from accepting any compensation for making speeches or writing articles, even if the subject of the speech or article has no connection with the employee's official duties. Executive Branch Employees below the grade of GS–16 sued to invalidate this law in *United States v. National Treasury Employees Union.*[25.10] In the past these plaintiffs had received compensation for writing or speaking about matters such as religion, history, dance, and the environment. Generally, neither the groups paying the plaintiffs nor the subjects discussed had any connection with their official duties.

Justice Stevens, for the Court, relying on cases such as *United States Civil Service Commission v. National Association of Letter Carriers* [25.15] and *United Public Workers v. Mitchell*,[25.20] held that § 501(b) violated the First Amendment rights of the plaintiffs. The employees were speaking on matters of public concern, not on matters of personal interest. Hence, the Government must show that the interests of the potential audiences and a "vast group" of present and future employees in a "broad range" of present and future expression are outweighed by that expression's "necessary impact on the actual operation" of the Government. The Government must demonstrate that the recited harms are real, not conjectural, and that the law will alleviate these harms in a direct and substantial way.

While § 501(b) did not restrict speech based on content or viewpoint, the prohibition on compensation did impose a significant disincentive on the plaintiffs and on the public's right to read and hear what these Government employees would otherwise have said or written. The Government, moreover, offered no evidence of misconduct by the vast number of employees (nearly 1.7 million) below the rank of GS–16. Such limited evidence of actual or apparent impropriety by high-level executives or Congressmen does not justify extension of the compensation ban to lower-level rank and file employees, because they have negligible power to grant favors to those who might pay to read their writings or hear them speak.

In addition, a careful look at the law and the regulations cast doubt on the claim that the compensation ban would be reasonable. For example, "a rather strange" section of the statute has the effect of allowing compensation for a *"series"* of articles if no nexus existed between the author's employment and either the subject matter of the expression or the identity of the payor. "For an *individual* article or speech, in contrast, pay is taboo even if neither the subject matter nor the payor bears any relationship at all to the author's duties." [25.25] Congress chose to single out and restrict only expressive activities, and did not ban other off-duty activities that are nonexpressive ways of collecting compensation, such as payment for services on corporate boards, travel, and sport and other entertainment expenses not reasonably necessary for the appearance involved. Anomalies such as these in the ineptly drafted statute and regulations indicate that "this crudely crafted burden" on the plaintiffs' free speech is not "as carefully tailored as it should have been," and hence § 501(b) violated the First Amendment.

The Court then ruled that the relief should be limited to the parties before the Court—Executive Branch employees below GS–16.[25.30] The Government, in a later case, might be able to advance a different justification of a compensation ban limited to more senior officials. The Court also refused to limit the statute's compensation ban to cases involving an undesirable nexus between the speaker's official duties and the subject matter of the expression or the identity of the payor because Congress should have the responsibility of redrafting the statute.

25.10 516 U.S. ___, 115 S.Ct. 1003, 130 L.Ed.2d 964 (1995). O'Connor, J., concurred in the judgment in part and dissented in part. She would hold the law unconstitutional only to the extent that it bars these lower level federal employees (below GS–16) from receiving compensation for nonwork-related speeches, appearances, and articles. Rehnquist, C.J., joined by Scalia & Thomas, JJ., dissented, arguing that the Court understated the Government's justifications and overstated the amount of speech actually deterred. Also, the dissent complained that the majority discussed the impact of the statute only as to a handful of its most appealing individual situations, but then invalidated the entire prohibition as to all employees below GS–16.

25.15 413 U.S. 548, 93 S.Ct. 2880, 37 L.Ed.2d 796 (1973).

25.20 330 U.S. 75, 67 S.Ct. 556, 91 L.Ed. 754 (1947).

25.25 516 U.S. at ___, 115 S.Ct. at 1016 (emphasis in original).

25.30 The lower court had also granted relief to a single GS–16 employee. The Supreme Court did not reverse that portion of the lower court order, even though the Supreme Court's holding was limited to employees *below* Grade GS–16. The majority sought to justify this action by stating: "the Government does not request, as part of its suggested alternative to outright reversal that we reverse the Court of Appeals judgment as to that one employee. Accordingly, we leave that part of the court's judgment intact." ___ U.S. at ___ n. 23, 115 S.Ct. at 1019 n. 23.

XVI. ASSEMBLY AND PETITION

§ 20.54 The Basic Legal Principles

Page 386, add to note 1:

1. Pollock, J., citing Treatise, in Snyder v. American Association of Blood Banks, 144 N.J. 269, 295, 676 A.2d 1036, 1049 (1996).

Page 391, add to note 26:

26. See, Professional Real Estate Investors, Inc. v. Columbia Pictures, Industries, Inc., 508 U.S. 49, 113 S.Ct. 1920, 123 L.Ed.2d 611 (1993). The Court held that an objectively reasonable effort to litigate cannot be a "sham" within the meaning of *Noerr*, regardless of plaintiff's subjective intent. The existence of probable cause to institute a civil proceeding precluded, as a matter of law, a finding that the plaintiff had engaged in sham litigation. To constitute "sham" litigation, the litigant's prior claims for judicial relief must have been so baseless that no reasonable litigant could reasonably have expected to secure favorable relief.

SLAPP Lawsuits. Some commentators have criticized law suits brought against persons who have brought political claims to the government. These commentators use the acronym, SLAPP, which stands for "Strategic Lawsuits Against Public Participation." These are described as "the use of litigation to derail political claims, moving a public debate from the political arena to the judicial arena, where the playing field appears to be more advantageous." Penelope Canan, The SLAPP from a Sociological Perspective, 7 Pace Environmental L.Rev. 23, 23 (1989). See also, Penelope Canan & George W. Pring, Studying Strategic Lawsuits Against Public Participation: Mixing Quantitative and Qualitative Approaches, 22 Law & Society Rev. 385 (1988). George W. Pring and Penelope Canan, SLAPPs: Getting Sued for Speaking Out (Temple U. Press, 1996).

However, this charge ignores the fact that a lawsuit is a form of public participation. If the lawsuit is baseless or sham, then a court may issue sanctions against the party and/or the party's lawyer. However, if the lawsuit is not baseless, then the litigant has a right to file suit. Calling the lawsuit a SLAPP suit does not add to the debate. The only question is whether the lawsuit is a sham, an objective question, not a subjective look at the plaintiff's motives. See, Professional Real Estate Investors, Inc. v. Columbia Pictures, Industries, Inc., 508 U.S. 49, 113 S.Ct. 1920, 123 L.Ed.2d 611 (1993).

Page 393, add to note 36:

36. Cf. National Organization for Women, Inc. v. Scheidler, 510 U.S. 249, 114 S.Ct. 798, 127 L.Ed.2d 99 (1994). A women's rights organization and abortion clinics brought a Racketeer Influenced and Corrupt Organizations (RICO) claim against a coalition of pro-life groups, who were alleged to be members of a nationwide conspiracy to shut down abortion clinics through a pattern of racketeering activity, including extortion. Plaintiffs alleged that respondents used threatened or actual force, violence, or fear to induce clinic employees, doctors, and patients to give up their right to provide or have abortions. The Court, with no dissent, held that RICCO does not require plaintiffs to prove that any racketeering enterprise or predicate acts of racketeering be motivated by economic purpose.

Souter, J., joined by Kennedy, J., concurring, added:

"it is important to stress that nothing in the Court's opinion precludes a RICO defendant from raising the First Amendment in its defense in a particular case. Conduct alleged to amount to Hobbs Act extortion, for example, or one of the other, somewhat elastic RICO predicate acts may turn out to be fully protected First Amendment activity, entitling the defendant to dismissal on that basis. See *NAACP v. Claiborne Hardware Co.* [E]ven in a case where a RICO violation has been validly established, the First Amendment may limit the relief that can be granted against an organization otherwise engaging in protected expression. [We] caution courts applying RICO to bear in mind the First Amendment interests that could be at stake." 510 U.S. at 265, 114 S.Ct. at 807. See,

Craig Bradley, NOW v. Scheidler: RICO Meets the First Amendment, 1994 Supreme Court Review 129 (1994).

Page 395, add to note 45:

45. Norman v. Reed, 502 U.S. 279, 112 S.Ct. 698, 116 L.Ed.2d 711 (1992), on remand 154 Ill.2d 77, 180 Ill.Dec. 685, 607 N.E.2d 1198 (1992), cert. denied 509 U.S. 906, 113 S.Ct. 3000, 125 L.Ed.2d 693 (1993), invalidated an Illinois law that broadly prohibited a new party from bearing the name of an established party. The state supreme court had read this statute so literally that it interpreted the statute to bar candidates running in one political subdivision from ever using the name of a political party established in another. As interpreted, this provision of the Illinois law was unconstitutional. The purpose of this law was to prevent voter confusion by precluding persons not affiliated with a party from latching on to a popular party name, but the interpretation of the Illinois Supreme Court did not further the purported purpose of the law: there was no danger of confusion in this case: the only Harold Washington Party (HWP) candidate to run in the most recent municipal election had in fact authorized the petitioners to use the HWP name. The state court's inhospitable reading of the statute "sweeps broader than necessary to advance electoral order and accordingly violates the First Amendment right of political association."

Prohibition of Write-in Votes. In Burdick v. Takushi, 504 U.S. 428, 112 S.Ct. 2059, 119 L.Ed.2d 245 (1992), the Court held that an Hawaiian law that prohibited write-in votes in both the primary and general elections did not violate any voter's right of expression and association. The state did provide easy access to the ballot until the cutoff for the filing of nominating petitions. Thus only voters who fail to identify their candidates until the days before the primary bear any burden. Justice White, for the Court, said that the interest in making a late, rather than early, choice is entitled to little weight. Whether categorized as a voting rights case or a ballot access case, the Court emphasized that reasonable, politically neutral regulations that have the effect of channeling expressive activity at the polls should be upheld. Hawaii has various interests to uphold, such as avoiding "unrestrained factionalism" at the general election, and permitting unopposed victors in certain primaries to be designated office holders. Thus, "when a State's ballot access laws pass constitutional muster as imposing only reasonable burdens on First and Fourteenth Amendment rights," then "a prohibition on write-in voting will presumptively be valid.... "

XVII. OBSCENITY

§ 20.56 Introduction

Page 401, add to note 1:

1. Sheldon H. Nahmod, Adam, Eve and the First Amendment: Some Thoughts on the Obscene as Sacred, 68 Chicago–Kent L.Rev. 377 (1992); James Lindgren, Defining Pornography, 141 U.Penn.L.Rev. 1153 (1993).

Media Violence and Obscenity. See, Thomas G. Krattenmaker & L.A. Powe, Jr., Televised Violence: First

Amendment Principles and Social Science Theory, 64 Va. L. Rev. 1123 (1978); Comment, View At Your Own Risk: Gang Movies and Spectator Violence, 12 Loyola Entertainment L.J. 477 (1992); Kevin W. Saunders, Media Violence and the Obscenity Exception to the First Amendment, 3 Wm. & Mary Bill of Rights J. 107 (1994).

§ 20.61   Special Considerations in Light of the *Miller* Case

(c) Prior Restraint

Page 425, add to note 33:

33. Informal Prior Restraint. Bantam Books, Inc. v. Sullivan, 372 U.S. 58, 83 S.Ct. 631, 9 L.Ed.2d 584 (1963) involved a system of informal coercion and prior restraint. A government commission would review books, identify those considered objectionable (either on grounds of obscenity or on other grounds), contact the distributor in writing that the books were considered "objectionable" and that the commission would recommend prosecution. The commission also thanked the distributors in advance for their cooperation. A police officer typically visited the distributors in person and asked what actions the distributors would be taking in connection with the objectionable books. Brennan, J., for the Court, concluded that, in context, the commission would be engaging in a system of administrative restraint and not merely offering legal advice.

Page 425, add to text after first paragraph of § 20.61(c):

Prior Restraint means that the court or another body, such as an administrator, issues an order that prevents communications (that are the subject of the prior restraint) prior to the time that the communications would occur, but for the order. The point of a prior restraint is to freeze (restrain) speech before (prior to the time) it occurs.[33.10] If a speaker must secure the prior approval of an agency or a court *before* speaking, that requirement would be a classic prior restraint.

33.10 Alexander v. United States, 509 U.S. 544, 549, 113 S.Ct. 2766, 2771, 125 L.Ed.2d 441 (1993), rehearing denied 510 U.S. 909, 114 S.Ct. 295, 126 L.Ed.2d 244 (1993).

Page 426, add to note 34 (which begins at p. 425):

34. No Prior Restraints for Books. The presumption against enjoining publication of books is very high, and it is unlikely that the Court would approve of a licensing scheme that would allow prior restraint of books on grounds of obscenity.

In Times Film Corp. v. City of Chicago, 365 U.S. 43, 81 S.Ct. 391, 5 L.Ed.2d 403 (1961), rehearing denied 365 U.S. 856, 81 S.Ct. 798, 5 L.Ed.2d 820 (1961), the Court split 5 to 4 on the question of whether the first amendment ever permitted a prior restraint of the exhibition of a movie. It is interesting that the dissent's much greater protection for speech came very close to becoming a majority. Clark, J., for the majority, held that there is no first amendment right to exhibit, at least once, any and every kind of motion picture. The majority carefully excluded books from the ruling. Warren, C.J., joined by Black, Douglas, & Brennan, JJ., dissented. While the majority did not apply its reasoning to other forms of expression, Warren's dissent expressed concern that the majority's opinion allowing some form of administrative licensing would be extended to other forms of communications, such as newspapers, journals, books, radio, television, or public speeches. Douglas, J., joined by Warren, C.J. & Black, J., also dissented, arguing that any censorship of movies is unconstitutional because it is a prior restraint.

No Prior Restraints of Non-obscene Movies that Advocate Unlawful Behavior. While the state may prosecute and restrain obscene movies, the state cannot constitutionally prosecute or restrain movies that advocate immoral or improper behavior, even if the behavior advocated is illegal. Advocacy of illegal conduct that falls short of *incitement* is constitutionally protected. Kingsley International Pictures v. Regents of the University of the State of

New York, 360 U.S. 684, 79 S.Ct. 1362, 3 L.Ed.2d 1512 (1959) held that New York may not refuse a movie licence to a motion picture entitled, *Lady Chatterley's Lover*. The state court found that the movie was not obscene but that it portrayed adultery as proper behavior. The U.S. Supreme Court held that New York acted unconstitutionally. It is basic first amendment doctrine that there is always freedom to advocate ideas. The state may not restrain a movie, or book, or other form of expression, that advocates ideas, even if the means of expression are eloquent and entertaining.

Page 428, add to end of page:

Forfeiture of Defendant's Assets in a RICO Prosecution. *Alexander v. United States*,[47.10] held that it was no violation of free speech when the government provided for the forfeiture of defendant's assets, used in the adult entertainment business, following defendant's conviction for participating in racketeering activities in violation of the Racketeer Influenced and Corrupt Organizations Act (RICO).[47.15]

The defendant in *Alexander* was convicted of violating federal obscenity laws, based on a finding that 7 items (4 magazines and 3 videotapes) sold at several of defendant's stores were constitutionally obscene. These obscenity convictions were also the predicates for his three RICO convictions. The trial court imposed a prison term of 6 years, fined defendant $100,000, and ordered him to pay the costs of prosecution, incarceration, and supervised release. Pursuant to his RICO conviction, the Government also sought forfeiture of his businesses and real estate that represented his interests in the racketeering enterprise. The trial court ultimately ordered defendant to forfeit his wholesale and retail businesses, and all their assets, and almost $9 million acquired through racketeering activity. (The Government destroyed these expressive materials that had been forfeited, after deciding that it did not want to go into the business of selling pornographic materials to the public, regardless of whether they were legally "obscene.")

Defendant argued that the RICO forfeiture provisions were a prior restraint on speech and overbroad. The lower courts and the Supreme Court, speaking through Chief Justice Rehnquist, rejected these arguments. First, the forfeiture is not a prior restraint on speech—there was no court or agency that prevented defendant from engaging in expressive activities in the future or that required defendant to secure prior approval before speaking. The forfeiture was a permissible criminal punishment. The courts imposed no legal restraint on defendant's ability to engage in any expressive activity. The forfeiture only prevents him from *financing* his expressive activities with assets derived from *prior* racketeering offenses.

The Government did not seize the materials because it suspected the materials to be obscene, without a prior judicial determination as to obscenity. Rather, defendant's RICO convictions caused his assets to be forfeited because they were directly related to his *past* racketeering violations. The majority found that the imposition of the forfeiture order had nothing to do with the expressive conduct of the materials; they were forfeited because they were assets *derived from prior* racketeering offenses. The forfeiture, in short, was a punishment for past conduct, not a restraint on future speech. Defendant "can go back into the adult entertainment business tomorrow, and sell as many sexually explicit magazines and videotapes as he likes, without any risk of being held in contempt for violating a court order." [47.20]

The Court also rejected defendant's argument that the law is "overbroad." The forfeiture may "chill" others from engaging in protected speech, because of the risk of forfeiture. But this result is no more chilling than the threat of a prison term or a large fine, yet these penalties are clearly constitutional. There is no "chill" in the sense that the law is unconstitutionally vague. [47.25]

To provide for forfeiture in this case is very different, the Court explained, from seizing materials pursuant to a general search warrant; nor did the government seize these materials on the suspicion of being obscene without a prior judicial determination of obscenity. Instead, the government gave the defendant a full trial, and the assets were forfeited because of defendant's *past* racketeering activities. The forfeiture provision of RICO provides for forfeiture because of the financial role that these assets played in the operation of the racketeering enterprise. [47.30]

47.10 509 U.S. 544, 113 S.Ct. 2766, 125 L.Ed.2d 441 (1993), rehearing denied 510 U.S. 909, 114 S.Ct. 295, 126 L.Ed.2d 244 (1993).

47.15 See, 18 U.S.C.A. § 1963.

47.20 509 U.S. at 549, 113 S.Ct. at 2771. See also, Arcara v. Cloud Books, Inc., 478 U.S. 697, 106 S.Ct. 3172, 92 L.Ed.2d 568 (1986), on remand 68 N.Y.2d 553, 510 N.Y.S.2d 844, 503 N.E.2d 492 (1986).

47.25 The Court then remanded so that the lower courts could determine whether the forfeiture, on top of his prison term and fine, is "excessive" within the meaning of the "excessive fines" clause of the Eighth Amendment.

Kennedy, J., joined by Blackmun & Stevens, JJ., and in part by Souter, J., dissented:

"The Court today embraces a rule that would find no affront to the First Amendment in the Government's destruction of a book and film business and its entire inventory of legitimate expression as punishment for a single past offense. Until now I had thought one could browse through any book or film store in the United States without fear that the proprietor had chosen each item to avoid risk to the whole inventory and indeed to the business itself. This ominous, onerous threat undermines free speech and press principles essential to our personal freedom."

509 U.S. at 559, 113 S.Ct. at 2776.

Souter, J., concurred in the judgment in part and dissented in part, arguing that the First Amendment forbids the forfeiture of defendant's expressive materials "in the absence of an adjudication that it is obscene or otherwise of unprotected character...." 509 U.S. at 559, 113 S.Ct. at 2776.

47.30 509 U.S. at 549–53, 113 S.Ct. at 2771–72. Compare, Marcus v. Search Warrants, 367 U.S. 717, 81 S.Ct. 1708, 6 L.Ed.2d 1127 (1961); Roaden v. Kentucky, 413 U.S. 496, 93 S.Ct. 2796, 37 L.Ed.2d 757 (1973).

(e) Obscenity and the Twenty–First Amendment

Page 435, replace the last sentence of the carryover paragraph at the top of the page with the following:

Rejecting the View that the Twenty–First Amendment Affects the Application of the First Amendment. In *44 Liquormart, Inc. v. Rhode Island*,[72] the Court invalidated a state law that banned accurate retail liquor advertisements except at the point of sale. The Court rejected the state's argument that it could limit truthful information in an effort to manipulate consumers and promote temperance. In the course of this opinion, in a portion of the decision that was an opinion of the Court, the Court emphatically disavowed the reasoning of cases like *Bellanca* and *LaRue*. Justice Stevens, for the Court, announced that the result in the earlier cases would have been "precisely the same" even if there had been no reliance on the 21st Amendment. He added:

"Without questioning the holding in *LaRue*, we now disavow its reasoning insofar as it relied on the Twenty-first Amendment. [W]e now hold that the Twenty-first Amendment does not qualify the constitutional prohibition against laws abridging the freedom of speech embodied in the First Amendment." [72.10]

The Twenty–First Amendment, in short, does not exclude an advertising ban from the protection of the First Amendment.

72. __ U.S. __, 116 S.Ct. 1495, 134 L.Ed.2d 711 (1996).

72.10 __ U.S. at __, 116 S.Ct. at 1514. The Court similarly rejected the reasoning of cases that had relied on *LaRue*, such as New York State Liquor Authority v. Bellanca, 452 U.S. 714, 101 S.Ct. 2599, 69 L.Ed.2d 357 (1981)(per curiam); Newport v. Iacobucci, 479 U.S. 92, 107 S.Ct. 383, 93 L.Ed.2d 334 (1986)(per curiam).

As the Court stated in another opinion, *LaRue* "did not involve commercial speech about alcohol, but instead concerned the regulation of nude dancing in places where alcohol was served." Rubin v. Coors Brewing Co., 514 U.S. __, __, 115 S.Ct. 1585, 1589, 131 L.Ed.2d 532 (1995).

(k) Feminism and Pornography

Page 441, add to end of page:

It would be a mistake to conclude that all feminists support censorship of speech that is demeaning to women. Many feminists oppose such censorship specifically from a feminist viewpoint. These commentators conclude that regulating "pornography" would undermine women's rights and interests. Such censorship, for example, perpetuates patronizing stereotypes about women and their alleged innate sexual vulnerability. Censorship also increases attention given to bigots and creates sympathy for them. If the censorship is effective, it drives the sexist expression underground, where it is harder to respond to it. And, there is no reason to believe that the censorship would not be broader than necessary.[105.10] In fact, if the censorship were narrowly and carefully implemented, it would probably be the first time in history that the censor continually exercises self-restraint and did not eventually use the heavy hand of suppression.[105.15]

105.10 For a particularly thoughtful article, see, Nadine Strossen, A Feminist Critique of "the" Feminist Critique of Pornography, 79 Va.L.Rev. 1099 (1993). Professor Strossen emphasizes that pornography is *allegedly* subordinating" to women because "subjective characterization is one with which many women, feminists, authors, and artists disagree." Strossen, A Feminist Critique of "the" Feminist Critique of Pornography, 79 Va.L.Rev. at 1105 (emphasis in original).

Other thoughtful commentary includes: Barry W. Lynn, "Civil Rights" Ordinances and the Attorney General's Commission: New Developments in Pornography Regulation, 21 Harv.Civ.Rts.–Civ.Lib.L.Rev. 27 (1986); Nadine Strossen, The Convergence of Feminist and Civil Liberties Principles in the Pornography Debate, 62 N.Y.U.L.Rev. 201 (1987); Mary C. Dunlap, Sexual Speech and the State: Putting Pornography in its Place, 17 Golden Gate U.L.Rev. 359 (1987); Kingsley R. Browne, Title VII as Censorship: Hostile–Environment Harassment and the First Amendment, 52 Ohio State L. J. 481 (1991); Jeanne L. Schroeder, The Taming of the Shrew: The Liberal Attempt to Mainstream Radical Feminist Theory, 5 Yale J.Law & Feminism 123 (1992); James Lind-

gren, Defining Pornography, 141 U.Penn.L.Rev. 1153 (1993); John M. Blim, Undoing Our Selves: The Error of Sacrificing Speech in the Quest for Equality, 56 Ohio State L.J. 428 (1995).

105.15 The Canadian Experience. The Supreme Court of Canada, in the case of Butler v. Her Majesty, 1 S.C.R. 452 (1992), decided in February, 1992, adopted the theories Catharine MacKinnon and Andrea Dworkin, who have argued that the government should ban sexually explicit or erotic words or images, even if not "obscene" in a constitutional sense, on the grounds that they "degrade" women and are harmful to women. The Canadian authorities have used this power to ban lesbian, gay, and feminist materials. Indeed, Canada even seized (as pornographic) two of Andrea Dworkin's books arguing that pornography should be banned! After a public outcry the authorities finally released the books. See, Leanne Katz, Censors' Helpers, New York Times, Dec. 4, 1993, at 15, col. 3–6. See also, Jeffrey G. Sherman, Love Speech: The Social Utility of Pornography, 47 Stanford L. Rev. 661 (1995), criticizing antipornography feminists for encouraging censorship, which results in censorship of gay and lesbian sexual expression and sexuality.

(l)Nude Dancing
Page 442, add to note 107:

107. Gardebring, J., citing Treatise in, Knudtson v. City of Coates, 519 N.W.2d 166, 170 (Minn.1994).

Page 444, add to end of page:
(m) Sexually Oriented Material on Broadcast or Cable Channels

Whatever the definition of "obscenity," if materials are found to be constitutionally "obscene," the Government can ban them from broadcast or cable channels, because the Government can ban completely any obscene materials. However, the Court has been unable to agree on the power of the Government to ban or restrict materials that are not "obscene" in the constitutional sense but are sexually oriented—often called "adult material"—when that material is broadcast over the airwaves or by cable.

In the major instances in which the Court has dealt with this issue, it has usually been unable to muster an opinion for the

Court. In *FCC v. Pacifica Foundation*,[115] a majority of the Court, but without a majority opinion, concluded that the FCC constitutionally could regulate "indecent" or "adult speech"[116] that was broadcast over the radio air waves in the early afternoon, when the Court assumed that children were more likely to be in the listening audience. The five Justices who voted to uphold the power of the FCC to sanction the radio station emphasized that their rule was very narrow and did not involve other means of broadcast, such as two-way radio or closed circuit transmission. Nor did the ruling, the Justices emphasized, cover broadcasts that had only an occasional expletive.[117]

Later, *Denver Area Educational Telecommunications Consortium, Inc. v. FCC*.[118] considered challenges to three sections of the 1992 Cable Act designed to regulate cable television broadcasting of "patently offensive" sex-related material. The very fragmented Court invalidated two provisions of the Cable Television Consumer Protection and Competition Act of 1992 and upheld one provision.

A majority of the Justices decided that a provision of the Act that *permitted* the cable operator to prohibit patently offensive or indecent programming on public access channels violated the First Amendment. "Public access channels" are channel capacity that cable operators agreed to reserve for public, governmental, and educational access as part of the consideration that municipalities obtained in exchange for awarding a cable franchise.

On the other hand, a majority of the Justices concluded that a provision *permitting* the operator to prohibit patently offensive or indecent programming on leased access channels was found to be constitutional. A "leased cable channel" is a channel that the relevant federal law required a cable system operator to reserve for commercial lease by unaffiliated third parties. Finally, the fragmented Court invalidated a third provision, that *required* leased channel operators to segregate "patently offensive" programming on a single channel and to block that channel from viewer access, and then to un-block it (or re-block it) within 30 days of a subscriber's written request.

Justice Kennedy's separate opinion concurring in the judgment would have invalidated all of the provisions of the law. Kennedy criticized the narrowness of the Breyer plurality. "When confronted with a threat to free speech in the context of an emerging technology, we ought to have the discipline to analyze the case by reference to existing elaborations of constant First Amendment principles."[119] Justice Breyer, in contrast, was unwilling to embrace any definite standard.

·115. 438 U.S. 726, 98 S.Ct. 3026, 57 L.Ed.2d 1073 (1978), rehearing denied, 439 U.S. 883, 99 S.Ct. 227, 58 L.Ed.2d 198 (1978). This case is discussed more thoroughly in § 20.18(a). Compare, Sable Communications of California, Inc. v. FCC, 492 U.S. 115, 109 S.Ct. 2829, 106 L.Ed.2d 93 (1989), where the Court ruled that the Communications Act imposed an outright ban on constitutionally obscene pre-recorded commercial telephone messages (so-called "dial-a-porn"), but the portion of the Act that banned "indecent" (but not constitutionally obscene) messages, regardless of age, was unconstitutional. The Government, in that instance, could have protected minors by a much more narrowly drafted statute. The FCC's own investigation showed that access codes and scrambling rules would have been sufficient to keep the indecent messages out of the reach of minors.

116. The speech in question is often called "adult," although it is callow speech and it might be more correct to call it "infantile."

117. Not only did the Justices in *Pacifica* announce that the decision was narrow, but later, in Sable Communications of California, Inc. v. FCC, 492 U.S. 115, 109 S.Ct. 2829, 106 L.Ed.2d 93 (1989), the Court described *Pacifica* was "an emphatically narrow holding."

118. Justice Breyer wrote plurality Opinion and the Opinion of the Court. Stevens, O'Connor, Kennedy, Souter, & Ginsburg JJ. joined the Opinion of the Court. Breyer also delivered an Opinion with respect to Parts I, II, & V (which Stevens, O'Connor & Souter, JJ., joined), and an Opinion with respect to Parts IV & VI (which Stevens & Souter, JJ., joined). Stevens, J., and Souter, J., filed concurring opinions. O'Connor, J., filed an Opinion concurring in part and dissenting in part. Kennedy, J., filed an Opinion concurring in part, concurring in the judgment in part, & dissenting in part (which Ginsburg, J., joined). Thomas, J., filed an Opinion concurring in the judgment in part & dissenting in part (which Rehnquist, C.J., & Scalia, J., joined). This case is discussed more thoroughly in § 20.18(a).

119. ___ U.S. at ___, 116 S.Ct. at 2404.

Chapter 21

FREEDOM OF RELIGION

WESTLAW Electronic Research

See WESTLAW Electronic Research Guide preceding the Summary of Contents.

I. INTRODUCTION

§ 21.1 The Natural Antagonism Between the Two Clauses

Page 447, add to note 6:

6. See generally, Douglas Laycock, Continuity and Change in the Threat to Religious Liberty: The Reformation Era and the Late Twentieth Century, 80 Minnesota L. Rev. 1047 (1996). Scott C. Idleman, Liberty in the Balance; Religion, Politics, and American Constitutionalism, 71 Notre Dame L.Rev. 991 (1996). In Board of Education of Kiryas Joel Village School District v. Grumet, 512 U.S. 687, 114 S.Ct. 2481, 129 L.Ed.2d 546 (1994), the Court, by a six to three vote of the Justices, invalidated a state law which created a separate school district for a Village that had been established by, and was inhabited only by, members of one religious sect. Six Justices believed that the state law violated the principle of religious neutrality; four of the Justices in the majority also believed that the state law improperly delegated government authority to a religious group. This decision is examined in § 21.3 of this Treatise.

In Lee v. Weisman, 505 U.S. 577, 112 S.Ct. 2649, 120 L.Ed.2d 467 (1992) the Supreme Court held that a public school graduation ceremony that included a "nonsectarian" prayer by a member of the clergy (in the particular case by a Rabbi) violated the establishment clause. The case was decided by a five to four vote of the Justices; Justice Kennedy wrote the majority opinion. Justice Souter wrote an opinion concurring in both the judgment and the majority opinion that was joined by Justices Stevens and O'Connor. Justice Souter found that one of the principal reasons for rejecting the arguments of "nonpreferentialists" (who would allow aid to all religion over nonreligion so long as the government aid did not include a sect preference) was the inability of courts to make decisions concerning the types of competing beliefs that would qualify as religions or theologies. 505 U.S. at 609, 112 S.Ct. at 2667, 2671 (Souter, J., joined by Stevens and O'Connor, JJ., concurring). Justice Blackmun also filed an opinion in the case in which he noted that nothing in this decision formerly altered, or was inconsistent with, the Court's establishment clause decisions during the previous two decades. 505 U.S. at 597, 112 S.Ct. at 2661 (Blackmun, J., joined by Stevens and O'Connor, JJ., concurring).

Page 447, add after note 6:

In at least one respect, the neutrality concept has given rise to a principle that applies in both establishment clause and free exercise clause cases. Both clauses will prevent the government from singling out specific religious sects for special benefits or burdens. If the government were to give benefits to a group of persons defined by their religious beliefs, it would have created a

85

sect preference that would violate the establishment clause unless it was necessary to promote a compelling interest.[6.5] If the government were to impose burdens on a group of persons solely because of their religious beliefs, its action would violate the free exercise clause unless the action was necessary to promote a compelling interest.[6.10]

6.5 See, e.g., Board of Education of Kiryas Joel Village School District v. Grumet, 512 U.S. 687, 114 S.Ct. 2481, 129 L.Ed.2d 546 (1994); Larson v. Valente, 456 U.S. 228, 102 S.Ct. 1673, 72 L.Ed.2d 33 (1982), rehearing denied 457 U.S. 1111, 102 S.Ct. 2916, 73 L.Ed.2d 1323 (1982). See § 21.3 of this Treatise.

6.10 See, e.g., Church of the Lukumi Babalu Aye, Inc. v. Hialeah, 508 U.S. 520, 113 S.Ct. 2217, 124 L.Ed.2d 472 (1993), on remand 2 F.3d 369 (11th Cir. 1993). See §§ 21.6, 21.8 of this Treatise. If a governmental entity denies an individual or group access to a public forum (otherwise open to all persons for expressive activities) on the basis that the individual or group will engage in religious speech, the government action may violate the free speech clause of the First Amendment. A denial of access to

a public forum could only be justified by an overriding or compelling interest. It is unlikely that a private group's activities on the government property would give rise to a government violation of the establishment clause. See, e.g., Widmar v. Vincent, 454 U.S. 263, 274, 102 S.Ct. 269, 276–77, 70 L.Ed.2d 440 (1981); Lamb's Chapel v. Center Moriches Union Free School District, 508 U.S. 384, 113 S.Ct. 2141, 124 L.Ed.2d 352 (1993); Rosenberger v. Rector and Visitors of the University of Virginia, ___ U.S. ___, 115 S.Ct. 2510, 132 L.Ed.2d 700 (1995). See §§ 21.3, 21.5(e) of this Treatise. See generally, Stephen Bainbridge, Student Religious Organizations and University Policies Against Discrimination on the Basis of Sexual Orientation: Implications of the Religious Freedom Restriction Act, 21 J. of College and Univ. Law 369 (1994).

II. THE ESTABLISHMENT CLAUSE

§ 21.3 Introduction

Page 455, add to the end of the carryover paragraph:

The Court in *Larson* chose to base its decision on the establishment clause. The law at issue in *Larson* also could have been invalidated under the free exercise clause, if the majority had chosen to categorize the law as being an attempt to suppress the activity of identifiable religious groups with a law that was not a religiously neutral law of general applicability.[2.5]

2.5 The Supreme Court relied on *Larson* in Church of the Lukumi Babalu Aye, Inc. v. Hialeah, 508 U.S. 520, 533, 535, 113 S.Ct. 2217, 2227, 2228, 124 L.Ed.2d 472 (1993), on remand 2 F.3d

369 (11th Cir.1993) when the Court held that a city law prohibiting the sacrifice of animals violated the free exercise clause because the law was designed to suppress a particular religion.

Page 455, add after the carryover paragraph:

In the 1990s, the Supreme Court moved away from applying the three part purpose–effect–and entanglement test without formally rejecting the test or the cases in which it had been used.[2.10] But the Justices remained committed to enforcing the concept of religious neutrality in establishment clause rulings; neither denominational preferences nor delegations of religious authority to religious sects would survive establishment clause review.

In *Board of Education of Kiryas Joel Village School District v. Grumet* [2.15] the Supreme Court invalidated a state law that created a separate school district for a small village that was inhabited entirely by members of one religious sect. Two decades before this Supreme Court case, members of the Satmar Hasidim, who are believers in a form of Judaism, moved to an undeveloped subdivision in New York. In 1977, employing a state law of general applicability, the Satmars separated from the town with which they had been associated and established the Village of Kiryas Joel.

The residents of the Village of Kiryas Joel educated their children at two religious schools, one for male students and one for female students. These schools were admittedly sectarian in nature, although they provided the students with instruction in general secular subjects (e.g., reading and mathematics) as well as religious courses. The Village of Kiryas Joel was in a general public school district. Parents who resided in the Village could have sent their children to public schools that were located outside the Village, but within the public school district.

The religious schools in the Village of Kiryas Joel did not offer any special services for handicapped children. At one time, the public school district which included the territory of the Village provided services for handicapped children who attended the two religious schools in the Village. These services were provided by the public school district at an annex to one of the religious schools. In 1985, the government services for the handicapped children in the religious schools were ended in response to United States Supreme Court decisions concerning the provision of services to children who attended religiously affiliated schools in other communities. [2.20]

Between 1985 and 1989, handicapped children from the Village of Kiryas Joel could only receive special educational services if they attended the public schools. But the Satmar children found that leaving their Village, with its distinctive life style, and attending the public schools was difficult to the point of being traumatic. In 1989, only one child from the Village still attended the public schools. All of the other handicapped children from the Village either received limited, privately funded services or they did not receive any special educational services.

The New York legislature, in 1989, passed a statute creating a separate school district that had boundaries identical to the Village of Kiryas Joel. The new Kiryas Joel Village School District had all of the powers and duties of any other school district; the state statute provided for a locally elected board to operate the school district. The Village School District was composed solely of persons who were a member of one religion. The persons elected to the school board were members of that religion. The Village School District then operated only a special education program for handicapped children; the District also accepted handicapped students from neighboring school districts. All of the children in the Village who were not handicapped continued to attend the religiously affiliated schools. The Kiryas Joel Village School District offered to send any child in the Village who was not handicapped, and who wanted to attend a public school, to a public school in the neighboring school district. The Village would pay the tuition and expenses for such a nonhandicapped child.[2.25]

Justice Souter wrote an opinion in the *Grumet* case that was, in part, a majority opinion and, in part, a plurality opinion. Writing for a majority of the Court, Justice Souter ruled that the New York law creating the Village School District was a sect preference that violated the neutrality principle, which is a core value of the establishment clause.[2.30] If the Village had been able to establish a school district by following laws of general applicability, the majority might have ruled that the mere existence of a public school district that primarily served children of one religion, in a local geographical area, did not violate the first amendment. The flaw in the New York law, according to the majority, was that the law creating the Village School District constituted a clear preference for one religious sect. New York had defended its law as a secular way of accommodating the desire of children and parents in the village to keep their children close to home and their religious way of life. The state believed that the law should be upheld because the public school operated by the Kiryas Joel Village School District did not have any religious characteristics. Justice Souter found that categorizing the law as an accommodation of religion would not save the state law from invalidation if the law gave preferential treatment to a religious sect. Justice Souter stated: "The fundamental source of constitutional concern here is that the legislature itself may fail to exercise governmental authority in a religiously neutral way." [2.35]

The state believed that the creation of the Village School District should be seen as a permissible accommodation for a small, unique group of children. The majority in *Grumet* refused to allow even this seemingly minor deviation from the neutrality principle. Justice Souter found that a sect preference given to a "small religious group causes no less a constitutional problem than would follow from aiding a sect with more members or religion as a whole." [2.40] The state could pursue other forms of accommodations for the children from the Village who needed special educational services. Justice Souter noted that earlier Supreme Court cases allowed for the provision of special education services "at a neutral site" near religiously affiliated schools.[2.45]

Justice Souter wrote a majority opinion in *Grumet* concerning New York's violation of the neutrality principle. But he wrote for only four Justices when he found that the New York law violated the establishment clause due to an improper delegation of governmental authority to a religious entity.[2.50] Justice Souter was joined by Justices Blackmun, Ginsburg and Stevens in finding that the state law could only be understood as delegating governmental power to a group of people defined by their membership in a religious sect. The Court had previously held that the establishment clause would prevent the government from delegating governmental authority to a religious organization, such as a church or the authorities who governed a religious community.[2.55]

The state had argued that there was no delegation of authority to a religious organization in this case because the new Village School District operated in presumably the same way any other school district in the State. Justice Souter, in the portion of his opinion that did not represent the views of the majority, found that there was no realistic difference between the granting of governmental power to "a group of religious individuals united by common doctrine" and a delegating governmental power to a religious group's official leadership or to a formal religious organization.[2.60] The plurality believed that the creation of the school district was "substantially equivalent to defining a political subdivision" in which the relevant governmental power was given to a religious sect. In their view, the state law created an unconstitutional "fusion of governmental and religious functions." [2.65]

Justice O'Connor concurred in the portion of Justice Souter's opinion that was a majority opinion, because she agreed that the New York law was an impermissible denominational preference.[2.70] However, Justice O'Connor did not join the portion of Justice Souter's opinion concerning whether the New York law constituted an improper delegation of governmental power to a religion. In her concurring opinion in *Grumet*, Justice O'Connor indicated that the Village of Kiryas Joel School District could have been created if the state had a generally applicable state law allowing local communities (regardless of any religious connection) to create a school district. She also reiterated her belief that the government should be able to provide special education services at private schools, including religious schools, so long as the services provided at the site of a religiously affiliated private school were nonreligious in character. Justice O'Connor believed that it might be impossible to create a "unitary test" for the wide range of cases that involved incidental government aid to religion, but she would find that laws which were not religiously neutral in character must be held to violate the establishment clause.

Justice Kennedy voted to invalidate the New York law creating the Kiryas Joel Village School District, but he did not join any portion of Justice Souter's opinion in *Grumet*.[2.75] He believed that a legislature might respond to the need of a group of persons who would not follow a generally applicable law because of their religious beliefs, so long as the legislature did not create a sect preference. But Justice Kennedy rejected the majority's position that the establishment clause should prohibit a legislature from passing a law to accommodate the needs of a particular religious group simply because, at some future date, the legislature might fail to provide a similar accommodation, if requested to do so, for members of another religion. Nevertheless, Justice Kennedy took the position that "a religious accommodation demands careful scrutiny" and that the New York law in *Grumet* was a sect preference that violated the establishment clause.

Justice Scalia, joined only by Chief Justice Rehnquist and Justice Thomas, dissented in *Grumet*.[2.80] These three Justices believed that the Supreme Court's rulings during the previous quarter century had improperly prevented government from engaging in religious accommodation. Chief Justice Rehnquist, and Justices Scalia and Thomas, might be joined by Justices O'Connor and Kennedy, in a future case, to government more power to accommodate the needs of members of a religious group to educate their children outside of the public school system, so long as the government did not employ a sect preference. There may be a new majority of Justices who will vote to uphold more types of government aid to religiously affiliated schools than would have been tolerated by a majority of the Justices during the Warren Court and Burger Court eras.[2.85]

2.10 In the 1980s and 1990s, the Supreme Court decided several establishment clause cases in which it ruled against the government without relying on the three–part purpose–effect–entanglement test. See, e.g., County of Allegheny v. American Civil Liberties Union, 492 U.S. 573, 109 S.Ct. 3086, 106 L.Ed.2d 472 (1989); Lee v. Weisman, 505 U.S. 577, 112 S.Ct. 2649, 120 L.Ed.2d 467 (1992).

2.15 Board of Education of Kiryas Joel Village School District v. Grumet, 512 U.S. 687, 114 S.Ct. 2481, 129 L.Ed.2d 546 (1994).

2.20 Grand Rapids School District v. Ball, 473 U.S. 373, 105 S.Ct. 3216, 87 L.Ed.2d 267 (1985); Aguilar v. Felton, 473 U.S. 402, 105 S.Ct. 3232, 87 L.Ed.2d 290 (1985).

2.25 The facts regarding the history of the Village of Kiryas Joel, and the local public school district, and the creation of the new school district are set forth in Board of Education of Kiryas Joel Village School District v. Grumet, 512 U.S. 687, ___, 114 S.Ct. 2481, 2485–87, 129 L.Ed.2d 546 (1994) (Part I of the opinion by Justice Souter).

2.30 Board of Education of Kiryas Joel Village School District v. Grumet, 512 U.S. 687, ___, 114 S.Ct. 2481, 2491–2493, 129 L.Ed.2d 546 (1994). This por-

tion of Justice Souter's opinion was joined by Justices Blackmun, Stevens, O'Connor, and Ginsburg.

2.35 512 U.S. at ___, 114 S.Ct. at 2491.

2.40 512 U.S. at ___, 114 S.Ct. at 2492.

2.45 512 U.S. at ___, 114 S.Ct. at 2493. For an examination of the aid that can be provided to students at religiously affiliated primary and secondary schools see § 21.4(a) of this Treatise.

2.50 Board of Education of Kiryas Joel Village School District v. Grumet, 512 U.S. 687, ___, 114 S.Ct. 2481, 2487–2490, 129 L.Ed.2d 546 (1994). This portion of Justice Souter's opinion was joined by Justices Blackmun, Stevens, and Ginsburg. Justice Blackmun wrote an opinion concurring in both the judgment and opinion of the Court in which he found that the Court's ruling in this case was consistent with the principles that formed the basis of the three part purpose–effect–entanglement test which had been used in most of the establishment clause cases of the Supreme Court after 1971. 512 U.S. at ___, 114 S.Ct. at 2494 (Blackmun, J., concurring). Justice Stevens was joined by Justices Blackmun and Ginsburg in stating the view that the special aid given to the children of the Village could not be char-

acterized as an accommodation of religion in any way because it was designed
to provide special aid to members of one
particular religious faith. 512 U.S. at
___, 114 S.Ct. at 2495 (Stevens, J.,
joined by Blackmun and Ginsburg, JJ.,
concurring).

2.55 512 U.S. at ___, 114 S.Ct. at
2487–90. The plurality likened the case
before it to Larkin v. Grendel's Den,
Inc., 459 U.S. 116, 103 S.Ct. 505, 74
L.Ed.2d 297 (1982) in which the Court
had invalidated a law giving religious
entities a power to veto applications for
liquor licenses in areas near the opera-
tions of those religious organizations.
The *Larkin* case is examined in this
section of the Treatise.

2.60 Board of Education of Kiryas
Joel Village School District v. Grumet,
512 U.S. 687, ___, 114 S.Ct. 2481, 2488,
129 L.Ed.2d 546 (1994) (opinion of Souter, J., joined by Blackmun, Stevens, and
Ginsburg, JJ.).

2.65 512 U.S. at ___, 114 S.Ct. at
2490 (internal citations and quotation
marks omitted).

2.70 Board of Education of Kiryas
Joel Village School District v. Grumet,
512 U.S. 687, ___, 114 S.Ct. 2481, 2495,
129 L.Ed.2d 546 (1994) (O'Connor, J.,
concurring in part and concurring in the
judgment).

2.75 512 U.S. at ___, 114 S.Ct. at
2500 (Kennedy, J., concurring in the
judgment).

2.80 512 U.S. at ___, 114 S.Ct. at
2505 (Scalia, J., joined by Rehnquist,
C.J., and Thomas, J., dissenting).

2.85 The permissible scope of government aid to religiously affiliated
schools is examined in § 21.4 of this
Treatise. See, Abner S. Greene, Kiryas
Joel and Two Mistakes About Equality,
94 Columbia L. Rev. 1 (1996). For responses to Professor Greene, see, Chris-
topher L. Eisgruber, The Constitutional
Value of Assimilation, 94 Columbia
L.Rev. 87 (1996), and Ira C. Lupu, Un-
covering the Village of Kiryas Joel, 94
Columbia L.Rev. 104 (1996).

**Page 463, add after the first full paragraph on this page
(and before § 21.4):**

In *Lee v. Weisman*,[27] the Court was presented with a challenge
to a government practice of having a prayer at a public middle
school graduation ceremony. School principals were permitted by
the public school regulations to invite members of the clergy to
offer invocation and benediction prayers at the start of formal
graduation ceremonies for high schools and middle schools. Clergy
who gave the prayers were provided with a document titled "Guidelines for Civic Occasions", which was prepared by the National
Conference of Christians and Jews, and which recommended that
prayers at nonsectarian ceremonies be designed so as to avoid
offending the sensibilities of any persons at the proceedings. In the
particular case before the Court, a middle school graduation had
included an invocation and benediction given by a Rabbi. The
Supreme Court found that the school policy permitting the prayer
at a school graduation violated the establishment clause.

The *Lee* decision helps clarify the Supreme Court's view of the
establishment clause in the early 1990s but it left open the question
of what specific test should be used in examining government
actions that are alleged to violate the establishment clause. The
case was decided by a five to four vote; the four dissenting Justices
were unsuccessful in their attempt to get the Court to approve
incidental aid to religion that did not favor a particular sect.[28] The
majority opinion by Justice Kennedy found that the government's
use of prayers at school graduations violated the "central principles" of the establishment clause so that the case did not require

the Justices to "revisit the difficult question dividing us in recent cases, questions of the definition and full scope of the principles governing the extent or permitted accommodation by the state for the religious beliefs and practices of many of its citizens ... we do not accept the invitation of petitions and amicus the United States to reconsider our decision in *Lemon v. Kurtzman*." [29]

The majority ruled that state sponsored and directed religious exercise constituted an involvement of government and religion that literally constituted the establishment of religion.   Justice Kennedy found that the principle of government neutrality was central to the establishment and free exercise clauses and that this principle was violated by the state directed prayer.[30] The majority opinion did not hold that only government actions that posed a danger of coercion of people's beliefs in religious matters would violate the establishment clause.   But Justice Kennedy's majority opinion stated government practices that coerced people to support, or participate in, religious activities would be violations of the establishment clause.[31]

The majority opinion in *Lee* did not give lower courts specific tests for reviewing every type of possible fact situation in which the government might be alleged to violate the establishment clause. The *Lee* majority opinion noted that the Court's concerns about coercion were "most pronounced" when reviewing the practices of public schools because the government subjecting children to the choice of participating in religious activities or missing classes, or graduation ceremonies, puts the young people in a real "conflict of conscience".[32] But the meaning of *Lee* outside the school setting is unclear. The majority concluded by noting: "We do not hold that every state action implicating religion is invalid if one or a few citizens find it offensive." [33]

The *Lee* decision demonstrated that the Court at the start of the 1990s was committed to defending establishment clause principles. A majority of the Justices were concerned about government neutrality in matters that would involve the religious beliefs of persons in our society; they rejected the argument that all nonsectarian or nonpreferential aid to religion generally was compatible with the establishment clause.[34] The *Lee* court did not reject the three part purpose, effect, and entanglement test used in earlier cases; it did not make "coercion" the touchstone of establishment clause analysis.[35]

The *Lee* Court's failure to endorse or revise specific standards set out in earlier majority opinions leaves lower courts facing new establishment clause cases somewhat adrift. But the *Lee* decision reaffirmed the role of the judiciary in examining on a case-by-case basis the question of whether government actions have violated the principles of neutrality and noncoercion so as to violate the establishment clause.[36] Unless the *Lemon* tests are overruled in the future, judicial review in establishment clause cases will involve the purpose, effect, and entanglement tests.[37]

In a series of cases, the Supreme Court has prohibited government entities from suppressing, or discriminating against, speech of religious organizations.[38] In each of these cases, a government entity attempted to deny access to government property to a religious group on the basis that, in the view of the government, the religious group's use of the public property would constitute a violation of the establishment clause. The Supreme Court, in these cases, ruled that allowing a religious organization to use a public forum for religiously oriented speech activities did not constitute a violation of the establishment clause, so long as the religious group was not given preferential treatment. However, in these cases, the Supreme Court was unable to identify a specific standard for determining if, or when, speech by private persons on government property would constitute a violation of the establishment clause. These cases did not formally reject the three-part *Lemon* Test, although several Justices in each case believed that the Court should employ an "endorsement test" for determining when government aid to religious activities or government connection to religious speech violated the First Amendment.

In *Lamb's Chapel v. Center Moriches Union Free School District*,[39] the Supreme Court ruled that a government school board violated the First Amendment freedom of speech when it denied a religious organization the right to conduct a meeting in a school building after school hours, at a time when the board allowed nonreligious groups to use the school premises for their meetings. Regardless of whether the school building was viewed as a "limited public forum" or a "nonpublic forum," the government's discrimination against religious speech constituted a form of viewpoint discrimination that violated the First Amendment.

The school board had attempted to justify its action by arguing that allowing the religious group to use the school property would violate the establishment clause. Justice White, writing for a majority in *Lamb's Chapel,* found that granting the religious organization equal access to the school would promote free speech values and would not violate the establishment clause. Justice White noted that the three-part *Lemon* test had never been overruled and that the *Lemon* test served, at that time, as the standard for determining if a government action violated the establishment clause.[40] Three concurring Justices in *Lamb's Chapel* agreed with the majority that the school board's discrimination against religious organizations violated the free speech clause, but these Justices objected to the majority opinion's reference to the *Lemon* tests.[41] Although the concurring Justices believed that the *Lemon* tests were not the proper basis for determining the compatibility of a government action with the establishment clause, these Justices were not clear regarding the establishment clause standards they would use in place of the *Lemon* tests.

The Supreme Court relied on *Lamb's Chapel* when the Justices, by a seven to two vote, ruled that allowing a private organization to place a religious symbol (a cross) in a public square, which was part of the state capitol grounds, would not violate the establishment clause. In *Capitol Square Review and Advisory Board v. Pinette* [42] the Court held that a state government would not violate the establishment clause if it permitted the Ku Klux Klan to place an unattended cross on public property that had been opened to private persons and organizations for the placement of signs and symbols. The government had denied the Klan's request on the basis that placing an unattended cross on the square would violate the establishment clause. The lower federal courts ruled that the government had violated the free speech rights of the Klan, because (1) the capitol grounds had become a "limited public forum" or "public forum," and (2) the display of a religious symbol in that setting would not violate the establishment clause.

Justice Scalia wrote an opinion in the *Capitol Square Review* case that was, in part, a majority opinion, and in part, a plurality opinion. Justice Scalia wrote for a majority when he held that the only question that had been properly presented to the Court in the *Capitol Square Review* case was the question of whether a cross being placed in a public forum by a private group violated the establishment clause. Justice Scalia wrote only for himself, Chief Justice Rehnquist, and Justices Kennedy and Thomas when he found that the Court had not adopted an "endorsement test" for resolving all establishment clause issues and refused to use an endorsement test to determine if the placement of the cross in the square would violate the establishment clause. According to the plurality opinion, if the endorsement test were to be used by the judiciary at all, its use should be limited to determining when the government's speech, or government grants of financial aid to religious organizations, linked the government with religious activity in a way that violated the establishment clause. Justice Scalia stated that the religious expression of private persons could not violate the First Amendment when the expression took place in a public forum that was open to all persons and speakers on equal terms. [43]

Justices O'Connor, Souter, and Breyer concurred in the part of Justice Scalia's opinion that framed the issues in the *Capitol Square* case. [44] However, they did not concur in the part of the plurality opinion in which Justice Scalia had discussed the establishment clause standards. These three Justices favored adopting the endorsement test that had been used in separate opinions by Justice O'Connor in earlier Supreme Court cases. [45] The three concurring Justices believed that the endorsement test was the proper test to use when determining whether there was a link between the government and religious activity by private persons that violated the establishment clause. The concurring Justices relied on the *Lamb's Chapel* decision because, in their view, it could be best understood as using the endorsement test, even though Justice White's majority opinion in *Lamb's Chapel* had specifically made use of the *Lemon* tests for determining whether granting a religious organization access to a public forum might violate the establishment clause.[46]

27. 505 U.S. 577, 112 S.Ct. 2649, 120 L.Ed.2d 467 (1992).

28. 505 U.S. at 630, 112 S.Ct. at 2678 (Scalia, J., joined by Rehnquist, C.J., and White and Thomas, JJ., dissenting).

29. Lee v. Weisman, 505 U.S. 577, 586, 112 S.Ct. 2649, 2655, 120 L.Ed.2d 467 (1992) citing Lemon v. Kurtzman, 403 U.S. 602, 91 S.Ct. 2105, 29 L.Ed.2d 745 (1971), rehearing denied 404 U.S. 876, 92 S.Ct. 24, 30 L.Ed.2d 123 (1971). The *Lemon* case created the three part (purpose, effect, entanglement) test that is examined at the start of this section of the Treatise and in § 21.4(A) of this Treatise.

30. Lee v. Weisman, 505 U.S. 577, 588, 112 S.Ct. 2649, 2656, 120 L.Ed.2d 467 (1992): "The First Amendment's Religion Clauses mean that religious beliefs and religious expression are too precious to be either proscribed or prescribed by the state."

31. The majority opinion stated: "It is beyond dispute that, at a minimum, the Constitution guarantees that the government may not coerce anyone to support or participate in religion or its exercise...." 505 U.S. at 587, 112 S.Ct. at 2655. "If citizens are subjected to state-sponsored religious exercises, the state disavows its own duty to guard and respect that sphere of inviolable conscience and belief which is the mark of a free people." 505 U.S. at 592, 112 S.Ct. at 2658.

32. Lee v. Weisman, 505 U.S. 577, 592–95, 112 S.Ct. 2649, 2658–60, 120 L.Ed.2d 467 (1992).

33. 505 U.S. at 597, 112 S.Ct. at 2661.

34. The rejection of the nonpreferentialist argument was stressed in Justice Souter's concurring opinion, which was joined by Justices Stevens and O'Connor. Lee v. Weisman, 505 U.S. 577, 609, 112 S.Ct. 2649, 2667, 120 L.Ed.2d 467 (1992) (Souter, J., joined by Stevens and O'Connor, JJ., concurring).

35. Justice Blackmun wrote an opinion concurring in the judgment and in the majority opinion that was joined by Justices Stevens and O'Connor. Justice Blackmun pointed out that in every establishment clause case decided after 1971 the Court had used the three part test known as the *Lemon* test because it came from the decision in Lemon v. Kurtzman, 403 U.S. 602, 91 S.Ct. 2105, 29 L.Ed.2d 745 (1971), rehearing denied 404 U.S. 876, 92 S.Ct. 24, 30 L.Ed.2d 123 (1971) except for the decision in Marsh v. Chambers, 463 U.S. 783, 103 S.Ct. 3330, 77 L.Ed.2d 1019 (1983) (which upheld a legislature's employment of a religious chaplain). Lee v. Weisman, 505 U.S. 577, 597, 603 n. 4, 112 S.Ct. 2649, 2661, 2663 n. 4, 120 L.Ed.2d 467 (1992) (Blackmun, J., joined by Stevens and O'Connor, JJ., concurring).

36. Lee v. Weisman, 505 U.S. 577, 597, 112 S.Ct. 2649, 2661, 120 L.Ed.2d 467 (1992): "Our jurisprudence in this area is of necessity one of line-drawing, of determining at what point a dissenter's rights of religious freedom are infringed by the State."

37. In the 1992–93 Term, the Supreme Court ruled on establishment clause issues without addressing the question of whether the *Lemon* tests should be overruled or modified. In Zobrest v. Catalina Foothills School District, 509 U.S. 1, 113 S.Ct. 2462, 125 L.Ed.2d 1 (1993), the Supreme Court found that the establishment clause did not create a barrier to a public school system providing an interpreter for a deaf child who attended a religiously affiliated high school. The majority opinion, by Chief Justice Rehnquist, found that the type of aid involved in the case was a type of neutral aid to all children and parents. The majority opinion did not use, or reject, the *Lemon* tests; the majority relied only upon a general analysis of the aid and a comparison of that aid to the types of aid to religious school students that had been upheld or invalidated in past cases. See § 21.4(a) of this Treatise.

38. See the cases discussed in § 21.5(e), such as Widmar v. Vincent, 454 U.S. 263, 102 S.Ct. 269, 70 L.Ed.2d 440 (1981), as well as the cases discussed in this section of the Treatise. See generally, Stephen Bainbridge, Student Religious Organizations and University Policies Against Discrimination on the Basis of Sexual Orientation: Implications of the Religious Freedom Restriction Act, 21 J. of College and Univ. Law 369 (1994).

39. 508 U.S. 384, 113 S.Ct. 2141, 124 L.Ed.2d 352 (1993).

40. 508 U.S. at 394 n. 7, 113 S.Ct. at 2148 n. 7.

41. Lamb's Chapel v. Center Moriches Union Free School District, 508 U.S. 384, 396, 113 S.Ct. 2141, 2149, 124 L.Ed.2d 352 (1993) (Kennedy, J., concurring in part and concurring in the judgment); 508 U.S. at 396, 113 S.Ct. at 2149 (Scalia, J., joined by Thomas, J., concurring in the judgment).

42. ___ U.S. ___, 115 S.Ct. 2440, 132 L.Ed.2d 650 (1995). Justice Thomas joined all of Justice Scalia's majority opinion, but he also wrote a concurring opinion. ___ U.S. at ___, 115 S.Ct. at 2450 (Thomas, J., concurring). Only Justices Stevens and Ginsburg dissented in *Capitol Square*. ___ U.S. at ___, 115 S.Ct. at 2464 (Stevens, J., dissenting); ___ U.S. at ___, 115 S.Ct. at 2474 (Ginsburg, J., dissenting).

43. ___ U.S. at ___, 115 S.Ct. at 2450 (opinion of Scalia, J., joined by Rehnquist, C.J., and Kennedy and Thomas, JJ.).

44. Capitol Square Review and Advisory Board v. Pinette, ___ U.S. ___, ___, 115 S.Ct. 2440, 2451, 132 L.Ed.2d 650 (1995) (O'Connor, J., joined by Souter and Breyer, JJ., concurring in part and concurring in the judgment); ___ U.S. at ___, 115 S.Ct. at 2457 (Souter, J., joined by O'Connor and Breyer, JJ., concurring in part and concurring in the judgment).

45. See, e.g., Lynch v. Donnelly, 465 U.S. 668, 690, 104 S.Ct. 1355, 1366, 79 L.Ed.2d 604 (1984) (O'Connor, J., concurring), rehearing denied 466 U.S. 994, 104 S.Ct. 2376, 80 L.Ed.2d 848 (1984); Witters v. Washington Department of Services for the Blind, 474 U.S. 481, 493, 106 S.Ct. 748, 755, 88 L.Ed.2d 846 (1986) (O'Connor, J., concurring), rehearing denied 475 U.S. 1091, 106 S.Ct. 1485, 89 L.Ed.2d 737 (1986); County of Allegheny v. American Civil Liberties Union, 492 U.S. 573, 623, 109 S.Ct. 3086, 3117, 106 L.Ed.2d 472 (1989) (O'Connor, J., concurring in part and concurring in the judgment).

46. Capitol Square Review and Advisory Board v. Pinette, ___ U.S. ___, ___, 115 S.Ct. 2440, 2451-53, 132 L.Ed.2d 650 (1995) (O'Connor, J., joined by Souter and Breyer, JJ., concurring in part and concurring in the judgment); ___ U.S. at ___, 115 S.Ct. at 2460 (Souter, J., joined by O'Connor and Breyer, JJ., concurring in part and concurring in the judgment). See footnote 40, and accompanying text, supra.

§ 21.4 Aid to Religious Institutions

(a) Primary and Secondary Schools

Page 464, add to the end of the carryover paragraph at the top of the page, after note 2:

The Supreme Court has not adopted a constitutional test that would separate unconstitutional aid to religiously affiliated schools from constitutional aid going to students or the parents of students who attend religiously affiliated schools. Instead of using a "student aid" versus "aid to religious schools" distinction, the Supreme Court has used the *Lemon* tests (the purpose-effect-entanglement tests) to determine the validity of each type of government aid that is given to religious schools or their students. Nevertheless, the following cases seem to demonstrate that the Supreme Court is most likely to uphold government student assistance programs if those programs are viewed primarily as aid to the individual students and their parents rather than a form of aid to the religious schools.[2.5]

2.5 Although the distinction between aid to students who may attend religious schools and the aid to the religious schools themselves has not been the adopted test of constitutionality, in three cases, the Supreme Court's majority opinion focused almost exclusively on the distinction. See, Mueller v. Allen, 463 U.S. 388, 103 S.Ct. 3062, 77 L.Ed.2d 721 (1983) (upholding a state tax statute allowing taxpayers to deduct from their state income tax certain school expenses including expenses in connection with providing children with an education at any private or public elementary or secondary school); Witters v. Washington Department of Services for the Blind, 474 U.S. 481, 106 S.Ct. 748, 88 L.Ed.2d 846 (1986), rehearing denied 475 U.S. 1091, 106 S.Ct. 1485, 89 L.Ed.2d 737 (1986) (upholding a state program that gave physically handicapped students payment to subsidize their education and the application of that system to the payment of aid to a blind student attending a religiously affiliated college); Zobrest v. Catalina Foothills School District, 509 U.S. 1, 113 S.Ct. 2462, 125 L.Ed.2d 1 (1993) (the Supreme Court rules that the establishment clause does not prohibit the government from providing for the services of a sign language and speech interpreter for a deaf student who was attending a religiously affiliated high school). Each of these three cases is analyzed in this section of the Treatise.

Page 471, add to note 32:

32. These decisions of the Supreme Court prohibited the government from providing religious school students with government health or educational services beyond testing services at religiously affiliated grade schools and high schools. However, these services could be provided to the religious school students at another site. Nevertheless, there is some doubt as to whether a majority of the Supreme Court Justices today believe that the state employed, or subsidized, health care workers may provide health services to students who attend a religiously affiliated school at the religious school premises. In Zobrest v. Catalina Foothills School District, 509 U.S. 1, 113 S.Ct. 2462, 125 L.Ed.2d 1 (1993) the Supreme Court, in a majority opinion written by Chief Justice Rehnquist, found that the establishment clause did not prohibit the government from providing a speech-sign language interpreter (or paying for interpreter services) for a student who was attending a religiously affiliated high school. Chief Justice Rehnquist indicated that the earlier Supreme Court cases concerning the provision of services to religious school students only prohibited the provision of educational services that would relieve sectarian schools of basic cost in educating the students. The Chief Justice described the Wolman decision as ruling that government health services could be provided to all school children "even when those services are provided within sectarian schools." 509 U.S. at 12 n. 10, 113 S.Ct. at 2469 n. 10. Justice Blackmun wrote the opinion in Wolman that was, in part, a majority opinion and, in part, a plurality opinion. In Zobrest, Justice Blackmun disagreed with the Chief Justice's interpretation of the earlier cases. Justice Blackmun believed that Wolman had allowed government employees "to administer diagnostic testing on the premises of the parochial schools while prohibiting the states from paying for providing remedial teachers or counsellors." Although he did not directly address this issue, Justice Blackmun appeared to disagree with the argument that the government could have provided health services beyond administering tests to students on parochial school premises. Zobrest v. Catalina Foothills School District, 509 U.S. at 16–22, 113 S.Ct. at 2471–74 (Blackmun, J., joined by Souter, dissenting). Justices O'Connor and Stevens joined part of Justice Blackmun's dissent but they did not join his discussion of the Court's establishment clause principles. These two justices believe that no constitutional issue had to be reached in this case. 509 U.S. at 24, 113 S.Ct. at 2475 (O'Connor, J., joined by Stevens, J., dissenting).

Page 473, add after the carryover paragraph at the top of the page:

The Supreme Court demonstrated a willingness to uphold religiously neutral government aid that was given to all school children when it upheld government programs that were designed to assist students in public and private schools to overcome physical or learning disabilities.[35.5] The Court's decisions concerning aid to students who have such disabilities do not clearly indicate whether, in the future, the Court will use more lenient establishment clause tests when reviewing government programs that provide more general forms of aid to children in religious schools. We will examine the Supreme Court decisions concerning aid to handicapped students after reviewing the Court's earlier rulings concerning assistance to religiously affiliated schools.

35.5 In Zobrest v. Catalina Foothills School District, 509 U.S. 1, 113 S.Ct. 2462, 125 L.Ed.2d 1 (1993) the Court ruled that the establishment clause would not prevent the government through a religiously neutral program, from providing a sign language-speech interpreter for a deaf student even though the deaf student was attending a religiously affiliated high school. The Zobrest case is examined in footnotes 55.5–55.40, and accompanying text, in this section of the Treatise. In Zobrest the Supreme Court relied on Witters v. Washington Department of Services for the Blind, 474 U.S. 481, 106 S.Ct. 748, 88 L.Ed.2d 846 (1986), rehearing denied 475 U.S. 1091, 106 S.Ct. 1485, 89 L.Ed.2d 737 (1986) and upheld the provision of state payments to blind students who were engaged in professional or vocational training and the provision of such payments to a handicapped student who was attending a religiously affiliated college. See footnotes 51–55, and accompanying text, in this section of the Treatise.

In Board of Education of Kiryas Joel Village School District v. Grumet, 512 U.S. 687, 114 S.Ct. 2481, 129 L.Ed.2d 546 (1994), the Supreme Court invalidated the creation of a separate school district for members of a religious community. However, as the Court did so, a majority of Justices, in concurring and dissenting opinions, indicated that the Court might in the future ease its establishment clause restrictions on the provision of aid to handicapped children at religiously affiliated school. See notes 50.5–50.35, and accompanying text, in this section of the Treatise.

Page 480, add after the carryover paragraph at the top of the page:

The *Wolman, Grand Rapids School District,* and *Aguilar* decisions appeared to make it virtually impossible for the government to provide even religiously neutral educational aid to students with special needs (such as physically handicapped children) on religious school property. Government sponsored education programs for such students could only be provided at sites that were not owned or operated by religious entities.

In *Board of Education of Kiryas Joel Village School District v. Grumet* [50.5] the Supreme Court invalidated a state law which created a separate school district for a Village composed of entirely of members of one religion. Justice Souter wrote an opinion that was, in part, a majority opinion and, in part, a plurality opinion in which he ruled that the state law constituted an improper sect preference that violated the establishment clause.[50.10] But the division of the Justices in *Grumet* made it appear that a majority of Justices were ready to depart from the view that any provision of on–site remedial services beyond educational testing, and some health related services, at religious schools would violate the establishment clause.

Justice O'Connor only joined part of Justice Souter's opinion in *Grumet.*[50.15] She believed the state statute creating the special school district for members of a particular religion violated the establishment clause. But in her concurring opinion, Justice O'Connor stated that, she would vote to uphold the provision of religiously neutral educational services "on–site" at religiously affiliated schools.[50.20]

Justice Kennedy concurred only in the judgment of the Court in *Grumet.*[50.25] Unlike Justice O'Connor, he did not clearly indicate that he would vote to overrule the *Grand Rapids* and *Aguilar* cases. But Justice Kennedy stated that those decisions "may have been erroneous" and that "it may be necessary for us to reconsider them." According to Justice Kennedy, the provision of religiously neutral aid to handicapped children who attended religious schools was the "preferable way" to address the problem of the students in *Grumet.*[50.30]

Justice Scalia, joined by Chief Justice Rehnquist and Justice Thomas, dissented in *Grumet.*[50.35] These three Justices would vote to allow the government to accommodate the needs of children for special educational services on the premises of a religiously affiliated school. It appears there are now five Justices (the three dissenters in *Grumet* and Justices O'Connor and Kennedy) who, in an appropriate case, would vote to overturn the 1985 decisions, or at least limit them, so that some forms of religiously neutral aid for students with special education needs could be provided at religiously affiliated schools.

50.5 Board of Education of Kiryas Joel Village School District v. Grumet, 512 U.S. 687, 114 S.Ct. 2481, 129 L.Ed.2d 546 (1994).

50.10 Justice Souter's opinion was joined in its entirety by Justices Blackmun, Stevens, and Ginsburg. Justice O'Connor joined only part of Justice Souter's opinion. The Court's ruling in *Grumet*, and the various opinions issued by the Justices in that case, are examined in § 21.3 of this Treatise.

50.15 512 U.S. at ___, 114 S.Ct. at 2495 (O'Connor, J., concurring in part and concurring in the judgment).

50.20 512 U.S. at ___, 114 S.Ct. at 2498 (O'Connor, J., concurring in part and concurring in the judgment).

50.25 512 U.S. at ___, 114 S.Ct. at 2500 (Kennedy, J., concurring in the judgment).

50.30 512 U.S. at ___, 114 S.Ct. at 2505 (Kennedy, J., concurring in the judgment).

50.35 Board of Education of Kiryas Joel Village School District v. Grumet, 512 U.S. 687, ___, 114 S.Ct. 2481, 2505, 129 L.Ed.2d 546 (1994) (Scalia, J., joined by Rehnquist, C.J., and Thomas, J., dissenting).

Page 481, add after the first full paragraph on this page, which ends with note 55:

In *Zobrest v. Catalina Foothills School District*,[55.5] the Supreme Court relied heavily on *Mueller* and *Witters* and ruled that the establishment clause did not prevent a public school district from providing a sign language interpreter to a deaf student who was attending a religiously affiliated school within the district's boundaries. This student had attended a school for the deaf during his early years of education; he had attended public schools operated by this school district for grades 6 through 8. While he was in the public schools, the district furnished him with a sign language interpreter. When the student entered a Catholic high school he claimed that the federal Individuals with Disabilities Education Act required the school district to provide him with a sign language interpreter. The school district refused to provide him with a sign language interpreter because, it claimed, that the provision of such aid to a religious school student would violate the establishment clause.

When the *Zobrest* case was before the United States Court of Appeals, the school district had failed to argue that the federal statute, and federal regulations implementing the statute, did not require the district to provide a student at a religious school be given a sign language interpreter. The school district, in the lower courts, also failed to assert the position that these federal statutes and regulations prevented the school district from providing sign language interpreters to students at religious schools. Because of the school district's failure to press its statutory arguments before the Court of Appeals, a majority of the Supreme Court Justices believed that they should assume that federal law would require the school district to provide a sign language interpreter to the student so long as this form of aid did not violate the establishment clause.

Two of the Justices refused to reach any constitutional issues because of their belief that the constitutional issue should be avoided and that the case should be remanded for an exploration of statutory issues.[55.10] Of the seven Justices who reached the constitutional issue in *Zobrest,* five justices rejected the school district's claim that the provision of a sign language interpreter for the religious school student would violate the establishment clause.

Chief Justice Rehnquist wrote for the majority in *Zobrest;* he cited and relied upon the *Mueller* and *Witters* cases. The Chief Justice found that the Supreme Court "[has] consistently held that government programs that neutrally provide benefits to a broad class of citizens defined without reference to religion are not readily subject to an establishment clause challenge because sectarian institutions may also receive an attenuated financial benefit." [55.15] The school district alleged that the provision of sign language interpreter services to the religious school student would be similar to the provision of teaching equipment (such as maps, charts, and tape recorders) or publicly paid teachers to teach the nonreligious subjects in religious schools. Those types of school aid programs had been invalidated in earlier Supreme Court cases.[55.20] The Chief Justice, in *Zobrest,* distinguished the provision of goods or services to religious schools on the basis that those invalidated government programs had "relieved sectarian schools of costs they otherwise would have borne in educating their students … handicapped children, not sectarian schools, are the primary beneficiaries of the [federal statute under which the child claimed a right to a sign language interpreter]; to the extent sectarian schools receive a benefit at all from [the statute and the sign language interpreter], they are only incidental beneficiaries." [55.25]

The dissenting Justices asserted that there was, or should be, an absolute prohibition against public employees providing services in religious schools,[55.30] but the majority in *Zobrest* rejected that position.   Chief Justice Rehnquist stated: "The establishment clause lays down no absolute bar to the placing of a public employee in a sectarian school." [55.35]   Because the majority viewed the program as "a neutral government program dispensing aid not to schools but to individual handicapped children," the majority found that the establishment clause would not prevent the government from providing a sign language interpreter to the deaf student at the Catholic high school.   The Chief Justice's opinion reached this result by finding that the nature of the aid to the deaf child should not be considered aid to the religious school or to religious activities.   The majority opinion did not make use of the three part *Lemon* test that had been used in most of the school aid cases decided by the Supreme Court during the previous two decades.[55.40]

55.5   509 U.S. 1, 113 S.Ct. 2462, 125 L.Ed.2d 1 (1993).   The majority in *Zobrest* found that the failure of the school board to press its statutory and regulatory issues before the Court of Appeals meant that "the prudential rule of avoiding constitutional questions has no application." 509 U.S. at 7, 113 S.Ct. at 2466.

55.10   Justices O'Connor and Stevens believed that the *Zobrest* case should be remanded to the lower courts for determination of whether federal statutes and regulations precluded the provision of aid to this student because, if the statute and regulations did so, there would be no need to reach a constitutional question.   These two justices joined only the portion of Justice Blackmun's dissent that dealt with the need to avoid constitutional issues and the need to have the statutory questions addressed in this case. 509 U.S. at 24, 113 S.Ct. at 2475 (O'Connor, J., joined by Stevens, J., dissenting).   Justices Blackmun dissented from both the majority's decision to consider the constitutional issues and the majority's ruling on the establishment clause issue. 509 U.S. at 12, 113 S.Ct. at 2469 (Blackmun, J., joined by Souter, J., dissenting; this dis-

senting opinion was joined in part by O'Connor and Stevens, JJ.).

55.15   Zobrest v. Catalina Foothills School District, 509 U.S. 1, 7, 113 S.Ct. 2462, 2466, 125 L.Ed.2d 1 (1993).

55.20   In making this argument before the United States Supreme Court, the school district relied on many of the cases that have been cited and discussed in this section of the Treatise.   The school district's principal argument was that the provision of an interpreter for a religious school student was similar to the aid that had been invalidated in Meek v. Pittenger, 421 U.S. 349, 95 S.Ct. 1753, 44 L.Ed.2d 217 (1975), rehearing denied 422 U.S. 1049, 95 S.Ct. 2668, 45 L.Ed.2d 702 (1975) and Grand Rapids School District v. Ball, 473 U.S. 373, 105 S.Ct. 3216, 87 L.Ed.2d 267 (1985).   The *Meek* and *Ball* cases are examined at footnotes 29–32, 44–48, and accompanying text, in this section of the Treatise.

55.25   Zobrest v. Catalina Foothills School District, 509 U.S. 1, 10–12, 113 S.Ct. 2462, 2468–69, 125 L.Ed.2d 1 (1993).

55.30   509 U.S. at 16–24, 113 S.Ct. at 2471–75 (Blackmun, joined by Souter,

J., dissenting). Justices O'Connor and Stevens did not join a portion of Justice Blackmun's dissent that involved an analysis of the establishment clause issue in this case.

55.35 Zobrest v. Catalina Foothills School District, 509 U.S. 1, 12, 113 S.Ct. 2462, 2469, 125 L.Ed.2d 1 (1993).

55.40 The three part test is known as the *Lemon* test because it was first clearly set forth in Lemon v. Kurtzman,

403 U.S. 602, 91 S.Ct. 2105, 29 L.Ed.2d 745 (1971). As noted in the earlier paragraphs of this subsection of the Treatise, the *Lemon* tests have been used in almost all of the Supreme Court establishment clause decisions since 1971. The nature of the three part test, and the division of the Justices concerning whether that test should be used to determine establishment clause violations, is examined in § 21.3 of this Treatise.

(c) Other Issues in Aid to Religious Institutions

(4) Government Payments of Money "Owned" by Private Individuals

Page 492, add to note 79:

79. In Zobrest v. Catalina Foothills School District, 509 U.S. 1, 113 S.Ct. 2462, 125 L.Ed.2d 1 (1993) the Court ruled that the establishment clause would not prevent the government from providing a sign language-speech interpreter for a deaf student even though the deaf student was attending a religiously affiliated high school.

The *Zobrest* case is examined in notes 55.5–55.40, and accompanying text, in this section of the Treatise.

(d) A Comment on the Emergence and Impact of the Excessive Entanglement Test

Page 504, add to note 113:

113. In Zobrest v. Catalina Foothills School District, 509 U.S. 1, 113 S.Ct. 2462, 125 L.Ed.2d 1 (1993) the Court ruled that the establishment clause would not prevent the government from providing a sign language-speech interpreter for a deaf student even though the deaf student was attending a religiously affiliated high school.

The *Zobrest* case is examined in notes 55.5–55.40, and accompanying text, in this section of the Treatise.

§ 21.5   Religion and the Public Schools

(a) Introduction

Page 505, add to note 1:

1. In Lee v. Weisman, 505 U.S. 577, 112 S.Ct. 2649, 120 L.Ed.2d 467 (1992) the Court, by a five to four vote of the Justices, found that school sponsored invocations and benediction prayers at graduation ceremonies violated the establishment clause. The majority opinion in *Lee,* found that this practice violated the "central principles" of the establishment clause, so that the Court would not "revisit the difficult questions dividing us in recent cases" concerning whether the three part (purpose, effect, entanglement) test should be used in all, or even some, establishment clause cases. 505 U.S. at 586, 112 S.Ct. at 2655. The *Lee* decision is examined in §§ 21.5(c), 21.3 of this Treatise.

Page 506, add after carryover paragraph:

The cases in this section of the Treatise involve issues concerning religious activities in government schools or other connections between government schools and religious beliefs. The situations in these cases differ from the situation confronted by the Court in *Board of Education of Kiryas Joel Village School District v. Grumet*.[1.5] The Supreme Court, in *Grumet*, invalidated a state law that created a separate public school district for a Village composed entirely of members of one religion. The only public school in the new Village School District was operated in a completely nonreligious manner for handicapped children within the district. The government school had no involvement with religion that would have violated the establishment clause. But a majority of the Justices in *Grumet* found that the state law creating the Village School District was a preference for members of one religious sect that violated the establishment clause's neutrality principle.[1.10]

1.5 512 U.S. 687, 114 S.Ct. 2481, 129 L.Ed.2d 546 (1994).

1.10 The *Grumet* decision is analyzed in § 21.3 of this Treatise.

(c) Prayers or Bible Reading

Page 512, add after the carryover paragraph—after note 22 and before subsection (d):

Even if the Court in the future abandons the *"Lemon* tests" [22.5] (the formal three part tests: purpose—effect—entanglement), the Court is unlikely to overrule its decisions finding that officially authorized prayers, or readings from religious texts, in government grade schools and high schools violate the establishment clause. This point was clearly made by the Court in *Lee v. Weisman*,[22.10] as the Court found that religious invocations at public school graduations violated the establishment clause.

Lee involved a school district policy that allowed high school and middle principals to have members of the clergy give invocations or benedictions at formal graduation ceremonies. Though the invocations or benedictions might be written with guidelines that were designed to avoid offending anyone, the practice could not withstand establishment clause analysis.[22.15] *Lee v. Weisman* was decided by a five to four vote of the Justices. But the strong support for basic establishment clause principles by a majority of the Justices is more important than the closeness of the vote. The four dissenting Justices would approve government involvement with religion that arguably is supported by historical practices in our country, at least so long as the government action at issue did not involve a preference for one religious sect over another.[22.20] Justice Kennedy wrote a majority opinion in *Lee,* even though he had dissented in cases in which the Court had invalidated government actions that aided religion, such as the government creation or toleration of religious symbols in holiday displays on government property.[22.25] Justice Kennedy, in *Lee,* found that the government practice of religious prayers at school graduations could not withstand any meaningful form of judicial review under basic establishment clause principles.

Justice Kennedy's majority opinion in *Lee v. Weisman* did not make use of the purpose, effect, or entanglement tests. The majority opinion stated:

> "The case does not require us to revisit the difficult cases dividing us in recent cases, questions of the definition in full scope of the principles governing the extent of permitted accommodation by the state for religious beliefs and practices.... for without reference to those principles and other contexts, the controlling precedence as they relate to prayer and religious exercise in primary and secondary public schools compel the holding here.... the State's involvement in the school prayers challenged today violates [the establishment clause] central principles." [22.30]

This majority opinion is a very strong endorsement of the concept that government neutrality in religious matters is a touchstone of establishment clause analysis; the concept of neutrality was clearly violated by government authorized prayers in public grade schools and high schools. Justice Kennedy's majority opinion did not find that coercion of individuals to give up or modify their religious beliefs, or to act inconsistently with their religious beliefs, was a prerequisite for an establishment clause violation.

The majority opinion stated that "it is beyond dispute that, at a minimum, the Constitution guarantees that the government may not coerce anyone to support or participate in religion or its exercise." [22.35] Justice Kennedy noted that "there are heightened concerns with protecting freedom of conscience from subtle coercive pressure in the elementary and secondary public schools." [22.40] Absent a significant change in the membership of the Court, the Justices will not accept the argument that government may authorize or endorse religious prayers, readings, or teachings in the public schools as a part of the official school day or school ceremonies. [22.45]

22.5 Lemon v. Kurtzman, 403 U.S. 602, 91 S.Ct. 2105, 29 L.Ed.2d 745 (1971), rehearing denied 404 U.S. 876, 92 S.Ct. 24, 30 L.Ed.2d 123 (1971).

22.10 505 U.S. 577, 112 S.Ct. 2649, 120 L.Ed.2d 467 (1992).

22.15 The majority opinion in *Lee* noted that guidelines were used by the school district for members of the clergy who gave invocations at school graduation ceremonies. Members of the clergy who were to give such invocations or benedictions were given a copy of a document entitled "Guidelines for Civic Occasions" that had been prepared by the National Conference of Christians and Jews for persons who were requested to give public prayers at nonsectarian civic ceremonies. Lee v. Weisman, 505 U.S.

577, 579, 112 S.Ct. 2649, 2652, 120 L.Ed.2d 467 (1992).

22.20 Lee v. Weisman, 505 U.S. 577, 629, 112 S.Ct. 2649, 2678, 120 L.Ed.2d 467 (1992) (Scalia, J., joined by Rehnquist, C.J., and White and Thomas, JJ., dissenting).

22.25 Justice Kennedy had dissented when the Court ruled that a county violated the establishment clause by having a creche display at a county courthouse that was set up by a Roman Catholic organization. County of Allegheny v. American Civil Liberties Union, 492 U.S. 573, 655, 109 S.Ct. 3086, 3134, 106 L.Ed.2d 472 (1989) (Kennedy, J., joined by Rehnquist, C.J., and White and Scalia, JJ., concurring in the judgment in part and dissenting in part), on remand 887 F.2d 260 (3d Cir.1989).

22.30 Lee v. Weisman, 505 U.S. 577, 586, 112 S.Ct. 2649, 2655, 120 L.Ed.2d 467 (1992). In a concurring opinion Justice Blackmun noted that the Court in *Lee* had taken a position that was consistent with the three part purpose—effect—entanglement test that the Supreme Court had used in every establishment clause case since 1971 (with the exception of the Court's decision upholding the use of a chaplain by a state legislature). 505 U.S. at 597, 603 n. 4, 112 S.Ct. at 2661, 2663 n. 4. The one post–1971 case in which the Court had not used the three part test was Marsh v. Chambers, 463 U.S. 783, 103 S.Ct. 3330, 77 L.Ed.2d 1019 (1983). The majority opinion in *Lee* found that the "inherent differences between the public school system and a session of the state legislature" made the Court's decision in *Marsh* irrelevant to the question of whether the government could have religious benedictions at school graduations that put students and their parents who disagreed with the religious prayers to the choice of either acting inconsistently with their beliefs or foregoing the graduation ceremony. Lee v. Weisman, 505 U.S. 577, 595–597, 112 S.Ct. 2649, 2660–61, 120 L.Ed.2d 467 (1992).

22.35 Lee v. Weisman, 505 U.S. 577, 586, 112 S.Ct. 2649, 2655, 120 L.Ed.2d 467 (1992).

22.40 505 U.S. at 592, 112 S.Ct. at 2658.

22.45 The Supreme Court in *Lee* did not rule that there would be a violation of the establishment clause whenever there was any involvement of government and religion. The majority opinion appears to endorse a case-by-case approach to protect the establishment clause values without establishing any clear tests. "We do not hold that every state action implicating religion is invalid if one or a few citizens find it offensive.... our jurisprudence in this area is of necessity one of line-drawing, of determining at what point a dissenter's rights of religious freedom are infringed." Lee v. Weisman, 505 U.S. 577, 597–98, 112 S.Ct. 2649, 2661, 120 L.Ed.2d 467 (1992).

Lee did not examine the issues or standards used in cases involving accommodation of religious beliefs of persons who wish to use government property and whose inability to use the property might inhibit their ability to carry out their beliefs. Statutes allowing for "equal access" to school facilities are examined in § 21.5(e) of this Treatise.

(e) Equal Access to School Facilities

Page 519, add after the carryover paragraph at the top of the page:

A state may not disfavor speakers, by punishing their speech or denying them the ability to speak, based upon the religious viewpoint expressed by that speaker. Although the government may not endorse or assist religious activities, including religious speech in a way that violates the establishment clause, the government is limited by the first amendment freedom of speech, as well as the free exercise clause, when it denies benefits to or imposes burdens on religious speakers. These principles, which were established in the *Widmar* and *Mergens* cases, were unanimously reaffirmed in *Lamb's Chapel v. Center Moriches Union Free School District.*[40]

A New York law allowed local school boards to adopt regulation for the use of school property, at times when schools were not in session, for specified purposes, including "social, civic, and recreational meetings and entertainments and other uses pertaining to the welfare of the community." The state law stated that the uses should be: "non-exclusive and open to the public" but it left the implementation of the law and the definition of permitted uses largely to the local school boards in the state. In the *Lamb's*

Chapel case, the school board for the Center Moriches Union Free School District authorized the use of school property, when it was not otherwise being used for school purposes, for social, civic, or recreational uses and for uses by political organizations. However, this school board denied a religious congregation the ability to use the school property at a time when classes were not in session and the school was not being used for previously scheduled activities.

In *Lamb's Chapel*, the Justices unanimously ruled that this school board regulation, as applied in this case, violated the free speech clause of the first amendment. Justice White wrote for seven members of the Court in finding that the board's action constituted viewpoint discrimination because the school board would have allowed groups to use the school property for discussions about childrearing and family values that were not connected to the views of a religious organization. Such viewpoint discrimination violates the first amendment freedom of speech even when the government is allegating access to a nonpublic forum.

The school board in the *Lamb's Chapel* case attempted to justify its action by alleging that it had a compelling interest in denying access to the religious organization in order to avoid violating the establishment clause of the first amendment. Justice White found that granting equal access to government property would not constitute a violation of the establishment clause tests adopted by the Supreme Court in earlier cases.[41] The school board also claimed that the particular church that wanted access to the property would be engaging in such highly sectarian proselytizing that the church's use of public property would lead to "threats of public unrest and even violence." However, the majority opinion found that there was "nothing in the record to support such a justification, which in any event would be difficult to defend as a reason to deny the presentation of a religious point of view about a subject that the [school district board] otherwise makes open to discussion on [school district] property."[42]

In *Rosenberger v. Rector and Visitors of the University of Virginia*,[43] the Justices, by a five to four vote, ruled that the University had violated the free speech clause when it refused to pay for a religious student organization's publication costs under a program that funded other student organization publications.

Under University of Virginia regulations, student groups were eligible to request for payment of bills from outside contractors that printed their newsletters. A group of students formed an organization named "Wide Awake Productions," which they registered as a student organization with the University. Because their registration met University standards, they qualified as a "contracted independent organization" that would be eligible for payment of its publication bills. However, the University refused this student organization's request for the University to pay for the publication of its newsletter, titled "Wide Awake: A Christian Perspective at the University of Virginia." The University asserted that the publication constituted religious literature that could not be funded because of the religious nature of the organization's expression in their newsletter. In the view of the University, government funding for a religious publication would violate the establishment clause. A majority of the Justices in *Rosenberger* relied on the principles established in the *Widmar, Mergens,* and *Lamb's Chapel* cases in ruling that the University's refusal to fund the student publication solely on the basis of the religious content of its speech constituted viewpoint discrimination that violated the free speech clause.[44]

The University had engaged in viewpoint discrimination when it refused to pay for the student organization's publication costs because of the religious nature of the organization's expression. This viewpoint discrimination could only be upheld if the University had a compelling interest in disfavoring the viewpoint. If a University payment for the religious organization's publication costs would violate the establishment clause, the University would have a compelling interest (the need to follow the Constitution) in refusing to subsidize the publication. The majority opinion in *Rosenberger,* written by Justice Kennedy, ruled that the University funding for the publication would not violate the establishment clause and that the refusal to fund the publication violated the free speech guarantee. The majority opinion did not specify a clear test to be used for determining whether a government action violated the establishment clause. Justice Kennedy stated that, in establishment clause cases, the Court "must in each case inquire first into the purpose and object of the government action in question and then into the practical details of the program's operation.... [a] central lesson of our decisions is that significant factor in upholding government programs in the face of establishment clause attack is their neutrality towards religion." [45] The majority found that the University program for funding students organizations was religiously neutral, and that "the neutrality of the program distinguishes the student fees from a tax levied for the direct support of a church or group of churches." [46]

In earlier cases, the Supreme Court had held that the establishment clause did not prohibit a government university from granting equal access to its facilities to a religious organization and that viewpoint discrimination against such organizations by a government university would violate the First Amendment free speech clause. The dissenters in *Rosenberger* believed that the establishment clause should be interpreted to prohibit all direct payments to religious organizations, or direct subsidies for the operational costs of religious organizations.[47] However, the majority ruled that: "there is no difference in logic or principle, and no difference of constitutional significance, between a school using its funds to operate a facility to which students have access, and a school paying a third-party contractor to operate the facility on its behalf." [48] Under the University regulations at issue in *Rosenberger,* the University would not make monetary payments to the religious organization. The University would pay the third party (the printer) who provided the printing services for student organizations. In the majority's opinion this payment system involved more separation between the University and the religious organization than would school policies that granted the religious organizations equal access to the university physical facilities. Therefore, in *Rosenberger,* the majority ruled that the First Amendment free speech clause prohibited the University from examining the content of publications for the purpose of denying funding to, and discriminating against, religious viewpoints and that there would be "no establishment clause violation in the University's honoring its duties under the free speech clause." [49]

40.　508 U.S. 384, 113 S.Ct. 2141, 124 L.Ed.2d 352 (1993).

41.　Justice White's majority opinion found that the intended use of the property "would not have been an establishment of religion under the three-part test articulated in Lemon v. Kurtzman, 403 U.S. 602, 91 S.Ct. 2105, 29 L.Ed.2d 745 (1971): The challenged governmental action has a secular purpose, does not have the principal or primary effect of advancing or inhibiting religion, and does not foster an excessive entanglement with religion." After this passage in his majority opinion, Justice White noted that, despite the statements in the concurring opinion, the *Lemon* tests had not been overruled. 508 U.S. at 394 n. 7, 113 S.Ct. at 2148 n. 7.

Three justices joined the Court's unanimous ruling concerning the school district's violation of the free speech clause, but they differed with the majority opinion insofar as Justice White continued to use the three-part *Lemon* tests. These three Justices believe that those tests unjustifiably restrict the actions of government that might assist religion. Lamb's Chapel v. Center Moriches Union Free School District, 508 U.S. 384, 396, 113 S.Ct. 2141, 2149, 124 L.Ed.2d 352 (1993) (Kennedy, J., concurring in part and concurring in the judgment). 508 U.S. at 396, 113 S.Ct. at 2149 (Scalia, J., joined by Thomas, J., concurring in the judgment).

42.　Lamb's Chapel v. Center Moriches Union Free School District, 508 U.S. 384, 394, 113 S.Ct. 2141, 2148, 124 L.Ed.2d 352 (1993).

43.　__ U.S. __, 115 S.Ct. 2510, 132 L.Ed.2d 700 (1995).

44.　__ U.S. at __, 115 S.Ct. at 2517.

45.　__ U.S. at __, 115 S.Ct. at 2521.

46.　__ U.S. at __, 115 S.Ct. at 2522.

47.　Rosenberger v. Rector and Visitors of the University of Virginia, __ U.S. __, __, 115 S.Ct. 2510, 2533, 132 L.Ed.2d 700 (1995) (Souter, J., joined by Stevens, Ginsburg, and Breyer, JJ., dissenting). Justice Thomas, who joined the majority opinion, also filed a concurring opinion in which he directly challenged the historical analysis used by the dissenting Justices. __ U.S. at __, 115 S.Ct. at 2528 (Thomas, J., concurring).

48.　Rosenberger v. Rector and Visitors of the University of Virginia, __ U.S. __, __, 115 S.Ct. 2510, 2524, 132 L.Ed.2d 700 (1995).

49.　Rosenberger v. Rector and Visitors of the University of Virginia, __ U.S. __, __, 115 S.Ct. 2510, 2525, 132 L.Ed.2d 700 (1995). Justice Kennedy's majority opinion in *Rosenberger* assumed that individual students did not have a right to a refund of their student activity fees, which were required to be paid by all students and which were used to fund the publication costs of student organizations including the religious student publication at issue in this case. "The fee is mandatory, and we do not have before us the question whether an objecting student has the first amendment right to demand a pro rata return to the extent the fee is expended for speech to which he or she does not describe." __ U.S. at __, 115 S.Ct. at 2522. Justice O'Connor joined the majority opinion and wrote a concurring opinion in which she stated that an objecting student might have a free speech right to refuse to be compelled to pay for the speech of student organizations with which the student disagreed and that "while the Court does not resolve the question ... the existence of such an opt-out possibility ... provides a potential basis for distinguishing proceeds of student fees in this case from proceeds of the general assessments in support of religion that lie at the core of the prohibition against religious funding." __ U.S. at __, 115 S.Ct. at 2525, 2527 (O'Connor, J., concurring).

See generally, Stephen Bainbridge, Student Religious Organizations and University Policies Against Discrimination on the Basis of Sexual Orientation: Implications of the Religious Freedom Restriction Act, 21 J. of College and Univ.Law 369 (1994).

III. THE FREE EXERCISE CLAUSE

§ 21.6   Introduction—Overview

Page 519, delete the second paragraph in this section; replace it with the following:

The first amendment provides, in part, that Congress shall make no law "prohibiting the free exercise" of religion.[2] The free exercise clause, like all of the guarantees of the first amendment, applies to state and local governments through the fourteenth amendment.[3]

Page 520, delete the last sentence of the first full paragraph and replace it with the following:

In *Church of the Lukumi Babalu Aye, Inc. v. Hialeah* [3.5] the Supreme court invalidated a city's ordinances prohibiting animal slaughter, insofar as they were applied to a particular religious sect, because the Justices unanimously found that these ordinances were passed for the sole purpose of excluding the religious sect from the city. The Justices avoided ruling on the issue of whether members of a religious sect that used animal slaughter in their rituals would be entitled by the free exercise clause to an exemption from a law prohibiting the slaughter of animals that was a religiously neutral law of general applicability. Instead, the Justices found that the city's ordinances (when all of the classifications and exemptions in the ordinances were combined) prohibited only the type of animal slaughter that was used in the ritual of the Santeria religion; the timing of the ordinances, and other facts in the record, demonstrated that the city had adopted these ordinances only after learning that members of the Santeria religion were going to establish a place of worship in the city.

Justice Kennedy wrote the majority opinion in *Church of the Lukumi Babalu Aye*. He began the opinion by noting that the Court was using a well established constitutional principle.

"The principle that government may not enact laws that suppress religious belief or practice is so well understood that few violations are recorded in our opinions.... Our review confirms that the laws in question were enacted by officials who did not understand, failed to perceive, or chose to ignore the fact that their official actions violated the Nation's essential commitment to religious freedom. The challenged laws had an impermissible object; and in all events the principle of general applicability was violated because the secular ends asserted in defense of the law, were pursued only with respect to conduct motivated by religious beliefs." [3.10]

The majority opinion in *Church of the Lukumi Babalu Aye,* found that the judiciary must examine laws regulating conduct of significance to persons because of their religious beliefs to ensure both that the conduct regulation was religiously neutral and that it was of general applicability. A law that failed the neutrality or general applicability standards would be subject to strict judicial scrutiny; it is doubtful that any such law would be truly necessary to a compelling government interest. Justice Kennedy's opinion summarized the Court's ruling as follows:

"[A] law that is neutral and of general applicability need not be justified by a compelling government interest even if the law has the incidental effect of burdening a particular religious practice.... A law failing to satisfy these requirements [the neutrality and general applicability requirements] must be justified by a compelling governmental interest and must be narrowly tailored to advance that interest." [3.15]

3.5 508 U.S. 520, 113 S.Ct. 2217, 124 L.Ed.2d 472 (1993), on remand 2 F.3d 369 (11th Cir.1993).

3.10 508 U.S. at 524, 113 S.Ct. at 2222.

3.15 508 U.S. at 531, 113 S.Ct. at 2226.

Page 522, add new sentence and note to the end of the third full paragraph (after note 8):

In 1993, the Supreme Court invalidated a city's law prohibiting animal slaughter insofar as those laws banned the ritual slaughter of animals by a specific religious sect.[8.5] The Justices unanimously concluded that the laws were not religiously neutral laws of general applicability and that the laws were only designed to suppress a particular sect. The Justices did not reach the issue of whether a religiously neutral law that banned all animal slaughter would have to allow exemptions from the slaughter of animals in religious rituals. A majority of the Justices found no reason to question the principle that a religiously neutral law of general applicability could be applied to persons whose religious beliefs prevented them from complying with the law.[8.10]

8.5 Church of the Lukumi Babalu Aye, Inc. v. Hialeah, 508 U.S. 520, 113 S.Ct. 2217, 124 L.Ed.2d 472 (1993), on remand 2 F.3d 369 (11th Cir.1993).

8.10 The Justices were unanimous in ruling that the City of Hialeah violated the free exercise clause by enacting ordinances designed solely to suppress a particular religious sect. But three of the Justices did not want to endorse the position that religiously neutral laws of general applicability need not provide exemptions for persons whose religious beliefs prevented their compliance. Justices Blackmun and O'Connor thought that the Court should return to using the compelling interest test that had been used in free exercise clause cases decided between 1963 and 1989. Justice Souter wished to reconsider this question in future cases. The majority reaffirmed the Court's earlier ruling, in Employment Division v. Smith, 494 U.S. 872, 110 S.Ct. 1595, 108 L.Ed.2d 876 (1990), denying religiously based exemptions from religiously neutral, generally applicable laws. Compare, Church of the Lukumi Babalu Aye, Inc. v. Hialeah, 508 U.S. 520, 531, 113 S.Ct. 2217, 2226, 124 L.Ed.2d 472 (1993), on remand 2 F.3d 369 (11th Cir.1993) (majority opinion by Justice Kennedy) and 508 U.S. at 557, 113 S.Ct. at 2239 (Scalia, J., joined by Rehnquist, C.J., concurring in part and concurring in the judgment), with 508 U.S. at 558, 113 S.Ct. at 2240 (Souter, J., concurring in part and concurring in the judgment) and, 508 U.S. at 577, 113 S.Ct. at 2250 (Blackmun, J., joined by O'Connor, J., concurring in the judgment).

Page 525, add to note 14:

14. In Church of the Lukumi Babalu Aye, Inc. v. Hialeah, 508 U.S. 520, 113 S.Ct. 2217, 124 L.Ed.2d 472 (1993), on remand 2 F.3d 369 (11th Cir.1993) the Court invalidated city laws prohibiting some forms of animal slaughter, insofar as the laws applied to a particular religious sect, because these laws were designed to suppress a particular religious sect by prohibiting the type of animal slaughter used in its religious rituals. In the course of making that ruling, the majority opinion noted that if the government chooses to grant exemptions from a regulation it cannot establish a rule that denies exemptions solely on the basis that the requested exemption is religiously motivated. The majority stated: "[I]n circumstances in which individualized exemptions from a general requirement are available, the government may not refuse to extend that system to cases of religious hardship without compelling reason." 508 U.S. at 536, 113 S.Ct. at 2229 (internal quotation marks and citations omitted).

Page 530, add to note 32:

32. In Lee v. Weisman, 505 U.S. 577, 112 S.Ct. 2649, 120 L.Ed.2d 467 (1992) the Supreme Court held that a public school graduation ceremony that included a "nonsectarian" prayer by a member of the clergy (in the particular case, by a Rabbi) violated the establishment clause. The case was decided by a five to four vote of the Justices; Justice Kennedy wrote the majority opinion. Justice Souter wrote an opinion concurring in both the judgment and the majority opinion that was joined by Justices Stevens and O'Connor. Justice Souter found that one of the principal reasons for rejecting the arguments of "nonpreferentialists" (who would allow aid to all religion over nonreligion so long as the government aid did not include a sect preference) was the inability of courts to make decisions concerning the types of competing beliefs that would qualify as religions or theologies. 505 U.S. at 609, 617, 112 S.Ct. at 2667, 2671 (Souter, J., joined by Stevens and O'Connor, JJ., concurring). Justice Blackmun also filed an opinion in the case in which he noted that nothing in this decision formally altered, or was inconsistent with, the Court's establishment clause decisions during the previous two decades. 505 U.S. at 597, 112 S.Ct. at 2661 (Blackmun, J., joined by Stevens and O'Connor, JJ., concurring).

Page 531, add to the end of the first full paragraph:

Although the Supreme Court's free exercise standards do not require the government to grant exemptions from neutral laws of general applicability, those standards prohibit government actions designed to suppress or burden a group of persons because of their religious beliefs. A law that bans certain actions only because they are of religious significance, and only to suppress a particular religious group, will violate the free exercise clause.[35.5] Cases wherein the Court invalidates a law because the Justices find that the law is designed to suppress religious beliefs or a religious sect are not likely to raise problems regarding the definition of religion or testing of sincerity.[35.10]

35.5 "The principle that government may not enact laws that suppress religious belief or practice is so well understood that few violations are recorded in our opinions." Church of the Lukumi Babalu Aye, Inc. v. Hialeah, 508 U.S. 520, 523, 113 S.Ct. 2217, 2222, 124 L.Ed.2d 472 (1993), on remand 2 F.3d 369 (11th Cir.1993). "[A] law that is neutral and of general applicability need not be justified by a compelling governmental interest even if the law has the incidental effect of burdening a particular religious practice.... A law failing to satisfy these requirements must be justified by a compelling governmental interest and must be narrowly tailored to advance that interest." 508 U.S. at 531, 113 S.Ct. at 2226.

35.10 For example, in Church of the Lukumi Babalu Aye, Inc. v. Hialeah, 508 U.S. 520, 113 S.Ct. 2217, 124 L.Ed.2d 472 (1993), on remand 2 F.3d 369 (11th Cir.1993) the Justices unanimously invalidated a city law prohibiting the slaughter of animals as it was applied to a particular religious sect because the law was designed only to prevent the practice of that religion within the city. In the course of making that ruling, the majority opinion noted: "The city does not argue that Santeria [the religious sect involved in this case] is not a 'religion' ... [n]or could it ... petitioners' assertion that animal sacrifice is an integral part of their religion 'cannot be deemed bizarre or incredible'.... Neither the city nor the courts below, moreover, have questioned the sincerity of petitioners' professed desire to conduct animal sacrifices." 508 U.S. at 530–31, 113 S.Ct. at 2225–26 (internal citation omitted).

Page 532, add new note to the end of the fourth sentence in the first full paragraph:

... or the endorsement of religious beliefs.[38.5]

38.5 Government accommodation of the needs of religious groups or persons affiliated with the religion must be done in a manner that does not violate the neutrality principle of the establishment clause. In Board of Education of Kiryas Joel Village School District v. Grumet, 512 U.S. 687, 114 S.Ct. 2481, 129 L.Ed.2d 546 (1994), the Supreme Court invalidated a state law creating a special school district for a Village that was composed of entirely of members of one religion. The Court found this to be an impermissible preference for members of a particular religious sect, rather than a permissible accommodation for persons confronted with special problems. The Grumet case is examined in § 21.3 of this Treatise.

See §§ 21.13, 21.15 of this Treatise regarding the accommodation of religious beliefs in statutes regulating the terms and conditions of private employment.

Page 532, add after the first full paragraph, to the end of the section:

In response to the Supreme Court's decision in Smith II, Congress passed, and the President signed into law, the "Religious Freedom Restoration Act of 1993." [39.5] If a case comes before the Supreme Court in which the constitutionality of the Act is brought into question, the Court will need to resolve several questions concerning the meaning of the Act prior to ruling on its constitutionality. For example, sections 2 and 3 of the Act state that the

Act applies to the action of any governmental entity (local, state, or federal) in the United States that would "substantially burden" a person's "free exercise of religion." But section 5 of the Act, which includes the statutory "definitions," does not clearly define those terms; prior Supreme Court decisions do not explain the extent to which any branch of government, including the judiciary, may define the concept of "religion" without violating the establishment clause.

Section 7 of the Act states that this law is not intended to modify establishment clause principles. The degree to which the Act requires the judiciary to grant exceptions from laws of general applicability to persons whose religious faith keeps them from following such laws should be a factor to consider in deciding whether the Religious Freedom Restoration Act itself violates the establishment clause. The Act does not use language that would provide benefits only to a particular religious denomination under the guise of providing an accommodation of religion.[39.10] However, the Act may raise establishment clause problems if the Act is seen as granting special advantages to believers of religious doctrines generally over nonbelievers.[39.15]

The standard set forth in Section 3 of the Religious Freedom Restoration Act mirrors the language used by the Supreme Court in free exercise clause cases between 1963 and 1989. During that time period, the Supreme Court found that if a person claiming a first amendment exemption from a generally applicable law could show that following the law was a substantial burden on his religious beliefs then the government could only deny him the exemption if it could show that the law was narrowly tailored to promote a compelling interest. But, during the quarter century in which the Court used that test, it almost always ruled in favor of the government.[39.20]

Two of the rare cases in which the Court found that the government had to grant a religiously based exemption from a law of general applicability were *Sherbert v. Verner*,[39.25] in which the Court found that states were required to waive certain conditions for unemployment compensation for persons who could not follow those conditions due to their religious beliefs, and *Wisconsin v. Yoder*,[39.30] in which the Court granted a limited exemption from a special type of compulsory education law to the parents of Amish children. Section 2 of the Act states that Congress' purpose was "to restore the compelling interest test as set forth in *Sherbert* and *Yoder*." If the Act were interpreted to require courts not only to use the analytical framework employed by the Supreme Court between 1963 and 1989, but also to grant exemptions from religiously neutral laws to persons who could not follow those laws because of their religious beliefs more easily, and more frequently, than the Supreme Court had during that time period, there may be significant questions concerning whether such a mandate would violate the establishment clause by granting special benefits to religious believers. Until such time as the Supreme Court considers the Act, we will not know whether the Constitution of 1787, the first amendment, or the fourteenth amendment allow Congress to expand the scope of civil liberties for individuals by mandating the judiciary to take a specific approach to free exercise clause issues.[39.35]

39.5 The following is the text of Pub.L. 103–141, H.R. 1038, S.578, 103 Cong. 1st Sess. (1993), 42 U.S.C.A. § 2000bb:

Be it enacted by the Senate and House of Representatives of the United States of America in Congress assembled, SECTION 1. SHORT TITLE.

This Act may be cited as the "Religious Freedom Act of 1993."

SEC. 2. CONGRESSIONAL FINDINGS AND DECLARATION OF PURPOSES.

(a) FINDINGS.—The Congress finds that—

(1) the framers of the Constitution, recognizing free exercise of religion as an unalienable right, secured its protection in the First Amendment to the Constitution;

(2) laws "neutral" toward religion may burden religious exercise as surely as laws intended to interfere with religious exercise;

(3) governments should not substantially burden religious exercise without compelling justification;

(4) in Employment Division v. Smith, 494 U.S. 872, 110 S.Ct. 1595, 108 L.Ed.2d 876 (1990) the Supreme Court virtually eliminated the requirement that the government justify burdens on religious exercise imposed by laws neutral toward religion; and

(5) the compelling interest test as set forth in prior Federal court rulings is a workable test for striking sensible balances between religious liberty and competing prior governmental interests.

(b) PURPOSES.—The purposes of the Act are—

(1) to restore the compelling interest test as set forth in Sherbert v. Verner, 374 U.S. 398, 83 S.Ct. 1790, 10 L.Ed.2d 965 (1963) and Wisconsin v. Yoder, 406 U.S. 205, 92 S.Ct. 1526, 32 L.Ed.2d 15 (1972) and to guarantee its application in all cases where free exercise of religion is substantially burdened; and

(2) to provide a claim or defense to persons whose religious exercise is substantially burdened by government.

SEC. 3. FREE EXERCISE OF RELIGION PROTECTED.

(a) IN GENERAL.—Government shall not substantially burden a person's exercise of religion even if the burden results from a rule of general applicability, except as provided in subsection (b).

(b) EXCEPTION.—Government may substantially burden a person's exercise of religion only if it demonstrates that application of the burden to the person—

(1) is in furtherance of a compelling governmental interest; and

(2) is the least restrictive means of furthering that compelling governmental interest.

(c) JUDICIAL RELIEF.—A person whose religious exercise has been burdened in violation of this section may assert that violation as a chain or defense in a judicial proceeding and obtain appropriate relief against a government. Standing to assert a claim or defense under this section shall be governed by the general rules of standing under article III of the Constitution.

SEC. 4. ATTORNEYS FEES.

(a) JUDICIAL PROCEEDINGS.— Section 722 of the Revised Statutes (42 U.S.C. 1988) is amended by inserting "the Religious Freedom Restoration Act of 1993," before "or title VI of the Civil Rights Act of 1964".

(b) ADMINISTRATIVE PROCEEDINGS.—Section 504(b)(1)(C) of title 5, United States Code, is amended—

(1) by striking "and" at the end of clause (ii);

(2) by striking the semicolon at the end of clause (iii) and inserting ",and"; and

(3) by inserting "(iv) the Religious Freedom Restoration Act of 1993;" after clause (iii).

SEC. 5. DEFINITIONS.

As used in the Act—

(1) the term "government" includes a branch, department, agency, instrumentality, and official (or other person acting under color of law) of the United States, a State, or subdivision of a State;

(2) the term "State" includes the District of Columbia, the Commonwealth of Puerto Rico, and each territory and possession of the United States;

(3) the term "demonstrates" means meets the burdens of going forward with the evidence and of persuasion; and

(4) the term "exercise of religion" means the exercise of religion under the First Amendment to the Constitution.

SEC. 6. APPLICABILITY.

(a) IN GENERAL.—This Act applies to all Federal and State law, and the implementation of that law, whether statutory or otherwise, and whether adopted before or after the enactment of this Act.

(b) RULE OF CONSTRUCTION.— Federal statutory law adopted after the date of the enactment of this Act is subject to this Act unless such law explicitly excludes such application by reference to this Act.

(c) RELIGIOUS BELIEF UNAFFECTED.—Nothing in this Act shall be construed to authorize any government to burden any religious belief.

SEC. 7. ESTABLISHMENT CLAUSE UNAFFECTED.

Nothing in this Act shall be construed to affect, interpret, or in any way address that portion of the First Amendment prohibiting laws respecting the establishment of religion (referred to in this section as the "Establishment Clause"). Granting government funding, benefits, or exemptions, to the extent permissible under the Establishment Clause, shall not constitute a violation of this Act. As used in this section, the term "granting", used with respect to governmental funding, benefits, or exemptions, does not include the denial of government funding, benefits, or exemptions.

Approved November 16, 1993

39.10 A denominational preference or a so–called sect preference would violate the establishment clause. See note 38.5, supra.

39.15 A law that does not include a sect preference may, under some circumstances, violate the establishment clause by providing aid to all persons who hold religious beliefs while denying similar aid to nonreligious persons. Compare, Estate of Thornton v. Caldor, Inc. 472 U.S. 703, 105 S.Ct. 2914, 86 L.Ed.2d 557 (1985) (invalidating a state law requiring all employers to honor every employee's desire to refuse work on "his Sabbath") with Corporation of Presiding Bishop of Church of Jesus Christ of Latter–day Saints, 483 U.S. 327, 107 S.Ct. 2862, 97 L.Ed.2d 273 (1987) (upholding the exemption of religious organizations from a statutory prohibition against religious discrimination) these cases are examined in §§ 21.13, 21.15 of this Treatise.

39.20 See § 21.8 for an analysis of the Supreme Court's free exercise clause decisions from 1960 to the present.

39.25 374 U.S. 398, 83 S.Ct. 1790, 10 L.Ed.2d 965 (1963).

39.30 406 U.S. 205, 92 S.Ct. 1526, 32 L.Ed.2d 15 (1972).

39.35 See note 39.15, supra. See generally, Jay S. Bybee, Taking Liberties with the First Amendment: Congress, Section 5, and the Religious Freedom Restoration Act, 48 Vanderbilt L.Rev. 1539 (1996) ; Keith Jaasma, Religious Freedom Restoration Act: Responding to *Smith*; Reconsidering *Reynolds*, 16 Whittier L.Rev. 211 (1995). See also, Steven D. Jamar, Accommodating Religion at Work: A Principled Approach to Title VII and Religious Freedom, 4 New York Law School Law Review 720 (1996). Issues concerning Congress' power to expand civil liberties through the use of the power granted to it by section 5 of the fourteenth amendment are examined in Chapter 19 of this Treatise.

§ 21.7   The Early Decisions

Page 532, add to note 1:

1. Torruella, C.J., citing Treatise in, Brown v. Hot, Sexy And Safer Productions, Inc., 68 F.3d 525, 533 n. 5 (1st

Cir.1995), cert. denied ___ U.S. ___, 116
S.Ct. 1044, 134 L.Ed.2d 191 (1996).

Page 533, add after note 4:

The laws at issue in these cases prohibited polygamy without banning the advocacy of polygamy. These laws did not punish only those persons who entered polygamous marriages on the basis of their religious beliefs. If a law punished the advocacy of polygamy, the law should be held to violate the freedom of speech.[4.5] If an anti-polygamy law, on its face, imposed penalties only on members of a specific religion, that law would violate the free exercise clause.[4.10]

4.5 In Romer v. Evans, ___ U.S. ___, 116 S.Ct. 1620, 134 L.Ed.2d 855 (1996) the Supreme Court invalidated a state constitutional amendment that prohibited any local or state legislative body from passing laws that protected people from discrimination on the basis of sexual orientation. The state, as well as dissenting Justices, argued that *Davis v. Beason* [cited in the previous footnote in this Treatise] should allow the state to punish any group that engaged in practices deemed immoral by the state. The majority opinion in *Romer* stated: "To the extent that *Davis* held that persons advocating a certain religious practice may be denied the right to vote, it is no longer good law. Brandenburg v. Ohio, 395 U.S. 444, 89 S.Ct. 1827, 23 L.Ed.2d 430 (1969) (per curiam). To the extent that it held that groups designated in the statute may be deprived of the right to vote because of their status, its ruling could not stand without surviving strict scrutiny, a most doubtful outcome." ___ U.S. at ___, 116 S.Ct. at 1628.

4.10 See generally, Church of Lukumi Babalu Aye, Inc. v. Hialeah, 508 U.S. 520, 113 S.Ct. 2217, 124 L.Ed.2d 472 (1993), (the Court invalidates a law regarding the treatment of animals that was designed to force a religious sect to leave the community). This case is examined in § 21.8 of this Treatise.

§ 21.8 The Modern Cases

Page 541, add after the third full paragraph:

Conclusion. Although none of the 1963–1990 free exercise clause decisions of the Supreme Court has been overruled, it is important to remember that the Supreme Court has disavowed the balancing test used in those decisions. In 1993, in *Church of Lukumi Babalu Aye, Inc. v. Hialeah*,[15.5] the majority opinion by Justice Kennedy summarized the current free exercise clause standards as follows:

"[A] law that is neutral and of general applicability need not be justified by a compelling government interest even if the law has the incidental effect of burdening a particular religious practice.... A law failing to satisfy these requirements [the neutrality and general applicability requirements] must be justified by a compelling governmental interest and must be narrowly tailored to advance that interest." [15.10]

The first part of this summary was an endorsement of *Smith II*, in which the Court refused to require religiously based exemptions for a religiously neutral, generally applicable law prohibiting the use of certain drugs.[15.15]

116

The second part of the summary was an endorsement of the principle, recognized in the *Smith II* decision, that a law that is designed to burden or suppress religious beliefs, or a law that prohibits an action solely because of its religious significance, violates the free exercise clause.[15.20] A law that is not a religiously neutral law of general applicability will be subject to strict judicial scrutiny and the compelling interest test. It is difficult to conceive of circumstances where a compelling interest of government would require the creation of a law designed to burden religious beliefs or to punish actions only because those actions were religiously motivated.

In *Church of the Lukumi Babalu Aye* the Court invalidated a city's ordinances prohibiting certain types of animal slaughter because the Justices unanimously found that the laws were solely designed to suppress a particular religious sect. The laws prohibited virtually no other types of animal slaughter except that used by the religious sect; the city did not adopt the laws until the religious sect planned to conduct its religious rituals in a building within the city. Because these city laws were obviously designed to suppress a particular religion, the Court did not need to explain in detail the difference between the requirement that a law be religiously "neutral" or that the law be one of "general applicability." [15.25] These city laws were invalidated by the Court, insofar as they were applied to the religious sect, because the city could not identify any compelling interest that would require banning only the type of animal slaughter used in the religion's rituals.

Let us assume that a jurisdiction had a religiously neutral law that was uniformly applied to all persons and organizations that forbid the slaughtering of animals. The law was not designed to suppress religiously motivated acts; the law was designed to promote both public health interests and to prevent the "cruel" treatment of animals. If members of a religious sect in religious rituals slaughtered animals in a manner that violated the law, could they be punished under that law? The Court in the *Church of the Lukumi Babalu Aye* case did not reach this question. The Court's ruling in *Smith II* would indicate that the religious sect would not have a constitutional right to an exemption from the law.[15.30]

15.5 508 U.S. 520, 113 S.Ct. 2217, 124 L.Ed.2d 472 (1993), on remand 2 F.3d 369 (11th Cir.1993).

15.10 508 U.S. at 531, 113 S.Ct. at 2226.

15.15 Employment Division v. Smith, 494 U.S. 872, 110 S.Ct. 1595, 108 L.Ed.2d 876 (1990). See footnotes 3–8, supra, and accompanying text, in this section of the Treatise.

15.20 See footnotes 6 and 7 and accompanying text, in this section of the Treatise regarding the recognition of this principle in *Smith II*.

In Church of the Lukumi Babalu Aye, Inc. v. Hialeah, 508 U.S. 520, 523, 113 S.Ct. 2217, 2222, 124 L.Ed.2d 472 (1993), on remand 2 F.3d 369 (11th Cir. 1993) the majority opinion stated:

"The principle that government may not enact laws that suppress religious

117

belief or practice is so well understood that few violations are recorded in our opinions.... Our review confirms that the laws in question were enacted by officials who did not understand, failed to perceive, or chose to ignore the fact that their official actions violated the Nation's essential commitment to religious freedom. The challenged laws had an impermissible object; and in all events the principle of general applicability was violated because the secular ends asserted in defense of the law, were pursued only with respect to conduct motivated by religious beliefs."

15.25 Perhaps the inquiry into "religious neutrality" would involve an inquiry into legislative motive or purpose, whereas an inquiry into general applicability might focus only on the scope of the statute. However, this point is not clear. Justice Kennedy wrote for five Justices in finding that the law was not religiously neutral because the ordinances exempted virtually all forms of animal sacrifice except those used by the Santeria religion. The object of the ordinances could only be understood as the symposium of religion. Church of the Lukumi Babalu Aye, Inc. v. Hialeah, 508 U.S. 520, 533, 113 S.Ct. 2217, 2227–30, 124 L.Ed.2d 472 (1993), on remand 2 F.3d 369 (11th Cir.1993). However, Justice Kennedy wrote only for himself and Justice Stevens when he stated that courts could determine religious neutrality, or the lack thereof, in the same manner in that courts would determine the existence of alleged discriminatory purpose in equal protection cases. 508 U.S. at 539–40, 113 S.Ct. at 2230–31 (opinion of Kennedy, J., joined by Stevens, J., as to part II–A–2). Justice Kennedy wrote for five Justices in finding that the Hialeah animal slaughter laws were not laws of general applicabil-

ity, 508 U.S. at 540–44, 113 S.Ct. at 2231–33.

Two concurring Justices noted that there might be no clear distinction between an inquiry into whether a law was religiously neutral and an inquiry into whether a law was one of general applicability. Church of the Lukumi Babalu Aye, Inc. v. Hialeah, 508 U.S. 520, 557, 113 S.Ct. 2217, 2239, 124 L.Ed.2d 472 (1993), on remand 2 F.3d 369 (11th Cir. 1993) (Scalia, J., joined by Rehnquist, C.J., concurring in part and concurring in the judgment).

15.30 Justices Blackmun and O'Connor agreed that the Hialeah ordinances violated the free exercise clause because these ordinances were designed to suppress religion. These two Justices wrote separately to restate their disagreement with the approach to free exercise issues adopted by the Court in *Smith II.* However, these two Justices did not reach the issue of whether a religious group must receive an exemption from a religiously neutral law prohibiting certain types of animal slaughter. It is possible that they would vote to deny such an exemption to religious sects even under the combined balancing test and compelling interest test. Church of the Lukumi Babalu Aye, Inc. v. Hialeah, 508 U.S. 520, 577–80, 113 S.Ct. 2217, 2250–52, 124 L.Ed.2d 472 (1993), on remand 2 F.3d 369 (11th Cir.1993) (Blackmun, J., joined by O'Connor, J., concurring in the judgment). Justice Souter wrote a concurring opinion to express his views that the Hialeah ordinances could be invalidated without reaffirming *Smith II;* he would consider reexamining the position the Court took in *Smith II* in a more appropriate case, such as a case involving a religiously neutral, generally applicable law. 508 U.S. at 558, 113 S.Ct. at 2240 (Souter, J., concurring in part and concurring in the judgment).

Page 554, add new note to the end of the carryover paragraph at the top of this page:

... interest in this case.[53.5]

53.5 See also, Sherwood v. Brown, 619 F.2d 47 (9th Cir.1980) (per curiam), cert. denied 449 U.S. 919, 101 S.Ct. 317, 66 L.Ed.2d 147 (1980), where the Court of Appeals upheld a Navy regulation that prohibited a Sikh sailor from wearing a turban after the court found that the turban prevented the sailor from wearing a helmet. In Khalsa v. Weinberger, 779 F.2d 1393 (9th Cir.1985),

affirmed 787 F.2d 1288 (9th Cir.1985) the court dismissed a claim of a Sikh who had sued the Army for refusing to process his enlistment application; the Army refused because he said that his religious beliefs did not allow him to comply with Army regulations governing appearance.

See generally, Vinet, Goldman v. Weinberger: Judicial Deference to Military Judgment in Matters of Religious Accommodation of Servicemembers, 36 Naval L.Rev. 257 (1986); Noone, Rendering Unto Caesar: Legal Responses to Religious Nonconformity in the Armed Forces, 18 St. Mary's L.Rev. 1233 (1987); Dwight H. Sullivan, The Congressional Response to Goldman v. Weinberger, 121 Military L.Rev. 125 (1988).

Congressional Response to *Goldman*. Congress responded to the Goldman decision by enacting legislation governing the wearing of religious apparel while in uniform. The statute, in general, allows members of the armed forces to wear items of religious apparel while in uniform unless the Secretary of Defense, pursuant to regulations, determines that wearing the item "would interfere with the performance of the member's military duties," or the item of apparel is "not neat and conservative." 10 U.S.C.A. § 774.

Government accommodation of the needs of religious groups or persons affiliated with the religion must be done in a manner that does not violate the neutrality principle of the establishment clause. In Board of Education of Kiryas Joel Village School District v. Grumet, 512 U.S. 687, 114 S.Ct. 2481, 129 L.Ed.2d 546 (1994), the Supreme Court invalidated a state law creating a special school district for a Village that was composed of entirely of members of one religion. The Court found this to be an impermissible preference for members of a particular religious sect, rather than a permissible accommodation for persons confronted with special problems. The *Grumet* case is examined in § 21.3 of this Treatise.

The federal "Religious Freedom Restoration Act of 1993" is examined in § 21.6.

See §§ 21.13, 21.15 regarding the accommodation of religious beliefs in statutes regulating the terms and conditions of private employment.

§ 21.9   Recurrent Free Exercise Problems

(b) Health and Medical Regulations

Page 563, delete the entire paragraph that appears immediately below this heading (and before subsection (1) Vaccinations); replace that paragraph with the following:

The decisions noted in this subsection involve claims by individuals that the free exercise clause entitled them to an exemption from a health or medical regulation. Today, the Supreme Court uses a free exercise clause test that would make it difficult, if not impossible, for an individual to prevail in such a case. The Court's free exercise clause standards were summarized by the Court as follows:

> "[A] law that is neutral and of general applicability need not be justified by a compelling government interest even if the law has the incidental effect of burdening a particular religious practice.... A law failing to satisfy [the neutrality and general applicability] requirements must be justified by a compelling governmental interest and must be narrowly tailored to advance that interest." [18.5]

So long as the health regulation at issue in a free exercise clause case is a generally applicable law that is religiously neutral, the Court would not require the government to grant religiously based exemptions for the law.

Some Justices believe that the Court should apply a balancing test or a compelling interest test in all free exercise cases.[18.10] If a majority of the Justices, in the future were to adopt any type of

119

case-by-case approach to free exercise clause claims, the Court might find that in some circumstances the social benefit of a particular health law are so slight that the government must grant exemption for persons whose religious beliefs prevent them from complying with the law. However, such an approach to these cases would represent a major departure from the Supreme Court's most recent free exercise clause rulings.[18.15]

18.5 Church of the Lukumi Babalu Aye, Inc. v. Hialeah, 508 U.S. 520, 531, 113 S.Ct. 2217, 2226, 124 L.Ed.2d 472 (1993), on remand 2 F.3d 369 (11th Cir. 1993). See §§ 21.6, 21.8.

18.10 See Church of the Lukumi Babalu Aye, Inc. v. Hialeah, 508 U.S. 520, 577, 113 S.Ct. 2217, 2250, 124 L.Ed.2d 472 (1993), on remand 2 F.3d 369 (11th Cir.1993) (Blackmun, J., joined by O'Connor, J., concurring). Between 1963 and 1989 the Supreme Court Justices, in majority opinions, used a free exercise clause test involving both a balancing of governmental interests against individual claims of religious suppression, and a search for "compelling interests" that might justify restrictions on religious activity. See §§ 21.6, 21.8.

18.15 In this Chapter we are only concerned with cases in which a individual seeks exemption from health or medical regulations on the basis of the free exercise clause. In limited circumstances an individual might claim that the due process clause of the fourteenth amendment gives him a right to refuse life sustaining medical treatment. See § 18.30(c) of this Treatise regarding the "right to die."

IV. OTHER ESTABLISHMENT— FREE EXERCISE PROBLEMS

§ 21.14 Prohibiting "Ministers" From Holding Public Office

Page 584, add to note 4:

4. The dispute between Justice Brennan and Chief Justice Burger regarding the proper basis for the Court's ruling in *McDaniel* may have been due to the fact that the Supreme Court rarely is called upon to review laws that are clearly intended to burden, punish or disfavor persons because of their religious beliefs. In Church of the Lukumi Babalu Aye, Inc. v. Hialeah, 508 U.S. 520, 113 S.Ct. 2217, 124 L.Ed.2d 472 (1993), on remand 2 F.3d 369 (11th Cir. 1993) the Court unanimously invalidated a city law that was designed to suppress a particular religion by outlawing its animal sacrifice ritual. The majority opinion begins with the following statement: "The principle that government may not enact laws that suppress religious belief or practice is so well understood that few violations are recorded in our opinion. Cf. *McDaniel v. Paty* . . . ." 508 U.S. at 523, 113 S.Ct. at 2222.

Chapter 22

NATURALIZATION AND CITIZENSHIP

WESTLAW Electronic Research

See WESTLAW Electronic Research Guide preceding the Summary of Contents.

I. INTRODUCTION

§ 22.1 Generally

Page 598, add to note 5:

5. Cf., Ann C. Barcher, First Asylum in Southeast Asia: Customary Norm or Ephemeral Concept?, 24 N.Y.U. J. of International L. & Politics 1253 (1992).

II. ADMISSION, IMMIGRATION, AND ACQUISITION OF CITIZENSHIP

§ 22.2 Admission

Page 600, add to note 5:

5. See also, Sale v. Haitian Centers Council, Inc., 509 U.S. 155, 113 S.Ct. 2549, 125 L.Ed.2d 128 (1993). The plaintiffs argued that the interdiction and repatriation of Haitian refugees on the high seas violated the Immigration and Nationality Act and an Article of the United Nations Protocol Relating to the Status of Refugees. The Court held (with only Blackmun, J., filing a dissenting opinion) that neither a federal statute (which generally prohibited the Attorney General from deporting or returning aliens to a country where the aliens' life or freedom would be threatened on account of the race, religion, nationality, membership in a particular social group, or political opinion), nor a parallel article in the United Nations Convention Relating to the Status of Refugees applied to actions that the Coast Guard took on the high seas.

IV. DEPORTATION

§ 22.7 Generally

Page 614, add new heading to beginning of paragraph that begins on the second to last line of the page:

Bail or Parole Pending Deportation.

Page 615, add to text after note 9:

In short, the Attorney General has broad discretion to determine whether and on what terms an alien who is arrested on suspicion of being deportable should be released pending a deportation hearing.[9.10]

9.10 Reno v. Flores, 507 U.S. 292, 113 S.Ct. 1439, 123 L.Ed.2d 1 (1993), on remand 992 F.2d 243 (9th Cir.1993). The Court (7 to 2) rejected constitutional challenges to a regulation of the Immigration and Naturalization Service (INS) governing release of detained *juvenile* aliens. The Court upheld the regulation that permitted detained juvenile aliens to be released only to their parents, close relatives, or legal guardians, except in unusual and compelling circumstances. The Court ruled that the responsibility for regulating the relationship between the United States "and our alien visitors has been committed to the political branches of the Federal Government."

The Court also rejected the argument that the government violated the equal protection component of due process by its disparate treatment between alien juveniles and citizen juveniles. Federal law allowed the release of *alien* juveniles only to close relatives or legal guardians, while another federal law allowed the release of non-alien juveniles (who were detained pending federal delinquency proceedings) to unrelated adults (e.g., the director of a shelter-care facility). The majority reasoned that the tradition of reposing custody in close relatives and legal guardians, and the difference between citizens and aliens is adequate to support the distinctions in the law.

Chapter 23

THEORIES AND METHODS OF CONSTITUTIONAL CONSTRUCTION AND INTERPRETATION IN THE CASE LAW AND THE LITERATURE

Table of New or Retitled Sections

WESTLAW Electronic Research

See WESTLAW Electronic Research Guide preceding the Summary of Contents.

II. THE SCHOOLS OF THOUGHT REGARDING CONSTITUTIONAL CONSTRUCTION AND INTERPRETATION

§ 23.2 The Movement Away From Natural Law and Contractual Theorists

Page 621, add to note 1:

1. For a thoughtful and interesting analysis of the process and theories of constitutional interpretation, see, William A. Kaplin, The Process of Constitutional Interpretation: A Synthesis of the Present and a Guide to the Future, 42 Rutgers L.Rev. 983 (1990). This article is also a useful bibliography to much of the literature in this area. See also, William A. Kaplin, The Concepts and Methods of Constitutional Law (1992).

Page 622, add to note 8:

8. **Oliver Wendell Holmes.** See, Patrick J. Kelley, Holmes' Early Constitutional Law Theory and Its Application in Takings Cases on the Massachusetts Supreme Judicial Court, 18 So.Ill.L.J. 357 (1994).

§ 23.5   Neutral Principles or Process Oriented Jurisprudence

(a) Legal Realism Versus Neutral Principles

Page 629, add to note 4:

4. Peter Linzer, The *Carolene Products* Footnote and the Preferred Position of Individual Rights: Louis Lusky and John Hart Ely vs. Harlan Fiske Stone, 12 Const.Commentary 277 (1995).

Page 631, add to note 13:

13. See also, Richard H. Fallon, Jr., Individual Rights and the Powers of Government, 27 Geo.L.Rev. 343 (1993); Barry Friedman, Trumping Rights, 27 Geo.L.Rev. 435 (1993); Richard H. Fallon, Jr., Dialogue and Judicial Review, 91 Mich.L.Rev. 577 (1993).

(b) The Interpretivist School

Page 633, add to note 14:

14. **Originalism.** Terry Brennan, Natural Rights and the Constitution: The Original "Original Intent," 15 Harv.J.L. & Public Policy 965 (1992); John O. McGinnis, The Original Constitution and Our Origins, 19 Harv.J. of L. & Pub. Policy 251 (1996).

Original Intent. Gerard Bradley, The Bill of Rights and Originalism, 1992 U.Ill.L.Rev. 417; John Nowak, The "Sixty Something" Anniversary of the Bill of Rights, 1992 U.Ill.L.Rev. 445; Roger Pilon, On the Folly and Illegitimacy of Industrial Policy, 5 Stanford L. & Policy Rev. 103 (1993); Roger Pilon, A Court without a Compass, 40 N.Y.L. School L. Rev. 999 (1996).

See the thoughtful essay by, Roger Pilon, Freedom, Responsibility, and The Constitution: On Recovering Our Founding Principles, 68 Notre Dame L.Rev. 507 (1993). See also, Michael Conant, The Constitution and the Economy (U.Okla. Press 1991).

The Second Amendment. Levin, The Right to Bear Arms: The Development of the American Experience, 48 Chi.–Kent L.Rev. 148 (1971); Sanford Levinson, The Embarrassing Second Amendment, 99 Yale L.J. 637 (1989); William Van Alstyne, The Second Amendment and the Personal Right to Arms, 43 Duke L.J. 1236 (1994).

(c) Value–Oriented Jurisprudence

Page 636, add to note 19:

19. Frederick Schauer, Constitutional Positivism, 25 Conn.L.Rev. 797 (1993); Randy E. Barnett, The Intersection of Natural Rights and Positive Constitutional Law, 25 Conn.L.Rev. 853 (1993).

Page 636, add to note 21:

21. Maxwell L. Stearns, The Misguided Renaissance of Social Choice, 103 Yale L.J. 1219 (1994).

(d) Neutral Principles as Related to Legal Realism

Page 638, add to note 25:

25. **Critical Legal Studies.** Cf. Anthony D. Taibi, Banking, Finance, and Community Economic Empowerment: Structural Economic Theory, Procedural Civil Rights, and Substantive Racial Justice, 107 Harv.L.Rev. 1463 (1994).

III.   THE HISTORICAL BACKGROUND BEHIND THE CONSTITUTION

§ 23.8   Principles of the Common Law

Page 648, note 3, 9th line from the bottom second column:

Replace "Yet the kind" with "Yet the king".

IV.   GENERAL RULES AND PRINCIPLES OF INTERPRETATION

§ 23.10   The Duty to Avoid Constitutional Issues

Page 651, add to end of carryover paragraph:

If the Court presumes that a law is constitutional—a presumption that courts often articulate—then it is reasonable to require that the legislature focus on the law in question, and really mean to enact that which has created the constitutional problem.[3.1]

3.1 NLRB v. Catholic Bishop of Chicago, 440 U.S. 490, 500, 99 S.Ct. 1313, 1318, 59 L.Ed.2d 533 (1979), holding that an "Act of Congress ought not be construed to violate the Constitution if any other possible construction remains available."

Page 653, add to text after note 13:

The duty to avoid constitutional issues is not an end in itself. If there is a case where the parties choose to litigate only the federal constitutional issues in the district court and in the Court of Appeals, where the respondent does not urge or offer any statutory ground to affirm the appellate court, and where the district court granting summary judgment addresses only the constitutional issues, the rule on the duty to avoid constitutional issues has no application. The fact that there might be buried in the record a nonconstitutional ground for decision does not require the Supreme Court to avoid the constitutional issue.[13.10]

13.10 Board of Airport Commissioners v. Jews for Jesus, 482 U.S. 569, 572, 107 S.Ct. 2568, 2571, 96 L.Ed.2d 500 (1987); Zobrest v. Catalina Foothills School District, 509 U.S. 1, 113 S.Ct. 2462, 125 L.Ed.2d 1 (1993).

VII. THE VIEWS OF THE CASE LAW ON CONTEMPORANEOUS AND SUBSEQUENT PRACTICAL CONSTRUCTION

§ 23.35   The Role of the Federalist Papers in the Courts

Page 679, change title of § 23.35 to:

§ 23.35   The Role of the Federalist Papers and the Declaration of Independence

Page 679, add new subheading:

(a) The Federalist Papers

Page 679, add to note 1:

1. See Symposium, The Legacy of the Federalist Papers, 16 Harv.J. of L. & Pub.Policy 1 (1993).

Page 680, add new subheading and text after first full paragraph:

(b) The Declaration of Independence

Courts rarely cite the Declaration of Independence and when they do, it is usually to make reference to it in a passing manner or to use it in order to date a moment in history, such as the moment that English case law ceased to operate as law in the ex- colonies.[6] In only a few cases has the Supreme Court referred to (and relied on) the Declaration in a more substantive manner, but this use is unusual.[7]

6. Robert J. Reinstein, Completing the Constitution: The Declaration of Independence, Bill of Rights and Fourteenth Amendment, 66 Temple L.Rev. 361, 361–62 & n. 2 (1993).

7. Some of the cases that have used the Declaration of Independence in more than a passing way include:

Voting. Reynolds v. Sims, 377 U.S. 533, 558, 84 S.Ct. 1362, 1380, 12 L.Ed.2d 506 (1964), rehearing denied 379 U.S. 870, 85 S.Ct. 12, 13 L.Ed.2d 76 (1964), where the majority referred to the Declaration of Independence in support of the one person, one vote principle. Gray v. Sanders, 372 U.S. 368, 381, 83 S.Ct. 801, 809, 9 L.Ed.2d 821 (1963), also referring to the Declaration of Independence in a one person, one vote case.

Treason. Cramer v. United States, 325 U.S. 1, 14–15, 65 S.Ct. 918, 925, 89 L.Ed. 1441 (1945), using the Declaration of Independence to show that the treason clause should be narrowly construed against the Government.

Trial by Jury. Adams v. United States ex rel. McCann, 317 U.S. 269, 276, 63 S.Ct. 236, 240, 87 L.Ed. 268 (1942), using the Declaration of Independence to demonstrate that the right of trial by jury in a criminal case is a fundamental right.

International and Foreign Affairs. United States v. Curtiss–Wright Export Corp., 299 U.S. 304, 316, 57 S.Ct. 216, 219, 81 L.Ed. 255 (1936), citing the Declaration of Independence to support its holding that the power to conduct foreign affairs moved from the British monarchy to the federal government, not the states; United States ex rel. Toth v. Quarles, 350 U.S. 11, 16 n. 9, 76 S.Ct. 1, 5 n. 9, 100 L.Ed. 8 (1955), relying on the Declaration of Independence to support the conclusion that civilian authority is superior to military authority; Reid v. Covert, 354 U.S. 1, 29, 77 S.Ct. 1222, 1237, 1 L.Ed.2d 1148 (1957), also citing the Declaration of Independence to support the conclusion that civilian authority is superior to military authority; Dames & Moore v. Regan, 453 U.S. 654, 661–62, 101 S.Ct. 2972, 2977–78, 69 L.Ed.2d 918 (1981), citing the Declaration of Independence to support the conclusion that the executive's power in foreign affairs is limited.

Property. Howard v. Ingersoll, 54 U.S. (13 How.) 381, 398, 14 L.Ed. 189 (1852), using the Declaration of Independence to conclude that any territory that was not apportioned to a specific state at the time of the Declaration of Independence belongs to the federal government; Allgeyer v. Louisiana, 165 U.S. 578, 589, 17 S.Ct. 427, 431, 41 L.Ed. 832 (1897), using the Declaration of Independence to support due process protection for property rights.

Appendix G

THE JUSTICES OF THE SUPREME COURT IN HISTORICAL PERSPECTIVE

Page 760, at end of chart, indicate the following:

Justice White retired in 1993, and was replaced by Justice Ginsburg;

Justice Blackmun retired in 1994, and was replaced by Justice Breyer.

Page 761,

> **Add the following information to,**
>
> BLACKMUN, HARRY A. (1908–___; Nixon, 1970–1994).
>
> **Add after,** BRADLEY, JOSEPH P.
>
> BREYER, STEPHEN GERALD (1937–___; Clinton, 1994–___); Mass. Dem.; U.S. *Judge, Court of Appeals* (13½).

Page 764,

> **Add after,** GOLDBERG, ARTHUR J.
>
> GINSBURG, RUTH BADER (1933–___; Clinton, 1993–___); N.Y. Dem.; U.S. *Judge, Court of Appeals* (13).

Page 769,

> **Add the following information to,**
>
> WHITE, BYRON R. (1917–___; Kennedy, 1962–1993).

128

Appendix K

THE PRESIDENTS AND VICE PRESIDENTS OF THE UNITED STATES IN HISTORICAL PERSPECTIVE

(As of January 1, 1995)

Page 776, replace line 41 with the following:

Order	President	Vice President	Service
41.	George H.W. Bush	James Danforth Quayle	1989–1993
42.	Bill Clinton	Al Gore	1993–

Appendix N

THE CONSTITUTION OF THE UNITED STATES

Page 808, Add to end of page:

INDEX TO THE CONSTITUTION AND AMENDMENTS *

	Article †	Section	Clause
A			
Abridged. The privileges or immunities of citizens of the United States shall not be. [Amendments]	14	1	....
Absent members, in such manner and under such penalties as it may provide. Each House is authorized to compel the attendance of	1	5	1
Accounts of receipts and expenditures of public money shall be published from time to time. A statement of the	1	9	7
Accusation. In all criminal prosecutions the accused shall be informed of the cause and nature of the. [Amendments]	6	....	....
Accused shall have a speedy public trial. In all criminal prosecutions the. [Amendments]	6	....	....
He shall be tried by an impartial jury of the State and district where the crime was committed. [Amendments]	6	....	....
He shall be informed of the nature of the accusation. [Amendments]	6	....	....
He shall be confronted with the witnesses against him. [Amendments]	6	....	....
He shall have compulsory process for obtaining witnesses in his favor. [Amendments]	6	....	....
He shall have the assistance of counsel for his defense. [Amendments]	6	....	....
Actions at common law involving over twenty dollars shall be tried by jury. [Amendments]	7	....	....
Acts, records, and judicial proceedings of another State. Full faith and credit shall be given in each State to the	4	1	....
Acts. Congress shall prescribe the manner of proving such acts, records, and proceedings	4	1	....
Adjourn from day to day. A smaller number than a quorum of each House may	1	5	1
Adjourn for more than three days, nor to any other place than that in which they shall be sitting. Neither House shall, during the session of Congress, without the consent of the other	1	5	4
Adjournment, the President may adjourn them to such time as he shall think proper. In case of disagreement between the two Houses as to	2	3	....
Admiralty and maritime jurisdiction. The judicial power shall extend to all cases of	3	2	1

* Adapted from House Document No. (1978). 95–256, 95th Congress, 1st Session

† Article of original Constitution or of Amendment.

130

	Article †	Section	Clause
Admitted by the Congress into this Union, but no new States shall be formed or erected within the jurisdiction of any other State. New States may be.........	4	3	1
Nor shall any State be formed by the junction of two or more States, or parts of States, without the consent of the legislatures and of Congress	4	3	1
Adoption of the Constitution shall be valid. All debts and engagements contracted by the confederation and before the..	6	....	1
Advice and consent of the Senate. The President shall have power to make treaties by and with the........	2	2	2
To appoint ambassadors or other public ministers and consuls by and with the	2	2	2
To appoint all other officers of the United States not herein otherwise provided for by and with the	2	2	2
Affirmation. Senators sitting to try impeachments shall be on oath or	1	3	6
To be taken by the President of the United States. Form of the oath or	2	1	7
No warrants shall be issued but upon probable cause and on oath or. [Amendments]	4	....	....
To support the Constitution. Senators and Representatives, members of State legislatures, executive and judicial officers, both State and Federal, shall be bound by oath or......................	6	....	3
Age. No person shall be a Representative who shall not have attained twenty-five years of	1	2	2
No person shall be a Senator who shall not have attained thirty years of........................	1	3	3
Right of citizens of the United States, who are eighteen years of age or older, to vote shall not be denied or abridged by the United States or any State on account of age. [Amendments]	26	1	....
Agreement or compact with another State without the consent of Congress. No State shall enter into any	1	10	3
Aid and comfort. Treason against the United States shall consist in levying war against them, adhering to their enemies, and giving them......................	3	3	1
Alliance or confederation. No State shall enter into any treaty of	1	10	1
Ambassadors, or other public ministers and consuls. The President may appoint	2	2	2
The judicial power of the United States shall extend to all cases affecting.....................	3	2	1
Amendments to the Constitution. Whenever two-thirds of both Houses shall deem it necessary, Congress shall propose	5	....	....
On application of the legislatures of two-thirds of the States, Congress shall call a convention to propose	5	....	....
Shall be valid when ratified by the legislatures of, or by conventions in, three-fourths of the States	5	....	....
Answer for a capital or infamous crime unless on presentment of a grand jury. No person shall be held to. [Amendments]	5	....	....
Except in cases in the land or naval forces, or in the militia when in actual service. [Amendments]...	5	....	....
Appellate jurisdiction both as to law and fact, with such exceptions and under such regulations as Congress shall make. In what cases the Supreme Court shall have...	3	2	2

† **Article of original Constitution or of Amendment.**

131

App. N   CONSTITUTION OF THE U.S.

	Article †	Section	Clause
Application of the legislature or the executive of a State. The United States shall protect each State against invasion and domestic violence on the	4	4	....
Application of the legislatures of two-thirds of the States, Congress shall call a convention for proposing amendments to the Constitution. On the	5	....	....
Appointment of officers and authority to train the militia reserved to the States respectively...............	1	8	16
Of such inferior officers as they may think proper in the President alone. Congress may by law vest the	2	2	2
In the courts of law or in the heads of departments. Congress may by law vest the	2	2	2
Of Presidential and Vice–Presidential electors. District of Columbia to have power of. [Amendments].......................................	23	1	....
Apportionment of representation and direct taxation among the several States. Provisions relating to the Congress shall have power to lay and collect taxes on incomes, from whatever source derived, without apportionment among the several States	1	2	3
	16	....	....
Of Representatives among the several States. Provisions relating to the. [Amendments]	14	2	....
Appropriate legislation. Congress shall have power to make all laws necessary and proper for carrying into execution the foregoing powers, and all other powers vested by the Constitution in the Government of the United States, or in any department or officer thereof	1	8	18
Congress shall have power to enforce the thirteenth article, prohibiting slavery by. [Amendments]	13	2	....
Congress shall have power to enforce the provisions of the fourteenth article by. [Amendments].....	14	5	....
Congress shall have power to enforce the provisions of the fifteenth article by. [Amendment]	15	2	....
Congress shall have power to enforce the provisions of the twenty-third article by. [Amendments]	23	2	....
Congress shall have power to enforce the provisions of the twenty-fourth article by. [Amendments]	24	2	....
Congress shall have power to enforce the provisions of the twenty-sixth article by. [Amendments]	26	2	....
Appropriation of money for raising and supporting armies shall be for a longer term than two years. But no...	1	8	12
Appropriations made by law. No money shall be drawn from the Treasury but in consequence of	1	9	7
Approve and sign a bill before it shall become a law. The President shall	1	7	2
He shall return it to the House in which it originated, with his objections, if he does not	1	7	2
Armies, but no appropriation for that use shall be for a longer term than two years. Congress shall have power to raise and support	1	8	12
Armies. Congress shall make rules for the government and regulation of the land and naval forces..........	1	8	14
Arms shall not be infringed. A well-regulated militia being necessary to the security of a free State, the right of the people to keep and bear. [Amendments]	2	....	....
Arrest during their attendance at the session of their respective Houses, and in going to and returning from the same. Members shall in all cases, except treason, felony, and breach of the peace, be privileged from...	1	6	1
Arsenals. Congress shall exercise exclusive authority over all places purchased for the erection of	1	8	17

† **Article of original Constitution or of Amendment.**

	Article [†]	Section	Clause
Articles exported from any State. No tax or duty shall be laid on	1	9	5
Arts by securing to authors and inventors their patent rights. Congress may promote the progress of science and the useful	1	8	8
Assistance of counsel for his defense. In all criminal prosecutions the accused shall have the. [Amendments]..	6	....	....
Assumption of the debt or obligations incurred in aid of rebellion or insurrection against the United States. Provisions against the. [Amendments]	14	4	....
Attainder or ex post facto law shall be passed. No bill of	1	9	3
Attainder, ex post facto law, or law impairing the obligation of contracts. No State shall pass any bill of	1	10	1
Attainder of treason shall not work corruption of blood or forfeiture, except during the life of the person attainted..	3	3	2
Authors and inventors the exclusive right to their writings and inventions. Congress shall have power to secure to...	1	8	8

B

	Article [†]	Section	Clause
Bail. Excessive bail shall not be required, nor excessive fines nor cruel and unusual punishments imposed. [Amendments]	8	....	....
Ballot for President and Vice President. The electors shall vote by. [Amendments].....................	12	....	....
Ballot. If no person have a majority of the electoral votes for President and Vice President, the House of Representatives shall immediately choose the President by. [Amendments]	12	....	....
Bankruptcies. Congress shall have power to pass uniform laws on the subject of	1	8	4
Basis of representation among the several States. Provisions relating to the. [Amendments]	14	2	....
Bear arms shall not be infringed. A well-regulated militia being necessary to the security of a free State, the right of the people to keep and. [Amendments]	2	....	....
Behavior. The judges of the Supreme and inferior courts shall hold their offices during good	3	1	....
Bill of attainder or ex post facto law shall be passed. No	1	9	3
Bill of attainder, ex post facto law, or law impairing the obligation of contracts. No State shall pass any	1	10	1
Bills of credit. No State shall emit	1	10	1
Bills for raising revenue shall originate in the House of Representatives. All.............................	1	7	1
Bills which shall have passed the Senate and House of Representatives shall, before they become laws, be presented to the President........................	1	7	2
If he approve, he shall sign them; if he disapprove, he shall return them, with his objections, to that House in which they originated	1	7	2
Upon the reconsideration of a bill returned by the President with his objections, if two-thirds of each House agree to pass the same, it shall become a law................................	1	7	2
Upon the reconsideration of a bill returned by the President, the question shall be taken by yeas and nays.......................................	1	7	2

[†] **Article of original Constitution or of Amendment.**

	Article [†]	Section	Clause
Not returned by the President within ten days (Sundays excepted), shall, unless Congress adjourn, become laws..............................	1	7	2
Borrow money on the credit of the United States. Congress shall have power to	1	8	2
Bounties and pensions, shall not be questioned. The validity of the public debt incurred in suppressing insurrection and rebellion against the United States, including the debt for. [Amendments]	14	4	....
Breach of the peace, shall be privileged from arrest while attending the session, and in going to and returning from the same. Senators and Representatives, except for treason, felony, and	1	6	1
Bribery, or other high crimes and misdemeanors. The President, Vice President, and all civil officers shall be removed on impeachment for and conviction of treason	2	4	....

C

	Article [†]	Section	Clause
Capital or otherwise infamous crime, unless on indictment of a grand jury, except in certain specified cases. No person shall be held to answer for a. [Amendments]	5	....	....
Capitation or other direct tax shall be laid unless in proportion to the census or enumeration. No	1	9	4
Captures on land and water. Congress shall make rules concerning....................................	1	8	11
Casting vote. The Vice President shall have no vote unless the Senate be equally divided	1	3	4
Census or enumeration of the inhabitants shall be made within three years after the first meeting of Congress, and within every subsequent term of ten years thereafter...	1	2	3
No capitation or other direct tax shall be laid except in proportion to the....................	1	9	4
Chief Justice shall preside when the President of the United States is tried upon impeachment. The......	1	3	6
Choosing the electors and the day on which they shall give their votes, which shall be the same throughout the United States. Congress may determine the time of	2	1	3
Citizen of the United States at the adoption of the Constitution shall be eligible to the office of President. No person not a natural-born	2	1	4
Citizen of the United States. No person shall be a Senator who shall not have attained the age of thirty years, and been nine years a	1	3	3
No person shall be a Representative who shall not have attained the age of twenty-five years, and been seven years a	1	2	2
Right to vote shall not be denied or abridged by the United States or any State for failure to pay any poll tax or other tax. [Amendments]	24	1	....
Right of citizens to vote shall not be denied or abridged by the United States or any State on account of sex. [Amendments]	19	....	....
Right to vote shall not be denied or abridged by the United States or any State to any citizen eighteen years or older, on account of age. [Amendments].......................................	26	1	....
Citizenship. Citizens of each State shall be entitled to all the privileges and immunities of citizens of the several States	4	2	1

† Article of original Constitution or of Amendment.

	Article †	Section	Clause
All persons born or naturalized in the United States, and subject to the jurisdiction thereof, are citizens of the United States and of the State in which they reside. [Amendments]	14	1	....
No State shall make or enforce any law which shall abridge the privileges or immunities of citizens of the United States. [Amendments]	14	1	....
Nor shall any State deprive any person of life, liberty, or property without due process of law. [Amendments]	14	1	....
Nor deny to any person within its jurisdiction the equal protection of the laws. [Amendments]	14	1	....
Citizens or subjects of a foreign state. The judicial power of the United States shall not extend to suits in law or equity brought against one of the States by the citizens of another State, or by. [Amendments]	11	....	....
Civil officers of the United States shall, on impeachment for and conviction of treason, bribery, and other high crimes and misdemeanors be removed. All.....	2	4	....
Claims of the United States or any particular State in the territory or public property. Nothing in this Constitution shall be construed to prejudice	4	3	2
Classification of Senators. Immediately after they shall be assembled after the first election, they shall be divided as equally as may be into three classes.......	1	3	2
Classification of Senators. The seats of the Senators of the first class shall be vacated at the expiration of the second year	1	3	2
The seats of the Senators of the second class at the expiration of the fourth year	1	3	2
The seats of the Senators of the third class at the expiration of the sixth year	1	3	2
Coin a tender in payment of debts. No State shall make anything but gold and silver..................	1	10	1
Coin money and regulate the value thereof and of foreign coin. Congress shall have power to	1	8	5
Coin of the United States. Congress shall provide for punishing the counterfeiting the securities and current	1	8	6
Color, or previous condition of servitude. The right of citizens of the United States to vote shall not be denied or abridged by the United States or by any State on account of race. [Amendments]	15	1	....
Comfort. Treason against the United States shall consist in levying war against them, and giving their enemies aid and	3	3	1
Commander in chief of the Army and Navy, and of the militia when in actual service. The President shall be	2	2	1
Commerce with foreign nations, among the States, and with Indian tribes. Congress shall have power to regulate	1	8	3
Commerce or revenue. No preference shall be given to the ports of one State over those of another by any regulation of	1	9	6
Vessels clearing from the ports of one State shall not pay duties in those of another	1	9	6
Commissions to expire at the end of the next session. The President may fill vacancies that happen in the recess of the Senate by granting....................	2	2	3
Common defense, promote the general welfare, &c. To insure the. [Preamble]	....	....	....
Common defense and general welfare. Congress shall have power to provide for the	1	8	1

† Article of original Constitution or of Amendment.

135

	Article †	Section	Clause
Common law, where the amount involved exceeds twenty dollars, shall be tried by jury. Suits at. [Amendments]	7	....	....
No fact tried by a jury shall be otherwise reexamined in any court of the United States than according to the rules of the. [Amendments]	7	....	....
Compact with another State. No State shall, without consent of Congress, enter into any agreement or	1	10	3
Compact with a foreign power. No State shall, without the consent of Congress, enter into any agreement or	1	10	3
Compensation of Senators and Representatives to be ascertained by law	1	6	1
Compensation of Senators and Representatives. No law varying the compensation for the services of. [Amendments]	27	....	....
Compensation of the President shall not be increased nor diminished during the period for which he shall be elected	2	1	6
Compensation of the judges of the Supreme and inferior courts shall not be diminished during their continuance in office	3	1	....
Compensation. Private property shall not be taken for public use without just. [Amendments]	5	....	....
Compulsory process for obtaining witnesses in his favor. In criminal prosecutions the accused shall have. [Amendments]	6	....	....
Confederation. No State shall enter into any treaty, alliance, or	1	10	1
Confederation. All debts contracted and engagements entered into before the adoption of this Constitution shall be valid against the United States under it, as under the	6	....	1
Confession in open court. Conviction of treason shall be on the testimony of two persons to the overt act, or upon	3	3	1
Congress of the United States. All legislative powers shall be vested in a	1	1	....
Shall consist of a Senate and House of Representatives	1	1	....
Shall assemble at least once in every year, which shall be on the first Monday of December, unless they by law appoint a different day	1	4	2
May at any time alter regulations for elections of Senators and Representatives, except as to the places of choosing Senators	1	4	1
Each House shall be the judge of the elections, returns, and qualifications of its own members	1	5	1
A majority of each House shall constitute a quorum to do business	1	5	1
A smaller number may adjourn from day to day and compel the attendance of absent members	1	5	1
Each House may determine the rules of its proceedings, punish its members for disorderly behavior, and, with the concurrence of two-thirds, expel a member	1	5	2
Each House shall keep a journal of its proceedings	1	5	3
Neither House, during the session of Congress, shall, without the consent of the other, adjourn for more than three days	1	5	4
Senators and Representatives shall receive a compensation to be ascertained by law	1	6	1
They shall in all cases, except treason, felony, and breach of peace, be privileged from arrest during			

† **Article of original Constitution or of Amendment.**

136

	Article †	Section	Clause
attendance at their respective Houses, and in going to and returning from the same	1	6	1
No Senator or Representative shall, during his term, be appointed to any civil office which shall have been created, or of which the emoluments shall have been increased, during such term	1	6	2
No person holding any office under the United States, shall, while in office, be a member of either House of Congress	1	6	2
All bills for raising revenue shall originate in the House of Representatives	1	7	1
Proceedings in cases of bills returned by the President with his objections	1	7	2
Shall have power to lay and collect duties, imposts, and excises, pay the debts, and provide for the common defense and general welfare	1	8	1
Shall have power to borrow money on the credit of the United States	1	8	2
To regulate foreign and domestic commerce, and with the Indian tribes	1	8	3
To establish uniform rule of naturalization and uniform laws on the subject of bankruptcies	1	8	4
To coin money, regulate its value and the value of foreign coin, and to fix the standard of weights and measures	1	8	5
To punish the counterfeiting of securities and current coin of the United States	1	8	6
To establish post-offices and post-roads	1	8	7
To promote the progress of science and the useful arts	1	8	8
To constitute tribunals inferior to the Supreme Court	1	8	9
To define and punish piracies and felonies on the high seas and to punish offenses against the law of nations	1	8	10
To declare war, grant letters of marque and reprisal, and make rules concerning captures on land and water	1	8	11
To raise and support armies, but no appropriations of money to that use shall be for a longer term than two years	1	8	12
To provide and maintain a Navy	1	8	13
To make rules for the government of the Army and Navy	1	8	14
To call out the militia to execute the laws, suppress insurrections, and repel invasions	1	8	15
To provide for organizing, arming, and equipping the militia	1	8	16
To exercise exclusive legislation over the District fixed for the seat of government, and over forts, magazines, arsenals, and dockyards	1	8	17
To make all laws necessary and proper to carry into execution all powers vested by the Constitution in the Government of the United States.........	1	8	18
No person holding any office under the United States shall accept of any present, emolument, office or title of any kind from any foreign state, without the consent of	1	9	8
May determine the time of choosing the electors for President and Vice President and the day on which they shall give their votes	2	1	3
The President may, on extraordinary occasions, convene either House of	2	3	....

† Article of original Constitution or of Amendment.

App. N CONSTITUTION OF THE U.S.

	Article [†]	Section	Clause
The manner in which the acts, records, and judicial proceedings of the States shall be prescribed by	4	1	....
New States may be admitted by Congress into this Union	4	3	1
Shall have power to make all needful rules and regulations respecting the territory or other property belonging to the United States.........	4	3	2
Amendments to the Constitution shall be proposed whenever it shall be deemed necessary by two-thirds of both Houses of	5	....	....
Persons engaged in insurrection or rebellion against the United States disqualified for Senators or Representatives in. [Amendments]	14	3	....
But such disqualification may be removed by a vote of two-thirds of both Houses of. [Amendments]	14	3	....
Shall have power to enforce, by appropriate legislation, the thirteenth amendment. [Amendments]	13	2	....
Shall have power to enforce, by appropriate legislation, the fourteenth amendment. [Amendments]	14	5	....
Shall have power to enforce, by appropriate legislation, the fifteenth amendment. [Amendments]	15	2	....
Shall have power to enforce, by appropriate legislation, the nineteenth amendment. [Amendments]	19	....	....
Sessions, time of assembling. [Amendments]	20	2	....
Shall have power to enforce, by appropriate legislation, the twenty-third amendment. [Amendments]..	23	2	....
Shall have power to enforce, by appropriate legislation, the twenty-fourth amendment. [Amendments]..	24	2	....
Shall have power to enforce, by appropriate legislation, the twenty-sixth amendment. [Amendments]..	26	2	....
To direct appointment of electors for President and Vice President by District of Columbia. [Amendments]....................................	23	1	....
Consent. No State shall be deprived of its equal suffrage in the Senate without its	5	....	....
Consent of Congress. No person holding any office of profit or trust under the United States shall accept of any present, emolument, office, or title of any kind whatever, from any king, prince, or foreign potentate, without the	1	9	8
No State shall lay any imposts, or duties on imports, except what may be absolutely necessary for executing its inspection laws, without the	1	10	2
No State shall lay any duty of tonnage, keep troops or ships of war in time of peace, without the	1	10	3
No State shall enter into any agreement or compact with another State, or with a foreign power, without the	1	10	3
No State shall engage in war unless actually invaded, or in such imminent danger as will not admit of delay, without the	1	10	3
No new State shall be formed or erected within the jurisdiction of any other State, nor any State be formed by the junction of two or more States, or parts of States, without the consent of the legislatures thereof, as well as the	4	3	1
Consent of the legislature of the State in which the same may be. Congress shall exercise exclusive authority over all places purchased for the erection of forts, magazines, arsenals, dockyards, and other needful buildings by the	1	8	17

† Article of original Constitution or of Amendment.

138

	Article †	Section	Clause
Consent of the legislatures of the States and of Congress. No States shall be formed by the junction of two or more States or parts of States without the	4	3	1
Consent of the other. Neither House, during the session of Congress, shall adjourn for more than three days, nor to any other place than that in which they shall be sitting, without the.........................	1	5	4
Consent of the owner. No soldier shall be quartered in time of peace in any house without the. [Amendments].......................................	3	....	....
Consent of the Senate. The President shall have power to make treaties, by and with the advice and	2	2	2
The President shall appoint ambassadors, other public ministers and consuls, judges of the Supreme Court and all other officers created by law and not otherwise herein provided for, by and with the advice and	2	2	2
Constitution, in the Government of the United States, or in any department or officer thereof. Congress shall have power to pass all laws necessary to the execution of the powers vested by the...............	1	8	18
Constitution, shall be eligible to the office of President. No person except a natural-born citizen, or a citizen at the time of the adoption of the...................	2	1	4
Constitution. The President, before he enters upon the execution of his office, shall take an oath to preserve, protect, and defend the...........................	2	1	7
Constitution, laws, and treaties of the United States. The judicial power shall extend to all cases arising under the...	3	2	1
Constitution shall be so construed as to prejudice any claims of the United States, or of any State (in respect to territory or other property of the United States). Nothing in the	4	3	2
Constitution. The manner in which amendments may be proposed and ratified.........................	5	....	....
Constitution as under the Confederation shall be valid. All debts and engagements contracted before the adoption of the	6	....	1
Constitution and the laws made in pursuance thereof, and all treaties made, or which shall be made, by the United States, shall be the supreme law of the land. The	6	....	2
The judges in every State, anything in the constitution or laws of a State to the contrary notwithstanding, shall be bound thereby	6	....	2
Constitution. All officers, legislative, executive, and judicial, of the United States, and of the several States, shall be bound by an oath to support the	6	....	3
But no religious test shall ever be required as a qualification for any office or public trust	6	....	3
Constitution between the States so ratifying the same. The ratification of the conventions of nine States shall be sufficient for the establishment of the	7	....	....
Constitution, of certain rights, shall not be construed to deny or disparage others retained by the people. The enumeration in the. [Amendments]................	9	....	....
Constitution, nor prohibited by it to the States, are reserved to the States respectively or to the people. Powers not delegated to the United States by the. [Amendments]	10	....	....
Constitution, and then engaged in rebellion against the United States. Disqualification for office imposed			

† Article of original Constitution or of Amendment.

139

	Article †	Section	Clause
Crimes and misdemeanors. The President, Vice President, and all civil officers shall be removed on impeachment for and conviction of treason, bribery, or other	2	4	
Crimes, except in cases of impeachment, shall be tried by jury. All	3	2	3
They shall be tried in the State within which they may be committed	3	2	3
When not committed in a State, they shall be tried at the places which Congress may by law have provided	3	2	3
Criminal prosecutions, the accused shall have a speedy and public trial by jury in the State and district where the crime was committed. In all. [Amendments]	6		
He shall be informed of the nature and cause of the accusation. [Amendments]	6		
He shall be confronted with the witnesses against him. [Amendments]	6		
He shall have compulsory process for obtaining witnesses in his favor. [Amendments]	6		
He shall have the assistance of counsel in his defense. [Amendments]	6		
Criminate himself. No person as a witness shall be compelled to. [Amendments]	5		
Cruel and unusual punishments inflicted. Excessive bail shall not be required, nor excessive fines imposed, nor. [Amendments]	8		

D

	Article †	Section	Clause
Danger as will not admit of delay. No State shall, without the consent of Congress, engage in war, unless actually invaded, or in such imminent	1	10	3
Day on which they shall vote for President and Vice President, which shall be the same throughout the United States. Congress may determine the time of choosing the electors, and the	2	1	3
Day to day, and may be authorized to compel the attendance of absent members. A smaller number than a quorum of each House may adjourn from	1	5	1
Death, resignation, or inability of the President, the powers and duties of his office shall devolve on the Vice President. In case of the	2	1	5
[Amendments]	25		
Death, resignation, or inability of the President. Congress may provide by law for the case of the removal [Amendments]	2	1	5
[Amendments]	25		
Debt of the United States, including debts for pensions and bounties incurred in suppressing insurrection or rebellion, shall not be questioned. The validity of the public. [Amendments]	14	4	
Debts. No State shall make anything but gold and silver coin a tender in payment of	1	10	1
Debts and provide for the common defense and general welfare of the United States. Congress shall have power to pay the	1	8	1
Debts and engagements contracted before the adoption of this Constitution shall be as valid against the United States, under it, as under the Confederation	6		1
Debts or obligations incurred in aid of insurrection or rebellion against the United States, or claims for the loss or emancipation of any slave. Neither the Unit-			

† **Article of original Constitution or of Amendment.**

141

† **Article of original Constitution or of Amendment.**

† Article of original Constitution or of Amendment.

143

	Article †	Section	Clause
But Congress may, at any time, alter such regulations, except as to the places of choosing Senators	1	4	1
Returns and qualifications of its own members. Each House shall be the judge of the............	1	5	1
Senators elected by the people. [Amendments]....	17	1	....
Election of Representatives shall have intervened. No law, varying the compensation for the services of Senators and Representatives, shall take effect, until an. [Amendments]	27	....	....
Electors for members of the House of Representatives. Qualifications of	1	2	1
Electors for Senators. Qualifications of. [Amendments]..	17	1	....
Electors for President and Vice President. Each State shall appoint, in such manner as the legislature thereof may direct, a number of electors equal to the whole number of Senators and Representatives to which the State may be entitled in the Congress	2	1	2
But no Senator or Representative, or person holding an office of trust or profit under the United States, shall be appointed an elector	2	1	2
Congress may determine the time of choosing the electors and the day on which they shall give their votes	2	1	3
Which day shall be the same throughout the United States	2	1	3
The electors shall meet in their respective States and vote by ballot for President and Vice President, one of whom, at least, shall not be an inhabitant of the same State with themselves. [Amendments]	12	....	....
District of Columbia to appoint, in such manner as the Congress may direct, a number of electors equal to the whole number of Senators and Representatives to which the District would be entitled if it were a State. [Amendments]	23	1	....
Electors shall name, in their ballots, the person voted for as President; and in distinct ballots the person voted for as Vice President. [Amendments].........	12	....	....
They shall make distinct lists of the persons voted for as President and of persons voted for as Vice President, which they shall sign and certify, and transmit sealed to the seat of government, directed to the President of the Senate. [Amendments]..	12	....	....
No person having taken an oath as a legislative, executive or judicial officer of the United States, or of any State, and afterwards engaged in insurrection or rebellion against the United States, shall be an elector	14	3	....
But Congress may, by a vote of two-thirds of each House remove such disability. [Amendments]	14	3	....
Emancipation of any slave shall be held to be illegal and void. Claims for the loss or. [Amendments]........	14	4	....
Emit bills of credit. No State shall	1	10	1
Emolument of any kind from any king, prince, or foreign state, without the consent of Congress. No person holding any office under the United States shall accept any	1	9	8
Enemies. Treason shall consist in levying war against the United States, in adhering to, or giving aid and comfort to their	3	3	1
Engagements contracted before the adoption of this Constitution shall be valid. All debts and.......	6	....	1

† Article of original Constitution or of Amendment.

	Article †	Section	Clause
Enumeration of the inhabitants shall be made within three years after the first meeting of Congress, and within every subsequent term of ten years thereafter	1	2	3
Ratio of representation not to exceed one for every 30,000 until the first enumeration shall be made	1	2	3
Income tax authorized without regard to. [Amendments]	16	....	....
Enumeration in the Constitution of certain rights shall not be construed to deny or disparage others retained by the people. The. [Amendments]	9	....	....
Equal protection of the laws. No State shall deny to any person within its jurisdiction the. [Amendments]	14	1	....
Equal suffrage in the Senate. No State shall be deprived without its consent, of its	5	....	....
Establishment of this Constitution between the States ratifying the same. The ratification of nine States shall be sufficient for the	7	....	....
Excessive bail shall not be required, nor excessive fines imposed, nor cruel and unusual punishments inflicted. [Amendments]	8	....	....
Excises. Congress shall have power to lay and collect taxes, duties, imposts, and	1	8	1
Shall be uniform throughout the United States. All duties, imposts, and	1	8	1
Exclusive legislation, in all cases, over such district as may become the seat of government. Congress shall exercise	1	8	17
Over all places purchased for the erection of forts, magazines, arsenals, dockyards, and other needful buildings. Congress shall exercise	1	8	17
Executive of a State. The United States shall protect each State against invasion and domestic violence, on the application of the legislature or the	4	4	....
Executive and judicial officers of the United States and of the several States shall be bound by an oath to support the Constitution	6	....	3
Executive departments. On subjects relating to their duties the President may require the written opinions of the principal officers in each of the	2	2	1
Congress may by law vest the appointment of inferior officers in the heads of	2	2	2
Executive power shall by vested in a President of the United States of America. The	2	1	1
Expel a member. Each House, with the concurrence of two-thirds, may	1	5	2
Expenditures of public money shall be published from time to time. A regular statement of the receipts and	1	9	7
Exportations from any State. No tax or duty shall be laid on	1	9	5
Exports or imports, except upon certain conditions. No State shall, without the consent of Congress, lay any duties on	1	10	2
Laid by any State, shall be for the use of the Treasury. The net produce of all duties on	1	10	2
Shall be subject to the revision and control of Congress. All laws of the States laying duties on	1	10	2
Ex post facto law shall be passed. No bill of attainder or	1	9	3
Ex post facto law, or law impairing the obligation of contracts. No State shall pass any bill of attainder	1	10	1
Extraordinary occasions. The President may convene both houses, or either House of Congress, on	2	3	....

† **Article of original Constitution or of Amendment.**

† **Article of original Constitution or of Amendment.**

	Article †	Section	Clause
Except in cases arising in the land and naval forces, and in the militia when in actual service. [Amendments]	5		
Guarantee to every State in this Union a republican form of government. The United States shall	4	4	
And shall protect each of them against invasion; and on application of the legislature or of the executive (when the legislature cannot be convened), against domestic violence	4	4	

H

	Article †	Section	Clause
Habeas corpus shall not be suspended unless in cases of rebellion or invasion. The writ of	1	9	2
Heads of departments. Congress may, by law, vest the appointment of inferior officers in the	2	2	2
On any subject relating to their duties, the President may require the written opinion of the principal officer in each of the executive departments	2	2	1
High crimes and misdemeanors. The President, Vice President, and all civil officers shall be removed on impeachment for and conviction of treason, bribery, or other	2	4	
House of Representatives. Congress shall consist of a Senate and	1	1	
Shall be composed of members chosen every second year	1	2	1
Qualifications of electors for members of the	1	2	1
No person shall be a member who shall not have attained the age of twenty-five years, and been seven years a citizen of the United States	1	2	2
The executives of the several States shall issue writs of election to fill vacancies in the	1	2	4
Shall choose their Speaker and other officers	1	2	5
Shall have the sole power of impeachment	1	2	5
Shall be the judge of the elections, returns, and qualifications of its own members	1	5	1
A majority shall constitute a quorum to do business	1	5	1
Less than a majority may adjourn from day to day, and compel the attendance of absent members	1	5	1
May determine its own rules of proceedings	1	5	2
May punish its members for disorderly behavior, and, with the concurrence of two-thirds, expel a member	1	5	2
Shall keep a journal of its proceedings	1	5	3
Shall not adjourn for more than three days during the session of Congress without the consent of the Senate	1	5	4
Members shall not be questioned for any speech or debate in either House or in any other place	1	6	1
No person holding any office under the United States shall, while holding such office, be a member, of the	1	6	2
No person, while a member of either House, shall be appointed to an office which shall have been created or the emoluments increased during his membership	1	6	2
All bills for raising revenue shall originate in the	1	7	1
The votes for President and Vice President shall be counted in the presence of the Senate and. [Amendments]	12		
If no person have a majority of electoral votes, then from the three highest on the list the House of			

† **Article of original Constitution or of Amendment.**

	Article †	Section	Clause
Representatives shall immediately, by ballot, choose a President. [Amendments]	12	....	
They shall vote by States, each State counting one vote. [Amendments]............................	12	....	
A quorum shall consist of a member or members from two-thirds of the States, and a majority of all the States shall be necessary to the choice of a President. [Amendments].......................	12	....	
No person having as a legislative, executive, or judicial officer of the United States, or of any State, taken an oath to support the Constitution, and afterwards engaged in insurrection or rebellion against the United States, shall be a member of the. [Amendments]	14	3	....
But Congress may, by a vote of two-thirds of each House, remove such disability. [Amendments]	14	3	....

I

	Article †	Section	Clause
Imminent danger as will not admit of delay. No State shall, without the consent of Congress, engage in war, unless actually invaded or in such	1	10	3
Immunities. Members of Congress shall, in all cases except treason, felony, and breach of the peace, be privileged from arrest during their attendance at the session of their respective houses, and in going and returning from the same	1	6	1
No soldier shall be quartered in any house without the consent of the owner in time of peace. [Amendments]	3	....	....
Immunities. No person shall be twice put in jeopardy of life and limb for the same offense. [Amendments]	5	....	
All persons born or naturalized in the United States, and subject to the jurisdiction thereof, are citizens of the United States and of the State in which they reside. [Amendments]	14	1	....
No State shall make or enforce any law which shall abridge the privileges or immunities of citizens of the United States. [Amendments]	14	1	....
Nor shall any State deprive any person of life, liberty, or property without due process of law. [Amendments]	14	1	....
Nor deny to any person within its jurisdiction the equal protection of the law. [Amendments]	14	1	....
Impeachment. The President may grant reprieves and pardons except in cases of	2	2	1
The House of Representatives shall have the sole power of	1	2	5
Impeachment for and conviction of treason, bribery, and other high crimes and misdemeanors. The President, Vice President, and all civil officers shall be removed upon	2	4	....
Impeachments. The Senate shall have the sole power to try all	1	3	6
The Senate shall be on oath, or affirmation, when sitting for the trial of............................	1	3	6
When the President of the United States is tried the Chief Justice shall preside..................	1	3	6
No person shall be convicted without the concurrence of two-thirds of the members present	1	3	6
Judgment shall not extend beyond removal from office and disqualification to hold office	1	3	7
But the party convicted shall be liable to indictment and punishment according to law	1	3	7

† **Article of original Constitution or of Amendment.**

	Article [†]	Section	Clause
Importation of slaves prior to 1808 shall not be prohibited by the Congress	1	9	1
But a tax or duty of ten dollars for each person may be imposed on such	1	9	1
Imports or exports except what may be absolutely necessary for executing its inspection laws. No State shall, without the consent of Congress, lay any imposts or duties on	1	10	2
Imports or exports laid by any State shall be for the use of the Treasury. The net produce of all duties on	1	10	2
Imports or exports shall be subject to the revision and control of Congress. All laws of States laying duties on	1	10	2
Imposts and excises. Congress shall have power to lay and collect taxes, duties	1	8	1
Shall be uniform throughout the United States. All taxes, duties	1	8	1
Inability of the President, the powers and duties of his office shall devolve on the Vice President. In case of the death, resignation, or	2	1	5
[Amendments]	25		
Inability of the President or Vice President. Congress may provide by law for the case of the removal, death, resignation, or	2	1	5
[Amendments]	25		
Income taxes. Congress shall have power to lay and collect without apportionment among the several States, and without regard to any census or enumeration. [Amendments]	16		
Indian tribes. Congress shall have power to regulate commerce with the	1	8	3
Indictment or presentment of a grand jury. No person shall be held to answer for a capital or infamous crime unless on. [Amendments]	5		
Except in cases arising in the land and naval forces, and in the militia when in actual service. [Amendments]	5		
Indictment, trial, judgment, and punishment, according to law. The party convicted in case of impeachment shall nevertheless be liable and subject to	1	3	7
Infamous crime unless on presentment or indictment of a grand jury. No person shall be held to answer for a capital or. [Amendments]	5		
Inferior courts. Congress shall have power to constitute tribunals inferior to the Supreme Court	1	8	9
Inferior courts as Congress may establish. The judicial power of the United States shall be vested in one Supreme Court and such	3	1	
The judges of both the Supreme and inferior courts shall hold their offices during good behavior	3	1	
Their compensation shall not be diminished during their continuance in office	3	1	
Inferior officers in the courts of law, in the President alone, or in the heads of Departments. Congress, if they think proper, may by law vest the appointment of	2	2	2
Inhabitant of the State for which he shall be chosen. No person shall be a Senator who shall not have attained the age of thirty years, been nine years a citizen of the United States, and who shall not, when elected, be an	1	3	3
Insurrection or rebellion against the United States. No person shall be a Senator or Representative in Congress, or presidential elector, or hold any office, civil			

† **Article of original Constitution or of Amendment.**

† **Article of original Constitution or of Amendment.**

	Article [†]	Section	Clause
It shall extend to all cases in law and equity arising under the Constitution, laws, and treaties of the United States	3	2	1
To all cases affecting ambassadors, other public ministers, and consuls...........................	3	2	1
To all cases of admiralty and maritime jurisdiction	3	2	1
To controversies to which the United States shall be a party..	3	2	1
To controversies between two or more States	3	2	1
To controversies between a State and citizens of another State	3	2	1
To controversies between citizens of different States	3	2	1
To citizens of the same State claiming lands under grants of different States	3	2	1
To controversies between a State or its citizens and foreign states, citizens, or subjects..............	3	2	1
In all cases affecting ambassadors, other public ministers and consuls, and those in which a State shall be a party, the Supreme Court shall have original jurisdiction	3	2	2
In all other cases before mentioned, it shall have appellate jurisdiction, both as to law and fact, with such exceptions and under such regulations as Congress shall make......................	3	2	2
The trial of all crimes, except in cases of impeachment, shall be by jury	3	2	3
The trial shall be held in the State where the crimes shall have been committed	3	2	3
But when not committed in a State, the trial shall be at such place or places as Congress may by law have directed	3	2	3
The judicial power of the United States shall not be held to extend to any suit in law or equity commenced or prosecuted against one of the United States by citizens of another State, or by citizens or subjects of any foreign State. [Amendments]	11	....	....
Judicial proceedings of every other State. Full faith and credit shall be given in each State to the acts, records, and..	4	1	....
Congress shall prescribe the manner of proving such acts, records, and proceedings	4	1	....
Judicial and executive officers of the United States and of the several States shall be bound by an oath to support the Constitution	6	....	3
Judiciary. The Supreme Court shall have original jurisdiction in all cases affecting ambassadors, other public ministers and consuls, and those in which a State may be a party...............................	3	2	2
The Supreme Court shall have appellate jurisdiction both as to law and fact, with such exceptions and regulations as Congress may make	3	2	2
Junction of two or more States or parts of States without the consent of the legislatures and of Congress. No State shall be formed by the	4	3	1
Jurisdiction of another State. No new State shall, without the consent of Congress, be formed or erected within the......................................	4	3	1
Jurisdiction, both as to law and fact, with such exceptions and under such regulations as Congress may make. The Supreme Court shall have appellate	3	2	2
Jurisdiction. In all cases affecting ambassadors and other public ministers and consuls, and in cases			

† Article of original Constitution or of Amendment.

† **Article of original Constitution or of Amendment.**

	Article †	Section	Clause
Legislature, or the Executive (when the legislature cannot be convened). The United States shall protect each State against invasion and domestic violence, on the application of the	4	4	
Legislatures of two-thirds of the States, Congress shall call a convention for proposing amendments to the Constitution. On the application of the	5		
Letters of marque and reprisal. Congress shall have power to grant	1	8	11
No State shall grant	1	10	1
Liberty to ourselves and our posterity, &c. To secure the blessings of. [Preamble]			
Life, liberty, and property without due process of law. No person shall be compelled in any criminal case to be a witness against himself, nor be deprived of. [Amendments]	5		
No State shall abridge the privileges or immunities of citizens of the United States, nor deprive any person of. [Amendments]	14	1	
Life or limb for the same offense. No person shall be twice put in jeopardy of. [Amendments]	5		
Loss or emancipation of any slave shall be held illegal and void. Claims for the. [Amendments]	14	4	

M

	Article †	Section	Clause
Magazines, arsenals, dock-yards, and other needful buildings. Congress shall have exclusive authority over all places purchased for the erection of	1	8	17
Majority of each House shall constitute a quorum to do business. A	1	5	1
But a smaller number may adjourn from day to day and may be authorized to compel the attendance of absent members	1	5	1
Majority of all the States shall be necessary to a choice. When the choice of a President shall devolve on the House of Representatives, a quorum shall consist of a member or members from two-thirds of the States; but a. [Amendments]	12		
When the choice of a Vice President shall devolve on the Senate, a quorum shall consist of two-thirds of the whole number of Senators, and a majority of the whole number shall be necessary to a choice. [Amendments]	12		
Maritime jurisdiction. The judicial power shall extend to all cases of admiralty and	3	2	1
Marque and reprisal. Congress shall have power to grant letters of	1	8	11
No State shall grant any letters of	1	10	1
Maryland entitled to six Representatives in the first Congress	1	2	3
Massachusetts entitled to eight Representatives in the first Congress	1	2	3
Measures. Congress shall fix the standard of weights and	1	8	5
Meeting of Congress. The Congress shall assemble at least once in every year, and such meeting shall be on the first Monday in December, unless they shall by law appoint a different day	1	4	2
Meeting of electors. District of Columbia, electors for President and Vice–President appointed by District. [Amendments]	23	1	

† **Article of original Constitution or of Amendment.**

153

	Article [†]	Section	Clause
Members of Congress and of State legislatures shall be bound by oath or affirmation to support the Constitution	6		3
Militia to execute the laws, suppress insurrections, and repel invasions. Congress shall provide for calling forth the	1	8	15
Congress shall provide for organizing, arming, and disciplining the	1	8	16
Militia to execute the laws, suppress insurrections, and repel invasions. Congress shall provide for governing such part of them as may be employed by the United States	1	8	16
Reserving to the States the appointment of the officers and the right to train the militia according to the discipline prescribed by Congress	1	8	16
A well-regulated militia being necessary to the security of a free State, the right of the people to keep and bear arms shall not be infringed. [Amendments]	2		
Misdemeanors. The President, Vice President, and all civil officers shall be removed on impeachment for and conviction of treason, bribery, or other high crimes and	2	4	
Money on the credit of the United States. Congress shall have the power to borrow	1	8	2
Regulate the value thereof and of foreign coin. Congress shall have power to coin	1	8	5
Shall be drawn from the Treasury but in consequence of appropriations made by law. No	1	9	7
Shall be published from time to time. A regular statement and account of receipts and expenditures of public	1	9	7
For raising and supporting armies. No appropriation of money shall be for a longer term than two years	1	8	12

N

	Article [†]	Section	Clause
Nations. Congress shall have power to regulate commerce with foreign	1	8	3
Congress shall provide for punishing offenses against the law of	1	8	10
Natural-born citizen, or a citizen at the adoption of the Constitution, shall be eligible to the office of President. No person except a	2	1	4
Naturalization. Congress shall have power to establish a uniform rule of	1	8	4
Naturalized in the United States, and subject to their jurisdiction, shall be citizens of the United States and of the States in which they reside. All persons born, or. [Amendments]	14	1	
Naval forces. Congress shall make rules and regulations for the government and regulation of the land and	1	8	14
Navy. Congress shall have power to provide and maintain a	1	8	13
New Hampshire entitled to three Representatives in the first Congress	1	2	3
New Jersey entitled to four Representatives in the first Congress	1	2	3
New States may be admitted by Congress into this Union	4	3	1

† **Article of original Constitution or of Amendment.**

† **Article of original Constitution or of Amendment.**

† **Article of original Constitution or of Amendment.**

	Article [†]	Section	Clause
Pennsylvania entitled to eight Representatives in the first Congress	1	2	3
People, peaceably to assemble and petition for redress of grievances, shall not be abridged by Congress. The right of the. [Amendments]	1	....	....
To keep and bear arms shall not be infringed. A well-regulated militia being necessary to the security of a free State, the right of the. [Amendments]..	2	....	....
To be secure in their persons, houses, papers, and effects, against unreasonable searches and seizures shall not be violated. The right of the. [Amendments]	4	....	....
People. The enumeration of certain rights in the Constitution shall not be held to deny or disparage others retained by the. [Amendments]	9	....	....
People. Powers not delegated to the United States, nor prohibited to the States, are reserved to the States or to the. [Amendments]	10	....	....
Perfect Union, &c. To establish a more. [Preamble]..	....	....	....
Persons, houses, papers, and effects against unreasonable searches and seizures. The people shall be secure in their. [Amendments].....................	4	....	....
Persons, as any State may think proper to admit, shall not be prohibited prior to 1808. The migration or importation of such	1	9	1
But a tax or duty of ten dollars shall be imposed on the importation of each of such	1	9	1
Petition for the redress of grievances. Congress shall make no law abridging the right of the people peaceably to assemble and to. [Amendments]	1	....	....
Piracies and felonies committed on the high seas. Congress shall define and punish	1	8	10
Place than that in which the two Houses shall be sitting. Neither House during the session shall, without the consent of the other, adjourn for more than three days, nor to any other....................	1	5	4
Places of choosing Senators. Congress may by law make or alter regulations for the election of Senators and Representatives, except as to the	1	4	1
Poll tax. The right of citizens of the United States to vote shall not be denied or abridged by the United States or any State by reason of failure to pay. [Amendments]	24	1	....
Ports of one State over those of another. Preference shall not be given by any regulation of commerce or revenue to the......................................	1	9	6
Vessels clearing from the ports of one State shall not pay duties in another	1	9	6
Post offices and post roads. Congress shall establish...	1	8	7
Powers herein granted shall be vested in Congress. All legislative......................................	1	1	....
Powers vested by the Constitution in the Government or in any Department or officer of the United States. Congress shall make all laws necessary to carry into execution the...	1	8	18
Powers and duties of the office shall devolve on the Vice President, on the removal, death, resignation, or inability of the President. The	2	1	5
[Amendments]	25	....	....
Powers not delegated to the United States nor prohibited to the States are reserved to the States and to the people. [Amendments].............................	10	....	....

† Article of original Constitution or of Amendment.

	Article †	Section	Clause
The enumeration of certain rights in this Constitution shall not be held to deny or disparage others retained by the people. [Amendments]	9	....	....
Preference, by any regulation of commerce or revenue, shall not be given to the ports of one State over those of another..	1	9	6
Prejudice any claims of the United States or of any particular State in the territory or property of the United States. Nothing in this Constitution shall	4	3	2
Present, emolument, office, or title of any kind whatever from any king, prince, or foreign State. No person holding any office under the United States shall, without the consent of Congress, accept any	1	9	8
Presentment or indictment of a grand jury, except in cases arising in the land or naval forces, or in the militia when in actual service. No person shall be held to answer for a capital or otherwise infamous crime unless on a. [Amendments]	5	....	....
President of the United States. The Senate shall choose a President pro tempore when the Vice President shall exercise the office of	1	3	5
Additional provision for succession through act of Congress. [Amendments]	20	4	....
Succession in case of death. [Amendments]	20	3	....
Succession in case of failure to be chosen or qualified. [Amendments]	20	3	....
Term of office, beginning and ending. [Amendments]...	20	1	....
The Chief Justice shall preside upon the trial of the	1	3	6
Shall approve and sign all bills passed by Congress before they shall become laws....................	1	7	2
Shall return to the House in which it originated, with his objections, any bill which he shall not approve......................................	1	7	2
If not returned within ten days (Sundays excepted), it shall become a law, unless Congress shall adjourn before the expiration of that time	1	7	2
Every order, resolution, or vote which requires the concurrence of both Houses, except on a question of adjournment, shall be presented to the	1	7	3
If disapproved by him, shall be returned and proceeded on as in the case of a bill..................	1	7	3
The executive power shall be vested in a	2	1	1
He shall hold his office during the term of four years	2	1	1
In case of the removal of the President from office, or of his death, resignation, or inability to discharge the duties of his office, the Vice President shall perform the duties of.....................	2	1	5
[Amendments]	25	....	....
Congress may declare by law, in the case of the removal, death, resignation, or inability of the President, what officer shall act as	2	1	6
[Amendments]	25	....	....
The President shall receive a compensation which shall not be increased nor diminished during his term, nor shall he receive any other emolument from the United States	2	1	6
Before he enters upon the execution of his office he shall take an oath of office	2	1	7
Shall be commander in chief of the Army and Navy and of the militia of the States when called into actual service	2	2	1

† **Article of original Constitution or of Amendment.**

	Article †	Section	Clause
He may require the opinion, in writing, of the principal officer in each of the Executive Departments	2	2	1
He may grant reprieves or pardons for offenses, except in cases of impeachment	2	2	1
He may make treaties by and with the advice and consent of the Senate, two-thirds of the Senators present concurring	2	2	2
He may appoint, by and with the advice and consent of the Senate, ambassadors, other public ministers and consuls, judges of the Supreme Court, and all other officers whose appointments may be authorized by law and not herein provided for	2	2	2
Congress may vest the appointment of inferior officers in the	2	2	2
He may fill up all vacancies that may happen in the recess of the Senate by commissions which shall expire at the end of their next session	2	2	3
He shall give information to Congress of the state of the Union, and recommend measures	2	3	....
On extraordinary occasions he may convene both Houses or either	2	3	....
In case of disagreement between the two Houses as to the time of adjournment, he may adjourn them to such time as he may think proper	2	3	....
He shall receive ambassadors and other public ministers	2	3	....
He shall take care that the laws be faithfully executed	2	3	....
He shall commission all the officers of the United States	2	3	....
On impeachment for, and conviction of, treason, bribery, or other high crimes and misdemeanors, shall be removed from office. The	2	4	....
No person except a natural-born citizen, or a citizen of the United States at the adoption of the Constitution, shall be eligible to the office of	2	1	4
No person shall be elected to office more than twice. [Amendments]	22	....	....
No person who shall not have attained the age of thirty-five years and been fourteen years a resident of the United States shall be eligible to the office of	2	1	4
President and Vice President. Manner of choosing. Each State by its legislature, shall appoint a number of electors equal to the whole number of Senators and Representatives to which the State may be entitled in the Congress	2	1	2
No Senator or Representative or person holding an office of trust or profit under the United States shall be an elector	2	1	2
Congress may determine the time of choosing the electors and the day on which they shall give their votes, which day shall be the same throughout the United States	2	1	3
The electors shall meet in their respective States and vote by ballot for President and Vice President, one of whom, at least, shall not be an inhabitant of the same State with themselves. [Amendments]	12	....	....
They shall name in distinct ballots the person voted for as President and the person voted for as Vice President. [Amendments]	12	....	....

† Article of original Constitution or of Amendment.

159

	Article †	Section	Clause
They shall make distinct lists of the persons voted for as President and as Vice President, which they shall sign and certify and transmit sealed to the President of the Senate at the seat of government. [Amendments]	12		
The President of the Senate shall, in the presence of the Senate and House of Representatives, open all the certificates, and the votes shall then be counted. [Amendments]	12		
The person having the greatest number of votes shall be the President, if such number be a majority of the whole number of electors appointed. [Amendments]	12		
If no person have such majority, then from the persons having the highest numbers, not exceeding three, on the list of those voted for as President, the House of Representatives shall choose immediately, by ballot, the President. [Amendments]	12		
In choosing the President, the votes shall be taken by States, the representation from each State having one vote. [Amendments]	12		
A quorum for this purpose shall consist of a member or members from two-thirds of the States, and a majority of all the States shall be necessary to a choice. [Amendments]	12		
But if no choice shall be made before the 4th of March next following, then the Vice President shall act as President, as in the case of the death or disability of the President. [Amendments]	12		
District of Columbia shall appoint a number of electors equal to the whole number of Senators and Representatives in Congress which the District would be entitled to if it were a State. [Amendments]	23	1	
President of the Senate, but shall have no vote unless the Senate be equally divided. The Vice President shall be	1	3	4
President pro tempore. In the absence of the Vice President the Senate shall choose a	1	3	5
When the Vice President shall exercise the office of President of the United States, the Senate shall choose a	1	3	5
Press. Congress shall pass no law abridging the freedom of speech or of the. [Amendments]	1		
Previous condition of servitude. The right of citizens of the United States to vote shall not be denied or abridged by the United States, or by any State on account of race, color, or. [Amendments]	15	1	
Primary elections. The right of citizens of the United States to vote in shall not be denied or abridged by the United States or any State by reason of failure to pay any poll tax or other tax. [Amendments]	24	1	
Private property shall not be taken for public use without just compensation. [Amendments]	5		
Privilege. Senators and Representatives shall, in all cases except treason, felony, and breach of the peace, be privileged from arrest during their attendance at the session of their respective Houses, and in going to and returning from the same	1	6	1
They shall not be questioned for any speech or debate in either House or in any other place	1	6	1
Privileges and immunities of citizens of the United States. The citizens of each State shall be entitled to			

† **Article of original Constitution or of Amendment.**

	Article †	Section	Clause
all the privileges and immunities of the citizens of the several States	4	2	1
No soldier shall be quartered in any house without the consent of the owner in time of peace. [Amendments]	3	....	....
No person shall be twice put in jeopardy of life or limb for the same offense. [Amendments]	5	....	....
All persons born or naturalized in the United States, and subject to the jurisdiction thereof, are citizens of the United States and of the State in which they reside. [Amendments]	14	1	....
No State shall make or enforce any law which shall abridge the privileges or immunities of citizens of the United States. [Amendments]	14	1	....
No State shall deprive any person of life, liberty, or property without due process of law. [Amendments]..	14	1	....
Nor deny to any person within its jurisdiction the equal protection of its laws. [Amendments].....	14	1	....
Prizes captured on land or water. Congress shall make rules concerning....................................	1	8	11
Probable cause. The right of the people to be secure in their persons, houses, papers, and effects, against unreasonable searches and seizures, shall not be violated. And no warrant shall issue for such but upon. [Amendments]	4	....	....
Process of law. No person shall be compelled in any criminal case to be a witness against himself, nor be deprived of life, liberty, or property, without due. [Amendments]	5	....	....
No State shall deprive any person of life, liberty, or property, without due. [Amendments]	14	1	....
Process for obtaining witnesses in his favor. In all criminal prosecutions the accused shall have. [Amendments]	6	....	....
Progress of science and useful arts. Congress shall have power to promote the	1	8	8
Property of the United States. Congress may dispose of and make all needful rules and regulations respecting the territory or................................	4	3	2
Property, without due process of law. No person shall be compelled in any criminal case to be a witness against himself; nor shall he be deprived of his life, liberty, or. [Amendments]	5	....	....
No State shall abridge the privileges or immunities of citizens of the United States; nor deprive any person of his life, liberty, or. [Amendments]	14	1	....
Prosecutions. The accused shall have a speedy and public trial in all criminal. [Amendments]..........	6	....	....
He shall be tried by a jury in the State or district where the crime was committed. [Amendments]	6	....	....
He shall be informed of the nature and cause of the accusation. [Amendments]....................	6	....	....
He shall be confronted with the witnesses against him. [Amendments]............................	6	....	....
He shall have compulsory process for obtaining witnesses. [Amendments]......................	6	....	....
He shall have counsel for his defense. [Amendments]..	6	....	....
Protection of the laws. No State shall deny to any person within its jurisdiction the equal. [Amendments]..	14	1	....

† Article of original Constitution or of Amendment.

† **Article of original Constitution or of Amendment.**

	Article [†]	Section	Clause
Quorum to elect a Vice President by the Senate. Two-thirds of the whole number of Senators shall be a. [Amendments]	12		
A majority of the whole number shall be necessary to a choice. [Amendments]	12		

R

	Article [†]	Section	Clause
Race, color, or previous condition of servitude. The right of citizens of the United States to vote shall not be denied or abridged by the United States or by any State on account of. [Amendments]	15	1	
Ratification of amendments to the Constitution shall be by the legislatures of three-fourths of the several States or by conventions in three-fourths of the States, accordingly as Congress may propose	5		
Ratification of the conventions of nine States shall be sufficient to establish the Constitution between the States so ratifying the same	7		
Ratio of representation until the first enumeration under the Constitution shall be made not to exceed one for every thirty thousand	1	2	3
Ratio of representation shall be apportioned among the several States according to their respective numbers, counting the whole number of persons in each State, excluding Indians not taxed. [Amendments]	14	2	
But when the right to vote for Presidential electors or members of Congress, or the legislative, executive, and judicial officers of the State, except for engaging in rebellion or other crime, shall be denied or abridged by a State, the basis of representation shall be reduced therein in the proportion of such denial or abridgement of the right to vote. [Amendments]	14	2	
Rebellion against the United States. Persons who, while holding certain Federal and State offices, took an oath to support the Constitution, afterward engaged in insurrection or rebellion, disabled from holding office under the United States. [Amendments]	14	3	
But Congress may by a vote of two-thirds of each House remove such disability. [Amendments]	14	3	
Rebellion against the United States. Debts incurred for pensions and bounties for services in suppressing the rebellion shall not be questioned. [Amendments]	14	4	
All debts and obligations incurred in aid of the rebellion, and all claims for the loss or emancipation of slaves, declared and held to be illegal and void. [Amendments]	14	4	
Rebellion or invasion. The writ of habeas corpus shall not be suspended except when the public safety may require it in cases of	1	9	2
Receipts and expenditures of all public money shall be published from time to time. A regular statement of	1	9	7
Recess of the Senate. The President may grant commissions, which shall expire at the end of the next session, to fill vacancies that may happen during the	2	2	3
Reconsideration of a bill returned by the President with his objections. Proceedings to be had upon the	1	7	2
Records, and judicial proceedings of every other State. Full faith and credit shall be given in each State to the acts	4	1	
Congress shall prescribe the manner of proving such acts, records, and proceedings	4	1	

† Article of original Constitution or of Amendment.

	Article †	Section	Clause
Redress of grievances. Congress shall make no law abridging the right of the people peaceably to assemble and to petition for the. [Amendments]	1		
Regulations, except as to the places of choosing Senators. The time, places, and manner of holding elections for Senators and Representatives shall be prescribed by the legislatures of the States, but Congress may at any time by law make or alter such	1	4	1
Regulations of commerce or revenue. Preference to the ports of one State over those of another shall not be given by any	1	9	6
Religion or prohibiting the free exercise thereof. Congress shall make no law respecting the establishment of. [Amendments]	1		
Religious tests shall ever be required as a qualification for any office or public trust under the United States. No	6		3
Removal of the President from office, the same shall devolve on the Vice President. In case of the	2	1	5
[Amendments]	25		
Representation. No State, without its consent, shall be deprived of its equal suffrage in the Senate	5		
Representation and direct taxation, how apportioned among the several States	1	2	3
Representation until the first enumeration under the Constitution not to exceed one for every thirty thousand. The ratio of	1	2	3
Representation in any State. The executive thereof shall issue writs of election to fill vacancies in the	1	2	4
Representation among the several States shall be according to their respective numbers, counting the whole number of persons in each State, excluding Indians not taxed. The ratio of. [Amendments]	14	2	
But where the right to vote in certain Federal and State elections is abridged for any cause other than rebellion or other crime, the basis of representation shall be reduced. [Amendments]	14	2	
Representatives. Congress shall consist of a Senate and House of	1	1	
Compensation of [Amendments]	27		
Qualifications of electors of members of the House of	1	2	1
No person shall be a Representative who shall not have attained the age of twenty-five years, been seven years a citizen of the United States, and an inhabitant of the State in which he shall be chosen	1	2	2
And direct taxes, how apportioned among the several States	1	2	3
Executives of the States shall issue writs of election to fill vacancies in the House of	1	2	4
Shall choose their Speaker and other officers. The House of	1	2	5
Shall have the sole power of impeachment. The House of	1	2	5
The times, places, and manner of choosing Representatives shall be prescribed by the legislatures of the States	1	4	1
But Congress may make by law at any time or alter such regulations except as to the places of choosing Senators	1	4	1
And Senators shall receive a compensation, to be ascertained by law	1	6	1

† **Article of original Constitution or of Amendment.**

164

	Article [†]	Section	Clause
Shall in all cases, except treason, felony, and breach of the peace, be privileged from arrest during attendance at the session of the House, and in going to and returning from the same	1	6	1
Shall not be questioned in any other place for any speech or debate. Members of the House of	1	6	1
No member shall be appointed during his term to any civil office which shall have been created, or the emoluments of which shall have been increased, during such term	1	6	2
No person holding any office under the United States shall, while holding such office, be a member of the House of............................	1	6	2
All bills for raising revenue shall originate in the House of	1	7	1
No Senator or Representative shall be an elector for President or Vice President.................	2	1	2
Representatives shall be bound by an oath or affirmation to support the Constitution of the United States. The Senators and	6		3
Representatives among the several States. Provisions relative to the apportionment of. [Amendments]	14	2	....
Representatives and Senators. Prescribing certain disqualifications for office as. [Amendments]	14	3	....
But Congress may, by a vote of two-thirds of each House, remove such disqualification. [Amendments]..	14	3	....
Representatives and Senators. No law varying compensation for services of. [Amendments]...............	27	....	....
Reprieves and pardons except in cases of impeachment. The President may grant	2	2	1
Reprisal. Congress shall have power to grant letters of marque and	1	8	11
No State shall grant any letters of marque and	1	10	1
Republican form of government. The United States shall guarantee to every State in this Union a	4	4	....
Republican form of government. And shall protect each of them against invasion; and on the application of the legislature, or of the executive (when the legislature cannot be convened), against domestic violence	4	4	....
Reserved rights of the States and the people. The enumeration in the Constitution of certain rights shall not be construed to deny or disparage others retained by the people. [Amendments]	9	....	....
The powers not delegated to the United States by the Constitution, nor prohibited by it to the States, are reserved to the States respectively, or to the people. [Amendments]..................	10	....	....
Resignation, or inability of the President, the duties and powers of his office shall devolve on the Vice President. In case of the death	2	1	5
[Amendments]	25	....	....
Resignation, or inability of the President. Congress may by law provide for the case of the removal, death	2	1	5
[Amendments]	25	....	....
Resolution, or vote (except on a question of adjournment) requiring the concurrence of the two Houses shall before it becomes a law, be presented to the President. Every order	1	7	3
Revenue shall originate in the House of Representatives. All bills for raising	1	7	1

† **Article of original Constitution or of Amendment.**

165

† **Article of original Constitution or of Amendment.**

	Article †	Section	Clause
If vacancies happen during the recess of the legislature of a State, the executive thereof may make temporary appointments until the next meeting of the legislature...............................	1	3	2
When vacancies happen the executive authority of the State shall issue writs of election to fill such vacancies; provided, that the legislature of any State may empower the executive thereof to make temporary appointment until the people fill the vacancies by election as the legislature may direct. [Amendments]	17	2	....
The Vice President shall be President of the Senate, but shall have no vote unless the Senate be equally divided	1	3	4
The Senate shall choose their other officers, and also a President pro tempore in the absence of the Vice President or when he shall exercise the office of President	1	3	5
The Senate shall have the sole power to try all impeachments. When sitting for that purpose they shall be on oath or affirmation	1	3	6
When the President of the United States is tried the Chief Justice shall preside; and no person shall be convicted without the concurrence of two-thirds of the members present	1	3	6
It shall be the judge of the elections, returns, and qualifications of its own members	1	5	1
A majority shall constitute a quorum to do business, but a smaller number may adjourn from day to day, and may be authorized to compel the attendance of absent members	1	5	1
It may determine the rules of its proceedings, punish a member for disorderly behavior, and with the concurrence of two-thirds expel a member	1	5	2
It shall keep a journal of its proceedings and from time to time publish the same, except such parts as may in their judgment require secrecy	1	5	3
It shall not adjourn for more than three days during a session without the consent of the other House	1	5	4
It may propose amendments to bills for raising revenue, but such bills shall originate in the House of Representatives......................	1	7	1
The Senate shall advise and consent to the ratification of all treaties, provided two-thirds of the members present concur	2	2	2
It shall advise and consent to the appointment of ambassadors, other public ministers and consuls, judges of the Supreme Court, and all other officers not herein otherwise provided for	2	2	2
It may be convened by the President on extraordinary occasions................................	2	3	1
No State, without its consent, shall be deprived of its equal suffrage in the Senate	5	....	....
Senators. They shall, immediately after assembling, under their first election, be divided into three classes, so that the seats of one-third shall become vacant at the expiration of every second year	1	3	2
No person shall be a Senator who shall not be thirty years of age, nine years a citizen of the United States, and an inhabitant when elected of the State for which he shall be chosen	1	3	3
The times, places, and manner of choosing Senators may be fixed by the legislature of a State,			

† **Article of original Constitution or of Amendment.**

167

	Article †	Section	Clause
but Congress may by law make or alter such regulations, except as to the places of choosing	1	4	1
If vacancies happen during the recess of the legislature of a State, the executive thereof may make temporary appointments until the next meeting of the legislature.............................	1	3	2
If vacancies happen the executive authority of the State shall issue writs of election to fill such vacancies; provided, that the legislature of any State may empower the executive thereof to make temporary appointment until the people fill the vacancies by election as the legislature may direct. [Amendments]	17	2	....
They shall in all cases, except treason, felony, and breach of the peace, be privileged from arrest during their attendance at the session of the Senate and in going to and returning from the same	1	6	1
Senators and Representatives shall receive a compensation to be ascertained by law	1	6	1
Senators and Representatives. No law varying the compensation for services. [Amendments]......	27	....	....
Senators and Representatives shall not be questioned for any speech or debate in either House in any other place.............................	1	6	1
No Senator or Representative shall, during the time for which he was elected, be appointed to any civil office under the United States which shall have been created, or of which the emoluments shall have been increased, during such term...................................	1	6	2
No person holding any office under the United States shall be a member of either House during his continuance in office.......................	1	6	2
No Senator or Representative or person holding an office of trust or profit under the United States shall be an elector for President and Vice President.....................................	2	1	2
Senators and Representatives shall be bound by an oath or affirmation to support the Constitution	6	....	3
No person shall be a Senator or Representative who, having, as a Federal or State officer, taken an oath to support the Constitution, afterward engaged in rebellion against the United States. [Amendments]	14	3	....
But Congress may, by a vote of two-thirds of each House, remove such disability. [Amendments]	14	3	....
Service or labor in one State, escaping into another State, shall be delivered up to the party to whom such service or labor may be due. Fugitives from	4	2	3
Servitude, except as a punishment for crime, whereof the party shall have been duly convicted, shall exist in the United States or any place subject to their jurisdiction. Neither slavery nor involuntary. [Amendments]	13	1	....
Servitude. The right of citizens of the United States to vote shall not be denied or abridged by the United States or by any State, on account of race, color, or previous condition of. [Amendments]	15	1	....
Sex. Right of citizens to vote shall not be denied or abridged by the United States or any State on account of sex. [Amendments]	19	....	....
Ships of war in time of peace, without the consent of Congress. No State shall keep troops or	1	10	3

† **Article of original Constitution or of Amendment.**

	Article [†]	Section	Clause
Silver coin a tender in payment of debts. No State shall make anything but gold and	1	10	1
Slave. Neither the United States nor any State shall assume or pay any debt or obligation incurred in aid of insurrection or rebellion, or any claim for the loss or emancipation of any. [Amendments]	14	4	....
Slavery nor involuntary servitude, except as a punishment for crime, whereof the party shall have been duly convicted, shall exist in the United States, or any places subject to their jurisdiction. Neither. [Amendments]	13	1	....
Slavery. Representatives apportioned by adding to number of free persons, including those bound to service for a term of years, ... three-fifths of all other persons.	1	2	3
Slavery. A tax or duty may be imposed on such Importation of Persons	1	9	1
Soldiers shall not be quartered, in time of peace, in any house without the consent of the owner. [Amendments]......................................	3	....	....
South Carolina entitled to five Representatives in the first Congress	1	2	3
Speaker and other officers. The House of Representatives shall choose their	1	2	5
Speech or of the press. Congress shall make no law abridging the freedom of. [Amendments]...........	1	....	....
Speedy and public trial by a jury. In all criminal prosecutions the accused shall have a. [Amendments]..	6	....	....
Standard of weights and measures. Congress shall fix the...	1	8	5
State of the Union. The President shall, from time to time, give Congress information of the	2	3	....
State legislatures, and all executive and judicial officers of the United States, shall take an oath to support the Constitution. All members of the several	6	....	3
States. When vacancies happen in the representation from any State, the executive authority shall issue writs of election to fill such vacancies	1	2	4
When vacancies happen in the representation of any State in the Senate, the executive authority shall issue writs of election to fill vacancies. [Amendments]	17	2	....
Congress shall have power to regulate commerce among the several	1	8	3
No State shall enter into any treaty, alliance, or confederation.................................	1	10	1
Shall not grant letters of marque and reprisal	1	10	1
Shall not coin money............................	1	10	1
Shall not emit bills of credit	1	10	1
Shall not make anything but gold and silver coin a tender in payment of debts	1	10	1
Shall not pass any bill of attainder, ex post facto law, or law impairing the obligation of contracts	1	10	1
Shall not grant any title of nobility	1	10	1
Shall not, without the consent of Congress, lay any duties on imports or exports, except what may be absolutely necessary for executing its inspection laws	1	10	2
Shall not, without the consent of Congress, lay any duty of tonnage, keep troops or ships of war in time of peace, enter into any agreement or compact with another State or with a foreign power,			

† **Article of original Constitution or of Amendment.**

169

	Article †	Section	Clause
or engage in war unless actually invaded or in such imminent danger as will not admit of delay	1	10	3
Full faith and credit in every other State shall be given to the public acts, records, and judicial proceedings of each State	4	1	....
Congress shall prescribe the manner of proving such acts, records, and proceedings	4	1	....
Citizens of each State shall be entitled to all privileges and immunities of citizens in the several States	4	2	1
New States may be admitted by Congress into this Union	4	3	1
But no new State shall be formed or erected within the jurisdiction of another State	4	3	1
Nor any State formed by the junction of two or more States or parts of States, without the consent of the legislatures as well as of Congress	4	3	1
No State shall be deprived, without its consent, of its equal suffrage in the Senate	5	....	....
Three-fourths of the legislatures of the States, or conventions of three-fourths of the States, as Congress shall prescribe, may ratify amendments to the Constitution	5	....	....
The United States shall guarantee a republican form of government to every State in the Union	4	4	....
They shall protect each State against invasion	4	4	......
And on application of the legislature, or the executive (when the legislature cannot be convened), against domestic violence	4	4	....
The ratification by nine States shall be sufficient to establish the Constitution between the States so ratifying the same	7	....	....
When the choice of President shall devolve on the House of Representatives, the vote shall be taken by States. [Amendments]	12	....	....
But in choosing the President the vote shall be taken by States, the representation from each State having one vote. [Amendments]	12	....	....
A quorum for choice of President shall consist of a member or members from two-thirds of the States, and a majority of all the States shall be necessary to a choice. [Amendments]	12	....	....
States or the people. Powers not delegated to the United States, nor prohibited to the United States, are reserved to the. [Amendments]	10	....	....
Suffrage in the Senate. No State shall be deprived without its consent of its equal	5	....	....
No denial of right to vote on account of sex. [Amendments]	19	....	....
Suits at common law, where the value in controversy shall exceed $20, shall be tried by jury. [Amendments]	7	....	....
In law or equity against one of the States, by citizens of another State, or by citizens of a foreign State. The judicial power of the United States shall not extend to. [Amendments]	11	....	....
Supreme Court. Congress shall have power to constitute tribunals inferior to the	1	8	9
Supreme Court, and such inferior courts as Congress may establish. The judicial power of the United States shall be vested in one	3	1	....
Supreme Court. The judges of the Supreme and inferior courts shall hold their offices during good behavior	3	1	......

† **Article of original Constitution or of Amendment.**

	Article †	Section	Clause
The compensation of the judges shall not be diminished during their continuance in office	3	1	. . . .
Shall have original jurisdiction. In all cases affecting ambassadors, other public ministers and consuls, and in which a State may be a party, the	3	2	2
Shall have appellate jurisdiction, both as to law and the fact, with such exceptions and regulations as Congress may make. The	3	2	2
Supreme law of the land. This Constitution, the laws made in pursuance thereof, and the treaties of the United States, shall be the	6	. . . .	2
The judges in every State shall be bound thereby . .	6	. . . .	2
Suppress insurrections and repel invasions. Congress shall provide for calling forth the militia to execute the laws	1	8	15
Suppression of insurrection or rebellion shall not be questioned. The public debt, including the debt for pensions and bounties, incurred in the. [Amendments]	14	4	. . . .

T

	Article †	Section	Clause
Tax shall be laid unless in proportion to the census or enumeration. No capitation or other direct	1	9	4
Tax on incomes authorized without apportionment among the several States, and without regard to any census or enumeration. [Amendments]	16	. . . .	. . . .
Tax or duty shall be laid on articles exported from any State. No	1	9	5
Tax. The right of citizens of the United States to vote shall not be denied or abridged by the United States or any State by reason of failure to pay. [Amendments]	24	1	. . . .
Taxes (direct) and Representatives, how apportioned among the several States	1	2	3
Taxes, duties, imposts, and excises. Congress shall have power to lay	1	8	1
They shall be uniform throughout the United States	1	8	1
Temporary appointments until the next meeting of the legislature. If vacancies happen in the Senate in the recess of the legislature of a State, the executive of the State shall make	1	3	2
Tender in payment of debts. No State shall make anything but gold and silver coin a	1	10	1
Terms of four years. The President and Vice President shall hold their offices for the	2	1	1
Term of office. President, not more than twice. [Amendments]	22	. . . .	. . . .
Term for which he is elected. No Senator or Representative shall be appointed to any office under the United States which shall have been created or its emoluments increased during the	1	6	2
Territory or other property of the United States. Congress shall dispose of and make all needful rules and regulations respecting the	4	3	2
Test as a qualification for any office or public trust shall ever be required. No religious	6	. . . .	3
Testimony of two witnesses to the same overt act, or on confession in open court. No person shall be convicted of treason except on the	3	3	1
Three-fourths of the legislatures of the States, or conventions in three-fourths of the States, as Congress			

† Article of original Constitution or of Amendment.

	Article [†]	Section	Clause
shall prescribe, may ratify amendments to the Constitution	5	....	....
Tie. The Vice President shall have no vote unless the Senate be equally divided.	1	3	4
Times, places, and manner of holding elections for Senators and Representatives shall be prescribed in each State by the legislature thereof	1	4	1
But Congress may at any time by law make or alter such regulations, except as to the places of choosing Senators	1	4	1
Title of nobility. The United States shall not grant any	1	9	8
No State shall grant any	1	10	1
Title of any kind, from any king, prince, or foreign state, without the consent of Congress. No person holding any office under the United States shall accept any	1	9	8
Tonnage without the consent of Congress. No State shall lay any duty of	1	10	3
Tranquility, provide for the common defense, &c. To insure domestic. [Preamble]	....	....	....
Treason shall consist only in levying war against the United States, or in adhering to their enemies, giving them aid and comfort	3	3	1
No person shall, unless on the testimony of two witnesses to the same overt act, or on confession in open court, be convicted of	3	3	1
Congress shall have power to declare the punishment of	3	3	2
Shall not work corruption of blood. Attainder of	3	3	2
Shall not work forfeiture, except during the life of the person attained. Attainder of	3	3	2
Treason, bribery, or other high crimes and misdemeanors. The President, Vice President, and all civil officers shall be removed from office on impeachment for and conviction of	2	4	1
Treason, felony, and breach of the peace. Senators and Representatives shall be privileged from arrest while attending or while going to or returning from the sessions of Congress, except in cases of	1	6	1
Treasury, but in consequence of appropriations made by law. No money shall be drawn from the	1	9	7
Treaties. The President shall have power, with the advice and consent of the Senate, provided two-thirds of the Senators present concur, to make	2	2	2
The judicial power shall extend to all cases arising under the Constitution, laws, and	3	2	1
They shall be the supreme law of the land, and the judges in every State shall be bound thereby	6	....	2
Treaty, alliance, or confederation. No State shall enter into any	1	10	1
Trial, judgment, and punishment according to law. Judgment in cases of impeachment shall not extend further than to removal from, and disqualification for, office; but the party convicted shall nevertheless be liable and subject to indictment	1	3	7
Trial by jury. All crimes, except in cases of impeachment, shall be tried by jury	3	2	3
Such trial shall be held in the State within which the crime shall have been committed	3	2	3
But when not committed within a State, the trial shall be at such a place as Congress may by law have directed	3	2	3
In all criminal prosecutions the accused shall have a speedy and public. [Amendments]	6	....	....

† **Article of original Constitution or of Amendment.**

	Article †	Section	Clause
Suits at common law, when the amount exceeds $20, shall be by. [Amendments]	7		
Tribunals inferior to the Supreme Court. Congress shall have power to constitute	1	8	9
Troops or ships of war in time of peace without the consent of Congress. No State shall keep	1	10	3
Trust or profit under the United States, shall be an elector for President and Vice President. No Senator, Representative, or person holding any office of	2	1	2
Two-thirds of the members present. No person shall be convicted on an impeachment without the concurrence of	1	3	6
Two-thirds, may expel a member. Each House, with the concurrence of	1	5	2
Two-thirds. A bill returned by the President with his objections, may be repassed by each House by a vote of	1	7	2
Two-thirds of the Senators present concur. The President shall have power, by and with the advice and consent of the Senate, to make treaties, provided	2	2	2
Two-thirds of the legislatures of the several States. Congress shall call a convention for proposing amendments to the Constitution on the application of	5		
Two-thirds of both Houses shall deem it necessary. Congress shall propose amendments to the Constitution whenever	5		
Two-thirds of the States. When the choice of a President shall devolve on the House of Representatives, a quorum shall consist of a member or members from. [Amendments]	12		
Two-thirds of the whole number of Senators. A quorum of the Senate, when choosing a Vice-President, shall consist of. [Amendments]	12		
Two-thirds, may remove the disabilities imposed by the third section of the fourteenth amendment. Congress, by a vote of. [Amendments]	14	3	
Two years. Appropriations for raising and supporting armies shall not be for a longer term than	1	8	12

U

	Article †	Section	Clause
Union. To establish a more perfect. [Preamble]			
The President shall, from time to time, give to Congress information of the state of the	2	3	1
New States may be admitted by Congress into this	4	3	1
But no new State shall be formed or erected within the jurisdiction of another	4	3	1
Unreasonable searches and seizures. The people shall be secure in their persons, houses, papers, and effects against. [Amendments]	4		
And no warrants shall be issued but upon probable cause, supported by oath or affirmation, and particularly describing the place to be searched, and the persons or things to be seized. [Amendments]	4		
Unusual punishments inflicted. Excessive bail shall not be required, nor excessive fines imposed, nor cruel and. [Amendments]	8		
Use without just compensation. Private property shall not be taken for public. [Amendments]	5		
Useful arts, by securing for limited times to authors and inventors the exclusive right to their writings and inventions. Congress shall have power to promote the progress of science and the	1	8	8

† **Article of original Constitution or of Amendment.**

† **Article of original Constitution or of Amendment.**

	Article †	Section	Clause
The President of the Senate shall, in the presence of the Senate and House of Representatives, open all the certificates, and the votes shall be then counted. [Amendments]	12		
The person having the greatest number of votes shall be Vice President, if such number be a majority of the whole number of electors. [Amendments]	12		
If no person have a majority, then from the two highest numbers on the list the Senate shall choose the Vice President. [Amendments]	12		
A quorum for this purpose shall consist of two-thirds of the whole number of Senators; and a majority of the whole number shall be necessary to a choice. [Amendments]	12		
But if the House shall make no choice of a President before the 4th of March next following, then the Vice President shall act as President, as in the case of the death or other constitutional disability of the President. [Amendments]	12		
No person constitutionally ineligible as President shall be eligible as. [Amendments]	12		
Vacancy in office of. President shall nominate a Vice President who shall take office upon confirmation by both Houses of Congress. [Amendments]	25		
Violence. The United States shall guarantee to every State a republican form of government, and shall protect each State against invasion and domestic	4	4	
Virginia entitled to ten Representatives in the first Congress	1	2	3
Vote. Each Senator shall have one	1	3	1
The Vice President, unless the Senate be equally divided, shall have no	1	3	4
Vote requiring the concurrence of the two Houses (except upon a question of adjournment) shall be presented to the President. Every order, resolution, or	1	7	3
Vote, shall not be denied or abridged by the United States or by any State on account of race, color, or previous condition of servitude. The right of citizens of the United States to. [Amendments]	15	1	
Vote, shall not be denied or abridged by the United States or any State by reason of failure to pay any poll tax or other tax. The right of citizens of the United States to. [Amendments]	24	1	
Vote. Right of citizens who are eighteen years of age or older to vote shall not be denied or abridged by the United States or any State, on account of age. [Amendments]	26	1	
Right of citizens to vote shall not be denied or abridged by the United States or any State on account of sex. [Amendments]	19		
Vote of two-thirds. Each House may expel a member by a	1	5	2
A bill vetoed by the President may be repassed in each House by a	1	7	2
No person shall be convicted on an impeachment except by a	1	3	6
Whenever both Houses shall deem it necessary, Congress may propose amendments to the Constitution by a	5		
The President may make treaties with the advice and consent of the Senate, by a	2	2	2

† **Article of original Constitution or of Amendment.**

	Article †	Section	Clause
Disabilities incurred by participation in insurrection or rebellion, may be relieved by Congress by a. [Amendments]	14	3	....

W

	Article †	Section	Clause
War, grant letters of marque and reprisal, and make rules concerning captures on land and water. Congress shall have power to declare	1	8	11
For governing the land and naval forces. Congress shall have power to make rules and articles of	1	8	14
No State shall, without the consent of Congress, unless actually invaded, or in such imminent danger as will not admit of delay, engage in	1	10	3
War against the United States, adhering to their enemies, and giving them aid and comfort. Treason shall consist only in levying........................	3	3	1
Warrants shall issue but upon probable cause, on oath or affirmation, describing the place to be searched, and the person or things to be seized. No. [Amendments]..	4	....	....
Weights and measures. Congress shall fix the standard of	1	8	5
Welfare and to secure the blessings of liberty, &c. To promote the general. [Preamble]	....	....	....
Welfare. Congress shall have power to provide for the common defense and general	1	8	1
Witness against himself. No person shall, in a criminal case, be compelled to be a. [Amendments]..........	5	....	....
Witnesses against him. In all criminal prosecutions the accused shall be confronted with the. [Amendments]	6	....	....
Witnesses in his favor. In all criminal prosecutions the accused shall have compulsory process for obtaining. [Amendments].................................	6	....	....
Witnesses to the same overt act, or on confession in open court. No person shall be convicted of treason unless on the testimony of two	3	3	1
Writ of habeas corpus shall not be suspended unless in case of rebellion or invasion the public safety may require it	1	9	2
Writs of election to fill vacancies in the representation of any State. The executives of the State shall issue	1	2	4
Written opinion of the principal officer in each of the Executive Departments on any subject relating to the duties of his office. The President may require the	2	2	1

Y

	Article †	Section	Clause
Yeas and nays of the members of either House shall, at the desire of one-fifth of those present, be entered on the journals	1	5	3
The votes of both Houses upon the reconsideration of a bill returned by the President with his objections shall be determined by	1	7	2

† Article of original Constitution or of Amendment.

TABLE OF CASES

TABLE OF CASES

178

C

TABLE OF CASES

Clements v. Fashing, 457 U.S. 957, 102 S.Ct. 2836, 73 L.Ed.2d 508 (1982)— **§ 2.13, n. 199.20.**

Codispoti v. Pennsylvania, 418 U.S. 506, 94 S.Ct. 2687, 41 L.Ed.2d 912 (1974)—**§ 15.6, n. 42.**

Cohen v. Beneficial Indus. Loan Corp., 337 U.S. 541, 69 S.Ct. 1221, 93 L.Ed. 1528 (1949)—**§ 2.12, n. 27.10; § 19.29, n. 19.**

Cohen v. Cowles Media Co., 501 U.S. 663, 111 S.Ct. 2513, 115 L.Ed.2d 586 (1991)—**§ 20.22, n. 14.15.**

Collins v. City of Harker Heights, Tex., 503 U.S. 115, 112 S.Ct. 1061, 117 L.Ed.2d 261 (1992)—**§ 14.6, n. 29; § 16.4, n. 28; § 19.39, n. 31.5.**

Colorado Republican Federal Campaign Committee v. Federal Election Com'n, __ U.S. __, 116 S.Ct. 2309, 135 L.Ed.2d 795 (1996)—**§ 18.25, n. 21.5; § 18.32, n. 59; § 20.51; § 20.51, n. 60.**

Comer v. Kemp, 37 F.3d 775 (2nd Cir. 1994)—**§ 18.4, n. 1.5.**

Commission on Judicial Qualifications, State ex rel. v. Rome, 229 Kan. 195, 623 P.2d 1307 (Kan.1981)—**§ 20.42, n. 67.15.**

Commonwealth of (see name of Commonwealth)

Compassion In Dying v. State of Wash., 49 F.3d 586 (9th Cir.1995)—**§ 18.30, n. 102.10.**

Complete Auto Transit, Inc. v. Brady, 430 U.S. 274, 97 S.Ct. 1076, 51 L.Ed.2d 326 (1977)—**§ 11.10; n. 11.10; § 13.1, n. 4; § 13.2; § 13.2, n. 23.5, 55, 111.5; § 13.4, n. 149.45, 149.80; § 13.6; § 13.6, n. 56, 79, 138.5.**

Concrete Pipe and Products of California, Inc. v. Construction Laborers Pension Trust for Southern California, 508 U.S. 602, 113 S.Ct. 2264, 124 L.Ed.2d 539 (1993)—**§ 15.4, n. 60; § 15.8, n. 76; § 15.9, n. 42; § 15.12, n. 9; § 17.8, n. 19.5.**

Conkle v. State, 677 So.2d 1211 (Ala.Cr. App.1995)—**§ 20.37, n. .5.**

Conley v. Gibson, 355 U.S. 41, 78 S.Ct. 99, 2 L.Ed.2d 80 (1957)—**§ 19.32, n. 17.10.**

Connecticut v. Indrisano, 228 Conn. 795, 640 A.2d 986 (Conn.1994)—**§ 20.12, n. 1.**

Connecticut v. Menillo, 423 U.S. 9, 96 S.Ct. 170, 46 L.Ed.2d 152 (1975)— **§ 18.29, n. 29.5.**

Connick v. Myers, 461 U.S. 138, 103 S.Ct. 1684, 75 L.Ed.2d 708 (1983)— **§ 17.4, n. 46, 46.15.**

Connor v. Williams, 404 U.S. 549, 92 S.Ct. 656, 30 L.Ed.2d 704 (1972)— **§ 9.4, n. 11.65.**

Container Corp. of America v. Franchise Tax Bd., 463 U.S. 159, 103 S.Ct. 2933, 77 L.Ed.2d 545 (1983)—**§ 13.4; § 13.4, n. 149.55, 149.65.**

Cooke v. United States, 267 U.S. 517, 45 S.Ct. 390, 69 L.Ed. 767 (1925)— **§ 17.9, n. 1.**

Cooper v. Oklahoma, __ U.S. __, 116 S.Ct. 1373, 134 L.Ed.2d 498 (1996)— **§ 14.6, n. 35; § 17.3, n. 16; § 17.4, n. 10; § 17.9, n. 38; § 18.41, n. 0.5.**

Corporation of Presiding Bishop of Church of Jesus Christ of Latter-day Saints, 483 U.S. 327, 107 S.Ct. 2862, 97 L.Ed.2d 273 (1987)—**§ 21.6, n. 39.15.**

Cory v. White, 457 U.S. 85, 102 S.Ct. 2325, 72 L.Ed.2d 694 (1982)—**§ 2.12, n. 49.15.**

County of (see name of county)

Cox v. New Hampshire, 312 U.S. 569, 61 S.Ct. 762, 85 L.Ed. 1049 (1941)— **§ 20.46, n. 11.10.**

Coyazo v. State, 120 N.M. 47, 897 P.2d 234 (N.M.App.1995)—**§ 18.25, n. .5.**

Craig v. Boren, 429 U.S. 190, 97 S.Ct. 451, 50 L.Ed.2d 397 (1976)—**§ 18.20, n. 20, 29; § 18.23, n. 52.**

Cramer v. United States, 325 U.S. 1, 65 S.Ct. 918, 89 L.Ed. 1441 (1945)— **§ 23.35, n. 7.**

Crane v. Logli, 1992 WL 70337 (N.D.Ill. 1992)—**§ 18.3, n. 5.**

Cross v. Cunningham, 87 F.3d 586— **§ 18.2, n. 5.**

CSX Transp., Inc. v. Easterwood, 507 U.S. 658, 113 S.Ct. 1732, 123 L.Ed.2d 387 (1993)—**§ 12.1, n. 10.**

Cupp v. Naughten, 414 U.S. 141, 94 S.Ct. 396, 38 L.Ed.2d 368 (1973)— **§ 17.4, n. 10.**

Curtiss–Wright Export Corporation, United States v., 299 U.S. 304, 57 S.Ct. 216, 81 L.Ed. 255 (1936)— **§ 6.7, n. 10; § 23.35, n. 7.**

D

Dalton v. Little Rock Family Planning Services, __ U.S. __, 116 S.Ct. 1063, 134 L.Ed.2d 115 (1996)— **§ 12.1, n. 3.20.**

Dalton v. Specter, 511 U.S. 462, 114 S.Ct. 1719, 128 L.Ed.2d 497 (1994)— **§ 2.11, n. 71; § 17.10, n. 15.**

Dames & Moore v. Regan, 453 U.S. 654, 101 S.Ct. 2972, 69 L.Ed.2d 918 (1981)—**§ 23.35, n. 7.**

Darusmont, United States v., 449 U.S. 292, 101 S.Ct. 549, 66 L.Ed.2d 513 (1981)—**§ 15.9, n. 28.15.**

Davis v. Michigan Dept. of Treasury, 489 U.S. 803, 109 S.Ct. 1500, 103

184

185

I

L

189

191

TABLE OF CASES

Nation Magazine v. United States Dept. of Defense, 762 F.Supp. 1558 (S.D.N.Y.1991)—§ **20.19, n. 33.10.**

Neal v. United States, ___ U.S. ___, 116 S.Ct. 763, 133 L.Ed.2d 709 (1996)— § **14.6, n. 22; § 15.6, n. 37; § 17.8, n. 22.**

Nebraska Dept. of Revenue v. Loewenstein, 513 U.S. 123, 115 S.Ct. 557, 130 L.Ed.2d 470 (1994)—§ **12.1, n. 10.**

Nebraska Press Ass'n v. Stuart, 427 U.S. 539, 96 S.Ct. 2791, 49 L.Ed.2d 683 (1976)—§ **20.17, n. 2.**

Nebraska Press Ass'n v. Stuart, 423 U.S. 1327, 96 S.Ct. 251, 46 L.Ed.2d 237 (1975)—§ **20.17, n. 32.**

Negonsott v. Samuels, 507 U.S. 99, 113 S.Ct. 1119, 122 L.Ed.2d 457 (1993)— § **4.2, n. 21.**

New Energy Co. of Indiana v. Limbach, 486 U.S. 269, 108 S.Ct. 1803, 100 L.Ed.2d 302 (1988)—§ **11.8, n. 7.05.**

New Mexico, United States v., 455 U.S. 720, 102 S.Ct. 1373, 71 L.Ed.2d 580 (1982)—§ **4.10, n. 50; § 13.9, n. 30.**

Newport, Ky., City of v. Iacobucci, 479 U.S. 92, 107 S.Ct. 383, 93 L.Ed.2d 334 (1986)—§ **20.31, n. 54.35; § 20.61, n. 72.10.**

Newville v. State, Dept. of Family Services, 267 Mont. 237, 883 P.2d 793 (Mont.1994)—§ **15.4, n. 1.**

New York, In re, 256 U.S. 490, 41 S.Ct. 588, 65 L.Ed. 1057 (1921)—§ **2.4, n. 8.**

New York v. United States, 505 U.S. 144, Nuclear Reg. Rep. P 20,553, 112 S.Ct. 2408, 120 L.Ed.2d 120 (1992)— § **2.13, n. 132; § 2.16, n. 68.5; § 4.9, n. 24; § 4.10; § 4.10, n. 21.30, 21.35, 21.40, 21.45, 21.55, 21.65, 21.75, 21.80, 24, 104.5, 104.15, 121, 122; § 5.7, n. 7; § 12.5, n. 24; § 13.9; § 13.9, n. 55, 171.5, 171.15, 171.25.**

New York State Conference of Blue Cross & Blue Shield Plans v. Travelers Ins. Co., ___ U.S. ___, 115 S.Ct. 1671, 131 L.Ed.2d 695 (1995)— § **12.1, n. 10.**

New York State Liquor Authority v. Bellanca, 452 U.S. 714, 101 S.Ct. 2599, 69 L.Ed.2d 357 (1981)—§ **20.31, n. 54.35; § 20.61, n. 72.10.**

Nichols v. Coolidge, 274 U.S. 531, 47 S.Ct. 710, 71 L.Ed. 1184 (1927)— § **15.9, n. 26.**

Nichols v. United States, 511 U.S. 738, 114 S.Ct. 1921, 128 L.Ed.2d 745 (1994)—§ **17.4; § 17.4, n. 54; § 17.10, n. 8; § 18.25, n. 16; § 18.41, n. 6.**

Niemotko v. Maryland, 340 U.S. 268, 71 S.Ct. 325, 95 L.Ed. 267 (1951)— § **20.39, n. 19.65.**

Nishitani v. Baker, 921 P.2d 1182 (Hawai'i App.1996)—§ **2.16, n. 0.05, 42.10.**

Nix v. Whiteside, 475 U.S. 157, 106 S.Ct. 988, 89 L.Ed.2d 123 (1986)—§ **17.9, n. 8.**

Nixon v. Fitzgerald, 457 U.S. 731, 102 S.Ct. 2690, 73 L.Ed.2d 349 (1982)— § **7.3; § 7.3, n. 11.30, 11.40, 21; § 19.29, n. 31.20.**

Nixon v. United States, 506 U.S. 224, 113 S.Ct. 732, 122 L.Ed.2d 1 (1993)— § **2.16; § 2.16, n. 92.10; § 8.10, n. 7.10; § 8.15; § 8.15, n. 5.10, 28.10, 29, 31.**

Nixon, United States v., 816 F.2d 1022 (5th Cir.1987)—§ **2.16, n. 92.15; § 8.15, n. 5.15.**

Nixon, United States v., 418 U.S. 683, 94 S.Ct. 3090, 41 L.Ed.2d 1039 (1974)—§ **1.4, n. 8; § 7.3; § 7.3, n. 11.10.**

N.L.R.B. v. Baptist Hosp., Inc., 442 U.S. 773, 99 S.Ct. 2598, 61 L.Ed.2d 251 (1979)—§ **20.47, n. 11, 103.79.**

N.L.R.B. v. Carroll Contracting and Ready–Mix, Inc., 636 F.2d 111 (5th Cir.1981)—§ **20.47, n. 103.50.**

N.L.R.B. v. Catholic Bishop of Chicago, 440 U.S. 490, 99 S.Ct. 1313, 59 L.Ed.2d 533 (1979)—§ **23.10, n. 3.1.**

Nollan v. California Coastal Com'n, 483 U.S. 825, 107 S.Ct. 3141, 97 L.Ed.2d 677 (1987)—§ **2.13, n. 131.10; § 15.12; § 15.12, n. 22.10, 56.25.**

Nordic Village Inc., United States v., 503 U.S. 30, 112 S.Ct. 1011, 117 L.Ed.2d 181 (1992)—§ **2.12, n. 52; § 7.3, n. 22; § 19.29, n. 31.25.**

Nordlinger v. Hahn, 505 U.S. 1, 112 S.Ct. 2326, 120 L.Ed.2d 1 (1992)— § **2.13, n. 269; § 13.7; § 13.7, n. 7, 22; § 18.3; § 18.3, n. 54.5, 54.15, 54.20; § 18.38, n. 61.**

Norman v. Reed, 502 U.S. 279, 112 S.Ct. 698, 116 L.Ed.2d 711 (1992)—§ **2.13, n. 70; § 18.32; § 18.32, n. 22.5, 68.15, 68.25, 68.30; § 20.41, n. 34; § 20.54, n. 45.**

Norris by Norris v. Board of Educ. of Greenwood Community School Corp., 797 F.Supp. 1452 (S.D.Ind.1992)— § **17.5, n. 6.**

North, In re, 10 F.3d 831, 304 U.S.App. D.C. 56 (D.C.Cir.1993)—§ **9.6, n. 41.10.**

Northeastern Florida Chapter of Associated General Contractors of America v. City of Jacksonville, Fla., 508 U.S. 656, 113 S.Ct. 2297, 124 L.Ed.2d 586 (1993)—§ **2.13, n. 59, 199.10, 234; § 18.10, n. 18.10.**

TABLE OF CASES

Richmond v. Lewis, 506 U.S. 40, 113 S.Ct. 528, 121 L.Ed.2d 411 (1992)—§ 17.3, n. 10.

Richmond, City of v. J.A. Croson Co., 488 U.S. 469, 109 S.Ct. 706, 102 L.Ed.2d 854 (1989)—§ 18.3, n. 15.5; § 18.10, n. 156.20.

Ridlen v. Four County Counseling Center, 809 F.Supp. 1343 (N.D.Ind. 1992)—§ 16.1, n. 1.

Riggins v. Nevada, 504 U.S. 127, 112 S.Ct. 1810, 118 L.Ed.2d 479 (1992)—§ 14.6, n. 35; § 17.3, n. 16; § 17.9, n. 38.

Riley v. National Federation of the Blind of North Carolina, Inc., 487 U.S. 781, 108 S.Ct. 2667, 101 L.Ed.2d 669 (1988)—§ 20.47, n. 103.30, 113.5.

Rivers v. Roadway Exp., Inc., 511 U.S. 298, 114 S.Ct. 1510, 128 L.Ed.2d 274 (1994)—§ 15.9; § 15.9, n. 57; § 19.10, n. 2.

Riverside Bayview Homes, Inc., United States v., 474 U.S. 121, 106 S.Ct. 455, 88 L.Ed.2d 419 (1985)—§ 15.12, n. 56.15.

Riverside, City of v. Rivera, 477 U.S. 561, 106 S.Ct. 2686, 91 L.Ed.2d 466 (1986)—§ 19.36, n. 50.25.

R.J. Reynolds Tobacco Co. v. Durham County, N.C., 479 U.S. 130, 107 S.Ct. 499, 93 L.Ed.2d 449 (1986)—§ 13.1, n. 2.

Roaden v. Kentucky, 413 U.S. 496, 93 S.Ct. 2796, 37 L.Ed.2d 757 (1973)—§ 20.61, n. 47.30.

Robertson v. City and County of Denver, 874 P.2d 325 (Colo.1994)—§ 17.4, n. 1.

Robertson v. Seattle Audubon Soc., 503 U.S. 429, 112 S.Ct. 1407, 118 L.Ed.2d 73 (1992)—§ 2.10, n. 25.

Rockford Life Ins. Co. v. Illinois Dept. of Revenue, 482 U.S. 182, 107 S.Ct. 2312, 96 L.Ed.2d 152 (1987)—§ 12.1, n. 10.

Roe v. Wade, 410 U.S. 113, 93 S.Ct. 705, 35 L.Ed.2d 147 (1973)—§ 15.5, n. 4; § 18.29; § 18.29, n. 27.5, 28.

Rogers v. Lodge, 458 U.S. 613, 102 S.Ct. 3272, 73 L.Ed.2d 1012 (1982)—§ 18.8, n. 116; § 18.10, n. 200.

Romano v. Oklahoma, 512 U.S. 1, 114 S.Ct. 2004, 129 L.Ed.2d 1 (1994)—§ 17.3, n. 13.

Rome, In re, 218 Kan. 198, 542 P.2d 676 (Kan.1975)—§ 20.42, n. 67.15.

Rome, State ex rel. Commission on Judicial Qualifications v., 229 Kan. 195, 623 P.2d 1307 (Kan.1981)—§ 20.42, n. 67.15.

Rome, City of v. United States, 446 U.S. 156, 100 S.Ct. 1548, 64 L.Ed.2d 119 (1980)—§ 18.4, n. 39, 64; § 18.8, n. 115, 117.25; § 18.10, n. 202; § 18.31, n. 86; § 18.36, n. 79.

Romer v. Evans, ___ U.S. ___, 116 S.Ct. 1620, 134 L.Ed.2d 855 (1996)—§ 15.4, n. 49; § 15.7, n. 33; § 15.12, n. 26; § 16.4; § 16.4, n. 21.5; § 18.3; § 18.3, n. 80, 82, 83, 84; § 18.8, n. 110; § 18.9, n. 107.5; § 18.27, n. 21; § 18.30; § 18.30, n. 45.5, 45.10, 45.30; § 21.7, n. 4.5.

Roosevelt, People ex rel. Hurley v., 179 N.Y. 544, 71 N.E. 1137 (N.Y.1904)—§ 7.3, n. 23.

Rosenberger v. Rector and Visitors of University of Virginia, ___ U.S. ___, 115 S.Ct. 2510, 132 L.Ed.2d 700 (1995)—§ 20.47; § 20.47, n. 98.20; § 21.1, n. 6.10; § 21.5; § 21.5, n. 43, 47, 48, 49.

Ross, State v., 230 Conn. 183, 646 A.2d 1318 (Conn.1994)—§ 15.9, n. 1.

Rotherham, State v., ___ N.M. ___, 923 P.2d 1131 (1996)—§ 15.4, n. 1.

Roulette v. City of Seattle, 850 F.Supp. 1442 (W.D.Wash.1994)—§ 20.47, n. 69.10.

Rowland v. California Men's Colony, Unit II Men's Advisory Council, 506 U.S. 194, 113 S.Ct. 716, 121 L.Ed.2d 656 (1993)—§ 14.5, n. 7; § 20.41, n. 7, 33.10.

Rubin v. Coors Brewing Co., ___ U.S. ___, 115 S.Ct. 1585, 131 L.Ed.2d 532 (1995)—§ 20.31; § 20.31, n. 41.10, 54.20; § 20.61, n. 72.10.

Ruckelshaus v. Monsanto Co., 467 U.S. 986, 104 S.Ct. 2862, 81 L.Ed.2d 815 (1984)—§ 2.13, n. 131.20.

Ruckelshaus v. Sierra Club, 463 U.S. 680, 103 S.Ct. 3274, 77 L.Ed.2d 938 (1983)—§ 2.12, n. 52.

Ryder v. Freeman, 918 F.Supp. 157 (W.D.N.C.1996)—§ 14.2, n. 3.

Ryder v. United States, ___ U.S. ___, 115 S.Ct. 2031, 132 L.Ed.2d 136 (1995)—§ 9.4, n. 11.75.

S

Sable Communications of California, Inc. v. F.C.C., 492 U.S. 115, 109 S.Ct. 2829, 106 L.Ed.2d 93 (1989)—§ 20.39, n. 19.75; § 20.61, n. 115, 116.

Sale v. Haitian Centers Council, Inc., 509 U.S. 155, 113 S.Ct. 2549, 125 L.Ed.2d 128 (1993)—§ 17.10, n. 15; § 18.11, n. 24; § 22.2, n. 5.

San Diego Bldg. Trades Council, Millmen's Union, Local 2020 v. Garmon, 359 U.S. 236, 79 S.Ct. 773, 3 L.Ed.2d 775 (1959)—§ 12.1, n. 10.

Sanner v. Patton, 155 Ill. 553, 40 N.E. 290 (Ill.1895)—§ 20.41, n. 52.5.

197

TABLE OF CASES

TABLE OF CASES

TABLE OF CASES

TABLE OF CASES

201

TABLE OF AUTHORITIES

TABLE OF AUTHORITIES

4 ROTUNDA PP - sig 8

TABLE OF AUTHORITIES

TABLE OF AUTHORITIES

TABLE OF AUTHORITIES

TABLE OF AUTHORITIES

TABLE OF AUTHORITIES

213

TABLE OF AUTHORITIES

214

INDEX

A

Abortion,
 Clinics and federal civil rights protection, § 19.9
 Informed consent, §§ 18.29(b)(2), 18.29(b)(3)
 Procedures, regulation of, § 18.29(b)(2)
 Undue burden, § 18.29(b)(1)(c)
Accountants, solicitation by, and compared with, attorney solicitation, § 20.31
Admission of Washington, D.C. as a state, § 3.6
Affirmative action,
 Voluntary remedial measures, § 18.19(a)(4)
Appeals,
 Absolute immunity of Government officials as final orders, §§ 2.4 note, 19.29
  note
 Denial of immunity under section 1983, § 19.29
 Eleventh Amendment claims as final orders, § 2.4 note appeal
Apportionment,
  See also, Reapportionment
 Affirmative action, §§ 18.10(a)(4), 18.10(c)
 Congressional districts among the states, §§ 2.16(c)(7), 18.35
 Nonretrogression principle in apportionment cases, § 19.12 note
Association, freedom of, and death penalty claims, § 17.3 note

B

Bankruptcy, and federal jurisdiction, § 2.10 note
Begging, § 20.47(c)
Bricker Amendment, § 6.5

C

Capital cases and freedom of association, §§ 17.3, 20.42(a)
Cargo container taxes, § 5.10(c)
Casus belli, and original jurisdiction of Supreme Court, § 2.3
Causality and equal protection, § 2.13(f)(2)
Certiorari pool, § 2.6
Closed rules, § 10.4(b)
Collateral Order Doctrine,
  Generally, § 2.12(b)
 Appeal, as final order, of denial of immunity, § 19.29
Colleges and equal protection, § 18.9(c)
Congress and open and closed rules, § 10.4(b)
Congressional districts, apportionment of, among the states, § 2.16(c)(7)
Congressional district residency requirements, § 9.19
Contrived litigation,
  And *Buchanan v. Warley,* § 2.13(c)
  And *Hylton v. United States,* § 2.13(c)
Court reporters and section 1983, § 19.23(d)

D

Death penalty and freedom of association, §§ 17.3, 20.42(a)

215

INDEX

INDEX

I

"Identifiable trifle" and standing, § 2.13(f)(2)
"Illegal war" defense and selective service prosecutions, § 6.13(b)
Immunity claims,
    Absolute or qualified immunity of government officials, §§ 2.4 note, 19.29 note
        Eleventh Amendment Immunity, §§ 2.4 note, 19.16
    Appealed as final orders,
        See also, Collateral Order Doctrine
    Section 1983,
        Attorney's fees and judicial immunity, § 19.23(b)
        Court reporters, § 19.23(d)
        Criminal prosecutions, § 19.23(c)
        Fabricating evidence, § 19.24
        Press conferences, § 19.24
        Reliance of counsel defense, § 19.28
Impeachment,
    Immunity, lack of, from criminal process prior to impeachment, § 8.10
    Proposals for reform, § 2.16(c)(5)
Imports from abroad and state taxing powers, § 13.2(c)(2)(a)
Injury in fact and Equal Protection, § 2.13(f)(2)

J

Judges and judicial speech, restrictions on, § 20.42(d)
Jurisdiction, and the domestic relations exception to diversity jurisdiction, § 2.15(e) note
Juveniles,
    Best interest of child, § 18.28 note
    Detention,
        Deportation cases, §§ 14.6, 17.4(b), 17.9(a), 18.13 note, 22.7

L

Legislation, and open and closed rules, § 10.4(b)
Lieber, Francis, § 1.5 note.

N

Nonretrogression principle in apportionment cases, § 19.12 note
Nuremberg War Crimes Tribunal, § 6.13(b)

O

Office of legal counsel, § 10.7(a)
Open rules, § 10.4(b)

P

Panama invasion of 1989, § 6.10
Press conferences,
    Attorney discipline and free speech, § 20.25
    Section 1983, § 19.24
Privacy, and Fourth Amendment, § 18.30(b)
Protective jurisdiction and bankruptcy, § 2.10 note
Protective jurisdiction and the *Tidewater* problem, § 2.6 note
Punitive damages under section 1983, § 19.34 (and accompanying appendix)

217

R

S

T

U

V